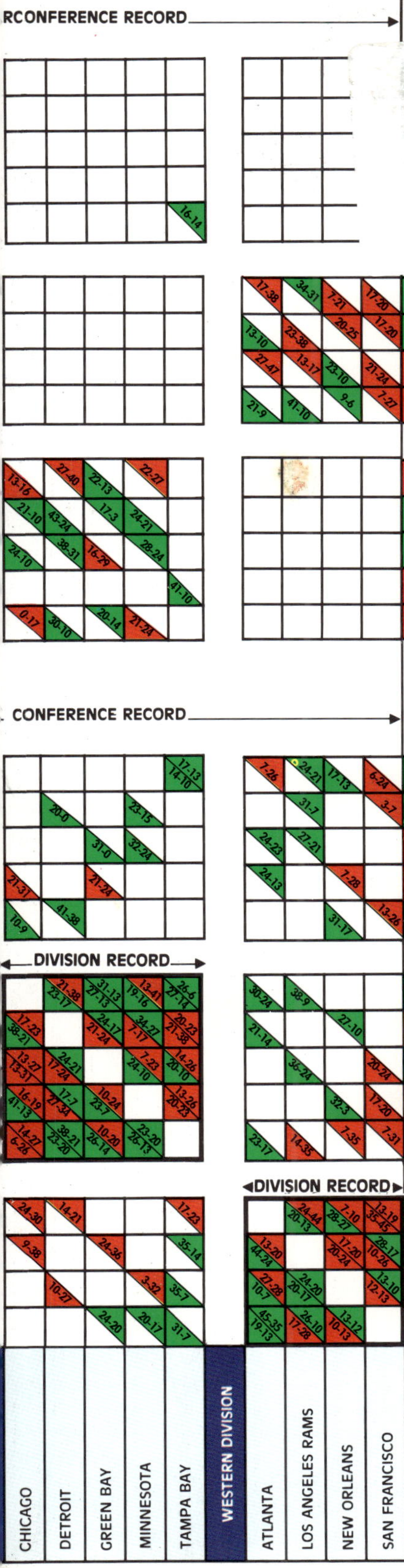

WEEK 1	WEEK 2	WEEK 3	WEEK 4	WEEK 5	WEEK 6	WEEK 7	WEEK 8	WEEK 9	WEEK 10	WEEK 11	WEEK 12	WEEK 13	WEEK 14	WEEK 15	WEEK 16	WEEK 17	Regular Season Record	Final Division Record	Final Conference Record	Final Inter Conference Record	Final Division Standing
											at HOU	PHI	at IND	at NYG	MIA	at WAS	13-3-0	7-1-0	10-2-0	3-1-0	1st
											at CIN	at PHX	BUF	at NYJ	WAS	at MIA	7-9-0	3-5-0	5-7-0	2-2-0	3rd
											at CLE	at WAS	PHIL	SEA	at BUF	IND	12-4-0	7-1-0	10-2-0	2-2-0	2nd
											at PHX	KC	at PIT	WAS	at NYJ	NYG	1-15-0	1-7-0	1-11-0	0-4-0	5th
											PIT	at SD		IND	NE	at TB	6-10-0	2-6-0	4-10-0	2-0-0	4th
NYJ	at SD	NE	at SEA	at RAM	at HOU	at CLE	at ATL	NO		PIT	IND	at PIT	SF	at RAD	HOU	CLE	9-7-0	.5-1-0	8-4-0	1-3-0	1st
PIT	at NYJ	SD	at KC	at DEN	at NO	CIN	at SF	BUF		HOU	MIA	RAM	at HOU	ATL	at PIT	at CIN	3-13-0	1-5-0	2-10-0	1-3-0	4th
at ATL	at PIT	IND	at SD	SF	CIN	NO	NYJ	at RAM		at CLE	BUF	at SEA	CLE	at KC	at CIN	PIT	9-7-0	4-2-0	8-4-0	1-3-0	2nd
at CLE	HOU	at RAD	MIA	SD	at DEN	at SF	RAM	ATL		at CIN	at NYJ	CIN	NE	at NO	CLE	at HOU	9-7-0	2-4-0	6-6-0	3-1-0	3rd
at RAD	KC	SEA	at BUF	CLE	PIT	at IND		at MIN	at SD	CHI	at DET	RAD	at KC	SD	at SEA	GB	5-11-0	3-5-0	4-8-0	1-3-0	5th
MIN	at DEN	at GB	CLE	at IND	DET	at SEA		RAD	SEA	SD	at RAD	at NE	DEN	HOU	at SD	at CHI	11-5-0	5-3-0	7-5-0	4-0-0	2nd
DEN	at SEA	PIT	CHI	at BUF	SEA	at SD		at KC	GB	at MIA	KC	at DEN	at DET	CIN	at MIN	SD	12-4-0	6-2-0	9-3-0	3-1-0	1st
at DAL	CIN	at CLE	HOU	at PIT	at NYJ	RAD	TB	at SEA	DEN	at KC	SEA	NYJ		at DEN	KC	at RAD	6-10-0	2-6-0	5-9-0	1-1-0	4th
at CHI	RAD	at DEN	CIN	at NE	at RAD	KC		SD	at KC	MIN	at SD	HOU	at GB	at MIA	DEN	DET	9-7-0	4-4-0	7-5-0	2-2-0	3rd
SD	NYG	at WAS	at NYG	TB	at PHX	at TB	PHI	at NYJ	SF	at RAM	WAS	NO		PHX	at PHI	at ATL	7-9-0	2-6-0	6-8-0	1-1-0	4th
PHI	at DAL	MIA	DAL		at WAS	PHX	WAS	at IND	at RAM	DET	at PHI	at SF	MIN	BUF	at PHX	at NE	13-3-0	7-1-0	10-2-0	3-1-0	1st
at NYG	PHX	at RAM	IND		MIN	at WAS	at DAL	NE	WAS	at ATL	NYG	at BUF	at MIA	GB	DAL	at PHX	10-6-0	5-3-0	9-3-0	1-3-0	2nd
at WAS	at PHI	at NO	WAS		DAL	at NYG	CHI	at MIA	at BUF	GB	NE	IND	at ATL	at DAL	NYG	PHI	5-11-0	2-6-0	3-9-0	2-2-0	5th
PHX	at SF	DAL	at PHX		NYG	PHI	at NYG	at DET	at PHI	NO	at DAL	MIA	CHI	at NE	at IND	BUF	10-6-0	4-4-0	7-5-0	3-1-0	3rd
SEA	at GB	MIN	at RAD	GB	RAM		at PHX	at TB	ATL	at DEN	at MIN	DET	at WAS	at DET	TB	KC	11-5-0	6-2-0	9-3-0	2-2-0	1st
TB	ATL	at TB	GB	at MIN	at KC		at NO	WAS	MIN	at NYG	DEN	at CHI	RAD	CHI	at GB	at SEA	6-10-0	3-5-0	5-7-0	1-3-0	3rd
RAM	CHI	KC	at DET	at CHI	at TB		MIN	SF	at RAD	at PHX	TB	at MIN	SEA	at PHI	DET	at DEN	6-10-0	3-5-0	5-7-0	1-3-0	4th
at KC	NO	at CHI	TB	DET	at PHI		at GB	DEN	at DET	at SEA	CHI	GB	at NYG	at TB	RAD	SF	6-10-0	3-5-0	4-8-0	2-2-0	5th
at DET	RAM	DET	at MIN	at DAL	GB	DAL	at SD	CHI	at NO	at SF	at GB	ATL		MIN	at CHI	NYJ	6-10-0	5-3-0	6-8-0	0-2-0	2nd
HOU	at DET	at SF		NO	SF	at RAM	CIN	at PIT	at CHI	PHI	at NO	at TB	PHX	at CLE	RAM	DAL	5-11-0	2-4-0	3-9-0	2-2-0	4th
at GB	at TB	PHI		CIN	at CHI	ATL	at PIT	HOU	NYG	DAL	at SF	at CLE	NO	SF	at ATL	at NO	5-11-0	2-4-0	3-9-0	2-2-0	3rd
SF	at MIN	PHX		at ATL	CLE	at HOU	DET	at CIN	TB	at WAS	ATL	at DAL	at RAM	PIT	at SF	RAM	8-8-0	4-2-0	6-6-0	2-2-0	2nd
at NO	WAS	ATL		at HOU	at ATL	PIT	CLE	at GB	at DAL	TB	RAM	NYG	at CIN	at RAM	NO	at MIN	14-2-0	4-2-0	10-2-0	4-0-0	1st

HINTS FOR INTERPRETING THE CHART

1. Identify a team from the left (vertical) column. The results of this team's games are set out in the horizontal row which corresponds with the team name. Buffalo's results appear along the very top horizontal row.
2. The result of a game against a team whose name is listed in the bottom horizontal row is indicated by a coloured triangle which appears in the square common to both teams.
3. Games won, lost or tied are colour-coded as follows:
   - Green triangle for a win
   - Red triangle for a loss
   - Yellow triangle for a tie
4. The score of a team which is listed in the vertical column **always** comes first. For this team, an away game is signified by a triangle in the top right of the square, and a home game is signified by a triangle in the bottom left of the square.
5. Examples using the Buffalo Bills: They won 24-14 at home to Miami but lost 7-30 away to Miami. Again, they defeated Denver 29-28 at home but lost 24-27 away to Houston.
6. The Bills' record for the 16-game regular season breaks down as follows: Divisional record 7-1-0; Conference record 10-2-0; Interconference record 3-1-0; Overall record 13-3-0.

THE OFFICIAL CHANNEL FOUR AMERICAN FOOTBALL ANNUAL 1991-92

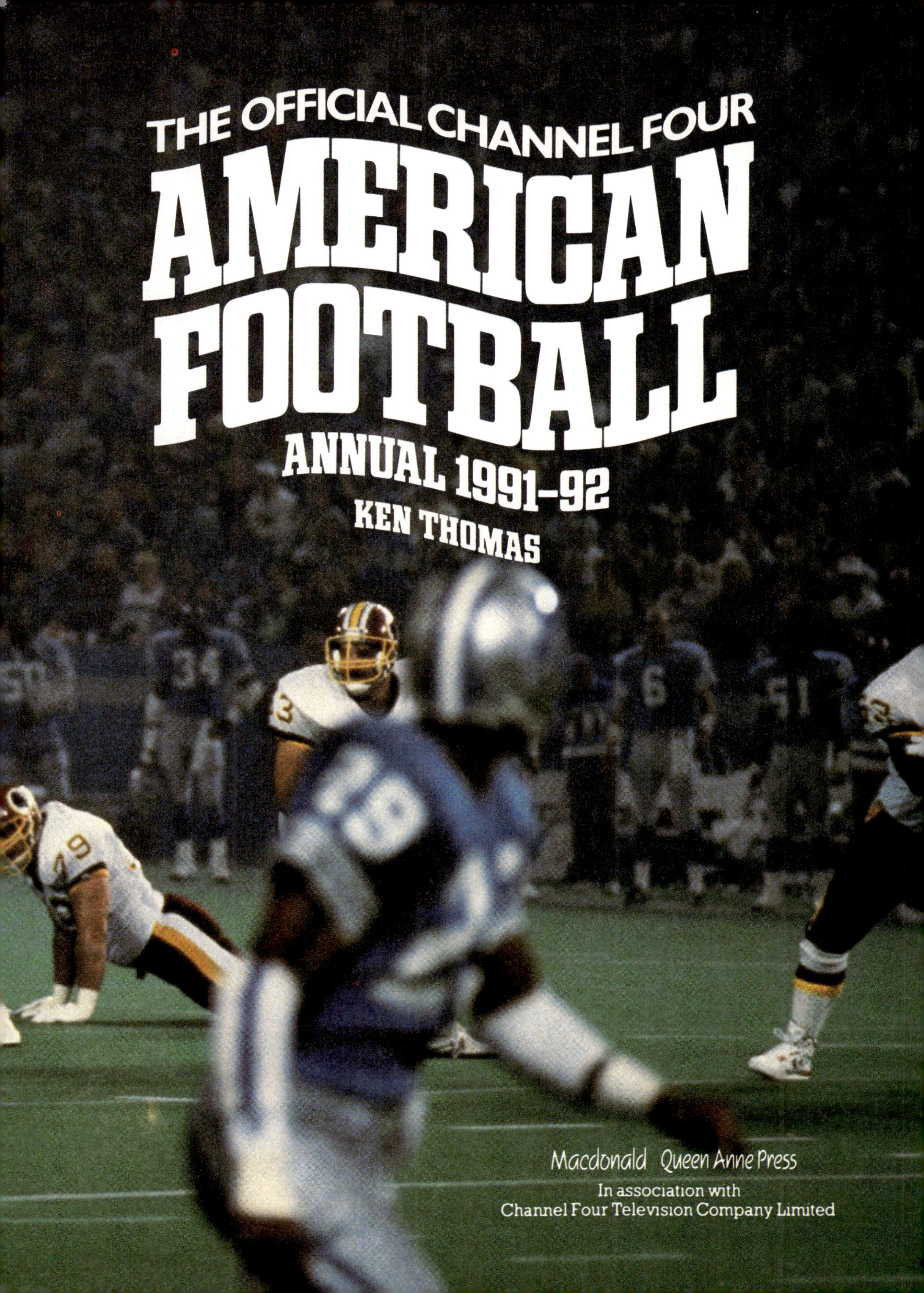

THE OFFICIAL CHANNEL FOUR

AMERICAN FOOTBALL

ANNUAL 1991-92

KEN THOMAS

Macdonald Queen Anne Press
In association with
Channel Four Television Company Limited

Acknowledgements

In one respect, expressing my thanks to the people who have been of incalculable assistance in the writing of this book is the most enjoyable part. For I am reminded of the friends I have gathered over the past decade.

For his knowledge of American Football, persistence, resilience and sheer hard work, Nick Wridgway deserves top billing. In several parts of the book which Nick organizes, in particular those tiresome rosters, I simply do as I am told. I hope that he'll continue to boss me around next year but, for the present, Nick, please accept my grateful thanks.

The American connection continues to expand. After nine years of friendship with Beau Riffenburgh, I should no longer be astounded at his insight and instant command of NFL history, but I am. It was through Beau that I met another of the same kind, Larry Eldridge, Jr., whose style, both personal and literary, I admire greatly. "If you need help, call Pete Abitante and Leslie Hammond," said Beau. So when I did need help, I called, and it came flowing in abundance. Pete has succeeded Jim Heffernan as the NFL Director of Public Relations while Leslie has taken over from Pete as the AFC Director of Information. It is with the same flawless efficiency and care that the photographic material comes from NFL Creative Services Division in Los Angeles. Paul Spinelli, Sandy Giornali, Kevin Terrell, Bob Kelly and the unflappable Stan James combine to ensure that the package always arrives ahead of schedule. John Herrera, a Senior Executive with the Los Angeles Raiders, is always on hand to offer help and advice. And while I appreciate greatly the technical explanations I have been given by former Raiders quarterback Daryle Lamonica, #3, who is my hero, I shall reserve judgement on his abilities as a fisherman. Naturally, I am indebted to them all.

A little closer to home, Susanna Yager and Sandy Holton, of Channel Four Television, have nudged the project along with their usual calm efficiency and understanding. Ian Marshall who, as editor, took on the onerous task of cleaning up my crude offerings, has been most kind. It goes without saying that Susanna, Sandy and Ian have both my respect and my thanks.

Finally, comes Janie my wife. Supportive as always, I really don't know how she puts up with me. Thanks love.

K.T., June 1991

A QUEEN ANNE PRESS BOOK

First published in Great Britain in 1991 by
Queen Anne Press, a division of
Macdonald & Co (Publishers) Ltd
165 Great Dover Street
London SE1 4YA

A member of Maxwell Macmillan Publishing Corporation

The Official Channel Four American Football Annual 1991-92 is associated with Channel Four Television coverage of the sport

NFL Properties (UK) Ltd

The Conference Record on the inside front cover and the Anatomy of Super Bowl XXV appear by kind permission of *Touchdown* magazine.

Cover photographs - Front: Super Bowl XXV Ottis Anderson of New York Giants (*Colorsport*)
Back: Super Bowl XXV (*Colorsport*)

Design: Peter Champion and Anne Samuel

A CIP catalogue record for this book is available from the British Library

ISBN 0-356-20259-3

Typeset in Great Britain by SB Datagraphics, Colchester
Printed and bound in Great Britain by BPCC Hazell Books, Aylesbury and Paulton

PHOTOGRAPHS

All photographs contained within this book have been supplied courtesy of the NFL. The following photographers took the pictures on the pages indicated: Bill Amatucci 68; Arthur Anderson 34, 77l; Bill Baptist 9; Tom Berg 81; John Betancourt 13; David Boss 65, 73; Peter Brouillet 17, 99; Rob Brown 24, 58b, 91, 151; Thomas J. Croke 80r; Dave Cross 40, 69, 88, 96; Scott Cunningham 2-3, 26, 50t, 135; Jonathan Daniel 30; Bruce Dierdorff 14; David Drapkin 29; Michael Fabus 109; George Gojkovich 18, 23; Pete J. Groh 20, 123; Michael Heinz 36, 84, 102; Dan Honda 25; Paul Jasienski 8, 11r, 19, 28, 58t, 77r, 105, 115, 139; Allen Kaye 75t; Perry McIntyre 147; Richard Mackson 16; Fred Matthes 5; Al Messerschmidt 6, 39, 45, 47, 53t, 101, 140; Vic Milton 60, 149; Mike Moore 79 (both), 133; Louis A. Raynor 33, 64; Russ Reed 72; Mitchell B. Reibel 153; John H. Reid III 37; Bob Rosato 21, 22, 83, 111, 121, 126; George Rose 43, 50b, 90; Manny Rubio 106; Chris Schwenk 11l; Owen Shaw 41; Aggie Skirball 31, 56l; Robert L. Smith 92; Jerry Soifer 49, 85; Paul Spinelli 27, 46, 78, 82, 95, 136; Brian Spurlock 10; Allen D. Steele 143; Sam Stone 117; Tony Tomsic 70, 74, 75b, 89, 119, 145; Greg Trott 32, 48, 124; Jim Turner 15, 56r, 71, 80l, 122, 129; Ron Vesely 125; Ed Webber 35; Herb Weitman 12, 38, 87, 113; Bill Wood 44; Ron Wyatt 42; Michael Zagaris 51, 52, 53br & bl; Joel Zwink 131.

CONTENTS

TITLE PAGE: Action from Super Bowl XXV.

PREVIOUS PAGE: From the hold of Jeff Hostetler, Matt Bahr drills the field goal which takes the Giants to Super Bowl XXV.

The face of Pittsburgh inside linebacker David Little is a model of intensity. As a tenth-year veteran in 1990, Little gained his first Pro Bowl selection.

INTRODUCTION

As I write, the London Monarchs have secured the WLAF European Division title. A loss to Barcelona on the final weekend was the only blemish on what would have been a perfect regular-season record but, more significant for the movement as a whole, the game was watched by a crowd of 50,835. Earlier, a World League-record 51,635 fans turned up to see Frankfurt lose to Sacramento when victory would have assured the Galaxy of the sole wild card spot in the playoffs.

It was on a late-March evening, in the rain uncharacteristic of Spain, that Barcelona began with a win over the New York/New Jersey Knights in the WLAF's inaugural game. Noted media personalities from the United States stood in line to express their 'astonishment' that as many as 19,000 fans were on hand to witness the event. How can it be that a surge of interest in American Football, stretching back at least to the mid-1980s and which has paused only occasionally before renewing its momentum, went unappreciated where recognition mattered the most? Perhaps some things just have to take time. But someone who counts really ought to accept as a sensible projection that, if 50,000 people will turn up to watch the WLAF Monarchs, an NFL Monarchs team would fill Wembley Stadium.

Doesn't time fly? This Annual is the ninth in the series and it has remained essentially unchanged, mostly because, in its present form, it has gathered together a loyal band of readers who share a common goal with the author. Over the years, there have been one or two changes in the formula and I hope that a new feature, a discussion of last year's rookie successes, will be found acceptable. The 25th Super Bowl stimulated the selection of an all-time Super Bowl squad and I could hardly miss the opportunity to talk about those players who have lent their greatness to the occasion.

In previous volumes I have explored the various ways of describing the pleasure I derive from writing this book. As a word, 'fun' doesn't tell the whole story, but it should be added to the list.

CHAPTER ONE

A Review Of The 1990 Season

Prologue

There was just a touch more than the usual anticipation in the air as the players went to camp in preparation for the NFL's 71st season, the main reason being that there was every prospect of the San Francisco 49ers winning the Super Bowl Championship for an unprecedented third consecutive year. Emulating the Pittsburgh Steelers of the 1970s, the 49ers had won the title four times in the 1980s, their most recent victory taking the form of a 55–10 rout of the Denver Broncos. With awesome power, elegance and dignity, San Francisco had established its authority, and there could be few who did not shelter hopes that the 49ers might succeed in their quest to write a unique chapter in NFL history. In the search for a slogan, American sportswriters never have been slow to adopt a term, and a corruption of the English language had led them to speculate on a so-called 'threepeat'!

Turning to the individual players who held out ambitions of breaking new ground, perhaps the most impressive quest was that of running back Eric Dickerson, who, with seven consecutive 1,000-yards-rushing seasons to his credit, needed one more to set the all-time record. However, it was a not unfamiliar story that this player of capricious genius was having difficulty with the club ownership – before the Colts it had been the Rams – and Dickerson would not be in uniform on opening day. Placekickers mostly endure the agony of rising tension as they wait in the wings before scurrying into the chilling isolation of the limelight. Nick Lowery had been doing that for ten years, in seven of which he had scored 100 or more points to share the NFL record. One more 'century' would take Lowery clear of the retired Jan Stenerud. In 1989, quarterbacks Dan Marino and Joe Montana had drawn alongside the retired Dan Fouts, forming a trio of the only players to have passed for 3,000-or-more yards in a campaign six times. It was one of the more likely prospects that both Marino and Montana would move into new territory.

Mike Webster was seeking to claim a longevity record as the postscript to a career of sustained greatness.

Less glamorous, but respected no less, former All-Pro center Mike Webster was a veteran of 236 regular-season games, a figure exceeded by only ten retired players in league history. He needed four games to displace Charlie Joiner from tenth position.

Webster had made his debut as a fifth-round selection in the 1974 draft, the annual process by which the league restocks its talent with collegiate seniors. Interestingly, there was a twist to the 1990 rite when, for the first time, the rules of access were expanded to include true juniors. Defined as those players still with one year of varsity eligibility remaining, only in the fullness of time could the wider impact of their premature entry into the pros be assessed and, for certain, there would be extra attention focused on the 18 young men who were drafted. Led by strong-armed Illinois quarterback Jeff George, who was the premier selection, eight juniors were snapped up with 24 of the available options in the first round.

A system designed to extend the freedom of player movement between clubs had been successfully introduced for the 1989 season. Known as Plan B, it was retained for 1990 and, of the 490 players declared unconditional free agents, 184 joined new teams. Dominating the market place, the Dallas Cowboys, a club in the process of reconstruction, seized the opportunity to sign 16 players. In contrast, the New England Patriots saw 17 players depart.

Of the head coaches there were three taking that responsibility for the first time. Bruce Coslet, who, as offensive coordinator, had fashioned the Cincinnati Bengals into a scoring machine, took his expertise to the New York Jets. By contrast, Rod Rust was a defensive specialist. Rust, who was the defensive coordinator of the New England team which went to Super Bowl XX and, subsequently, had held that office for one-year terms with Kansas City and Pittsburgh, rejoined the Patriots. Joe Bugel had been a truly outstanding offensive line coach for the Washington Redskins, tutoring the famous 'Hogs'. Bugel brought this expertise to Phoenix, where the Cardinals were expected to answer the call. For Jerry Glanville, the Atlanta Falcons offered a new challenge. As the head coach of the Oilers for the previous four seasons, Glanville's aggressive style had attracted some criticism. But his was the kind of approach which might just reinvigorate the Falcons. The role of head coach was not new to Jack Pardee, who had served in that position for both the Chicago Bears and Washington. More recently, he had developed an expressive passing offense as head coach of the University of Houston Cougars. Succeeding Glanville in charge of the Oilers, Pardee promised to fill the air with passes. Finally, Art Shell, who had established a platform by winning seven of 12 games after taking over from Mike Shanahan in 1989, was expected to be no less successful in his first full season with the Raiders.

Jerry Glanville ponders his prospects as the new head coach of the Atlanta Falcons.

Always alert to opportunities for enhancing the appeal of its product, the NFL came up with a new formula which admitted an extra wild-card team to the playoffs. Also, in moves designed to trim the duration of a game, there were minor adjustments in managing the time inbetween plays. For the television moguls, an extra weekend of games was generated by extending the regular season to 17 weeks, meaning that each club would have the benefit of a one-week break for rest and recuperation. A consequence was the disappearance of the usual weekend off for the teams contesting the Super Bowl. And when thoughts turned to predicting the winner, few observers looked beyond the 49ers, who, it was widely felt, might even be coming to their best.

WEEK ONE

American Football Conference
Denver 9 at Los Angeles Raiders 14
Indianapolis 10 at Buffalo 26
Miami 27 at New England 24
New York Jets 20 at Cincinnati 25
Pittsburgh 3 at Cleveland 13

National Football Conference
Los Angeles Rams 24 at Green Bay 36
Philadelphia 20 at New York Giants 27
Phoenix 0 at Washington 31
San Francisco 13 at New Orleans 12
Tampa Bay 38 at Detroit 21

Interconference Games
Houston 27 at Atlanta 47
Minnesota 21 at Kansas City 24
San Diego 14 at Dallas 17
Seattle 0 at Chicago 17

Interconference Play
AFC 1 – NFC 3

Game of The Week
New York Jets 20 - Cincinnati 25

"I'm very proud of my players. They played their guts out. We just didn't get it done, but give Cincinnati credit. They have a damned good football team," said Jets head coach Bruce Coslet after an emotional loss to his former club on his debut.

Earlier that day, the Jets had stood their ground in the face of Cincinnati's offensive power, and had given every sign of bringing off an upset. Quarterback Ken O'Brien combined with wide receiver Al Toon for touchdown plays covering 46 and nine yards to give New York a 17–10 lead, 10:16 into the third quarter. On the Bengals' return drive, New York strong safety Brian Washington intercepted a Boomer Esiason pass and carried the ball down to the Cincinnati 37-yard line, offering the prospect of further points as the period ended. 1:17 inside the final quarter, placekicker Pat Leahy duly completed a nine-play drive with his 26-yard field goal, extending the Jets' lead to ten points.

With the game on the line, Cincinnati's Esiason clicked into gear, completing passes of 24 and 16 yards on a quick-fire drive culminating in running back James Brooks' three-yard touchdown catch. Less than a minute later, the Bengals trailed by only one point after strong safety David Fulcher had tackled O'Brien in the end zone for a safety.

The Jets' defense firmed up but not quite well enough, as Cincinnati twice moved into position for Jim Breech field goals of 44 and 37 yards, leaving the Bengals needing to protect a five-point lead with just over two minutes remaining.

Still there was time for the Jets to mount one final effort, but the touch which had seen O'Brien pass for 300 yards on the day evaporated in the heat of the occasion, as did the Jets' final hopes when Fulcher capped an All-Pro performance with his end-zone pass interception that settled the issue.

The Road To Super Bowl XXV
Facing an Indianapolis team without star running back Eric Dickerson and with Colts rookie quarterback Jeff George making his NFL debut, the Bills were not troubled in easing to a 26–10 win.

Linebacker Lawrence Taylor had three quarterback sacks and forced a fumble as the Giants struck an early blow against an Eagles team which was strongly fancied to contend.

Anthony Dilweg threw three touchdown passes in his first NFL start, leading the Packers to victory over the Rams.

ABOVE: *Al Toon made a fast start in the Jets' losing cause.*

RIGHT: *Safety David Fulcher helped to keep the Jets at bay.*

Outstanding Individual Performances

100 Yards Rushing
Sammie Smith (Miami) 23-159-27-1
Neal Anderson (Chicago) 20-101-17t-2

100 Yards Pass Receiving
Flipper Anderson (L.A. Rams) 5-128-40t-1
Mark Jackson (Denver) 7-121-41-0
Al Toon (N.Y. Jets) 8-118-46t-2
Robert Clark (Detroit) 6-117-26t-2
Ernest Givins (Houston) 4-109-80t-2
Henry Ellard (L.A. Rams) 6-106-30-0

Passing
Vinny Testaverde (Tampa Bay) 21-16-237-1-54t-3
Anthony Dilweg (Green Bay) 32-20-248-0-50-3
Mark Rypien (Washington) 31-17-240-0-43t-3
Steve Grogan (New England) 28-17-217-0-48-2
Jim Kelly (Buffalo) 37-28-283-0-25-1
Steve DeBerg (Kansas City) 28-16-196-0-29-2

Standings

AFC East	W	L	T	PF	PA	Pct.
Buffalo	1	0	0	26	10	1.000
Miami	1	0	0	27	24	1.000
Indianapolis	0	1	0	10	26	0.000
New England	0	1	0	24	27	0.000
N.Y. Jets	0	1	0	20	25	0.000

AFC Central	W	L	T	PF	PA	Pct.
Cincinnati	1	0	0	25	20	1.000
Cleveland	1	0	0	13	3	1.000
Houston	0	1	0	27	47	0.000
Pittsburgh	0	1	0	3	13	0.000

AFC West	W	L	T	PF	PA	Pct.
Kansas City	1	0	0	24	21	1.000
L.A. Raiders	1	0	0	14	9	1.000
Denver	0	1	0	9	14	0.000
San Diego	0	1	0	14	17	0.000
Seattle	0	1	0	0	17	0.000

NFC East	W	L	T	PF	PA	Pct.
Dallas	1	0	0	17	14	1.000
N.Y. Giants	1	0	0	27	20	1.000
Washington	1	0	0	31	0	1.000
Philadelphia	0	1	0	20	27	0.000
Phoenix	0	1	0	0	31	0.000

NFC Central	W	L	T	PF	PA	Pct.
Chicago	1	0	0	17	0	1.000
Green Bay	1	0	0	36	24	1.000
Tampa Bay	1	0	0	38	21	1.000
Detroit	0	1	0	21	38	0.000
Minnesota	0	1	0	21	24	0.000

NFC West	W	L	T	PF	PA	Pct.
Atlanta	1	0	0	47	27	1.000
San Francisco	1	0	0	13	12	1.000
L.A. Rams	0	1	0	24	36	0.000
New Orleans	0	1	0	12	13	0.000

Week Two

American Football Conference

Buffalo 7 at Miami 30
Cincinnati 21 at San Diego 16
Cleveland 21 at New York Jets 24
Houston 9 at Pittsburgh 20
Kansas City 23 at Denver 24
Los Angeles Raiders 17 at Seattle 13
New England 16 at Indianapolis 14

National Football Conference

Atlanta 14 at Detroit 21
Chicago 31 at Green Bay 13
Los Angeles Rams 35 at Tampa Bay 14
New Orleans 3 at Minnesota 32
New York Giants 28 at Dallas 7
Phoenix 23 at Philadelphia 21
Washington 13 at San Francisco 26

Interconference Play

AFC 1 – NFC 3

Game of The Week
Kansas City 23 - Denver 24

Denver quarterback John Elway may go down in NFL history as one whose team was beaten in three Super Bowls in four successive years, but also he will be remembered for an almost unparalleled ability to snatch victory in the final few seconds of a game. This was one of those games.

After losing to the Raiders on opening day, the odds were that the reigning AFC Western division champions Denver would balance the account, even against a Kansas City club which was a gathering force and had started out well by beating the powerful Minnesota Vikings.

It was no surprise, then, that the Broncos ended the third quarter leading comfortably by the score of 21–9. Second-year running back Bobby Humphrey was scything towards a game total of 132 yards on 19 carries, while Elway had completed passes of 24 and 43 yards in the drives for Humphrey's touchdown runs of 37 and six yards. Elway's two-yard touchdown run, the only scoring play of the third quarter, appeared to have placed the issue beyond reasonable doubt.

Until then, the Chiefs had been forced to settle for three Nick Lowery field goals. And even when wide receiver Stephone Paige caught a 16-yard touchdown pass, it was hardly a sign of shifting fortunes, coming as it did after a blocked punt had given Kansas City possession just 17 yards from the Denver end zone. However, with only 1:44 left in the game, Chiefs veteran quarterback Steve DeBerg, a former Broncos player who had helped to nurse Elway through his 1983 rookie campaign, combined with Paige for a second touchdown, this time on a stunning, 83-yard play. For Denver, there was worse to come.

With time ebbing away, a marauding Chiefs defense turned the screw, leaving Denver at fourth-and-10 on its own 17-yard line, trailing by the score of 23–21. So what did John Elway do? He dropped back, surveyed the scene, selected a target, wide receiver Vance Johnson, and calmly completed a 49-yard pass down to the Kansas City 34-yard line. There still was work to do but, six plays later, after Elway had nudged the Broncos into field goal range, placekicker David Treadwell chipped the winner from 22 yards as the final gun sounded.

The Road To Super Bowl XXV

The Giants allowed themselves the luxury of spurning several opportunities and, still, they were able to beat Dallas with some ease, holding the Cowboys to just Alexander Wright's touchdown on a 90-yard kickoff return.

Miami took advantage of a fumble recovery and three Buffalo turnovers, handing Don Shula his 200th regular-season victory as Dolphins head coach. For the Bills, it was an early reminder that, in Miami, they had a serious challenger for supremacy in the AFC East.

Ten receptions for 206 yards and two touchdowns by wide receiver Stephone Paige almost saw Kansas City home against Denver.

Outstanding Individual Performances

100 Yards Rushing

Bobby Humphrey (Denver) 19-132-37t-2
Marion Butts (San Diego) 18-103-28-0

100 Yards Pass Receiving

Stephone Paige (Kansas City) 10-206-83t-2
Eddie Brown (Cincinnati) 10-178-30t-2
John Taylor (San Francisco) 8-160-49t-1
Vance Johnson (Denver) 6-150-49-0
Anthony Miller (San Diego) 9-137-30-0
Gary Clark (Washington) 7-106-40-0
Hassan Jones (Minnesota) 4-103-42-0

Passing

Jim Everett (L.A. Rams) 25-18-269-0-42t-4
Wade Wilson (Minnesota) 24-16-212-0-42-3
Jim Harbaugh (Chicago) 14-11-161-1-40t-2
Jay Schroeder (L.A. Raiders) 17-10-236-0-46-1
Phil Simms (N.Y. Giants) 21-16-208-0-29-1
Steve DeBerg (Kansas City) 45-26-395-0-83t-2
Dan Marino (Miami) 26-18-177-0-23-1

Denver quarterback John Elway wrote another chapter in his treatise on escapology.

Standings

AFC East	**W**	**L**	**T**	**PF**	**PA**	**Pct.**
Miami	2	0	0	57	31	1.000
Buffalo	1	1	0	33	40	.500
New England	1	1	0	40	41	.500
N.Y. Jets	1	1	0	44	46	.500
Indianapolis	0	2	0	24	42	0.000
AFC Central	**W**	**L**	**T**	**PF**	**PA**	**Pct.**
Cincinnati	2	0	0	46	36	1.000
Cleveland	1	1	0	34	27	.500
Pittsburgh	1	1	0	23	22	.500
Houston	0	2	0	36	67	0.000
AFC West	**W**	**L**	**T**	**PF**	**PA**	**Pct.**
L.A. Raiders	2	0	0	31	22	1.000
Denver	1	1	0	33	37	.500
Kansas City	1	1	0	47	45	.500
San Diego	0	2	0	30	38	0.000
Seattle	0	2	0	13	34	0.000

NFC East	**W**	**L**	**T**	**PF**	**PA**	**Pct.**
N.Y. Giants	2	0	0	55	27	1.000
Dallas	1	1	0	24	42	.500
Phoenix	1	1	0	23	52	.500
Washington	1	1	0	44	26	.500
Philadelphia	0	2	0	41	50	0.000
NFC Central	**W**	**L**	**T**	**PF**	**PA**	**Pct.**
Chicago	2	0	0	48	13	1.000
Detroit	1	1	0	42	52	.500
Green Bay	1	1	0	49	55	.500
Minnesota	1	1	0	53	27	.500
Tampa Bay	1	1	0	52	56	.500
NFC West	**W**	**L**	**T**	**PF**	**PA**	**Pct.**
San Francisco	2	0	0	39	25	1.000
Atlanta	1	1	0	61	48	.500
L.A. Rams	1	1	0	59	50	.500
New Orleans	0	2	0	15	45	0.000

Week Three

American Football Conference

Buffalo 30 at New York Jets 7
Indianapolis 10 at Houston 24
New England 7 at Cincinnati 41
Pittsburgh 3 at Los Angeles Raiders 20
San Diego 24 at Cleveland 14
Seattle 31 at Denver 34 (OT)

National Football Conference

Atlanta 13 at San Francisco 19
Dallas 15 at Washington 19
Detroit 20 at Tampa Bay 23
Minnesota 16 at Chicago 19
Philadelphia 27 at Los Angeles Rams 21
Phoenix 7 at New Orleans 28

Interconference Games

Kansas City 17 at Green Bay 3
Miami 3 at New York Giants 20

Interconference Play

AFC 2 – NFC 4

Outstanding Individual Performances

100 Yards Rushing

Thurman Thomas (Buffalo) 18-214-60-0
Derrick Fenner (Seattle) 22-144-28-3
Bobby Humphrey (Denver) 25-129-26-0
Christian Okoye (Kansas City) 23-122-32-1
Anthony Toney (Philadelphia) 24-103-20-0

100 Yards Pass Receiving

Jerry Rice (San Francisco) 8-171-42-1
Tim McGee (Cincinnati) 6-163-52-0
Henry Ellard (L.A. Rams) 7-145-50t-1
Mervyn Fernandez (L.A. Raiders) 5-130-66t-1
Andre Rison (Atlanta) 11-128-27-0
Brent Jones (San Francisco) 5-125-67t-1
Drew Hill (Houston) 10-123-23-0
Vance Johnson (Denver) 9-120-22-0

Passing

Joe Montana (San Francisco) 36-24-398-0-67t-2
John Elway (Denver) 40-30-297-0-29t-3
Warren Moon (Houston) 39-29-308-1-28-3
Dave Krieg (Seattle) 28-20-213-0-28-1
Boomer Esiason (Cincinnati) 26-15-271-1-52-2
Vinny Testaverde (Tampa Bay) 22-13-181-0-26-1

Game of The Week
Minnesota 16 - Chicago 19

After having lost on opening day, the Minnesota Vikings had reverted to type as they rebounded to register a thumping, 32–3 victory over New Orleans. There seemed little doubt that the reigning NFC Central division champions were back in business. That also was the case for the Chicago Bears, one of the NFL's most powerful teams during the second half of the 1980s but which had closed out that decade with six straight losses. They had opened by stifling Seattle and followed up with another show of tough defense as Green Bay were dismissed 31–13. A titanic struggle was in prospect.

For lovers of old-style, rushing football, the Bears put on a show. In one memorable period, they rushed on 19 consecutive plays from scrimmage. And for much of the time, the formula worked, as they ground out 16 points. With running backs Neal Anderson and Brad

Muster rushing for 91 and 90 yards respectively, the Bears would total 215 yards in that category while passing for just 40 net yards. But they hadn't put the Vikings away. Short-range, Donald Igwebuike field goals had rewarded Minnesota drives of 47, 38 and 66 yards. Remaining calm in the face of a defensive onslaught, Vikings quarterback Wade Wilson led his team down the field – a pass completion to wide receiver Hassan Jones gaining 17 yards and running back Herschel Walker clawing for three yards on a critical fourth-and-one play. One minute and 55 seconds remained when Jones caught the 17-yard touchdown pass which, with the ensuing extra point, levelled the scores.

But the drama was only beginning. First Chicago were held and, in turn, so were Minnesota. As punter Harry Newsome lined up on fourth down the prospect of overtime loomed large. Tragically for the Vikings, Newsome fumbled the snap, handing possession to Chicago on the Minnesota 39-yard line. It came down to one final swing of the boot by Chicago kicker Kevin Butler. Earlier, he had kicked a 51-yard field goal and now, with just four seconds remaining, he landed a 52-yarder to send the Bears into Week Four as one of the NFL's five unbeaten teams. Remarkably, it was Butler's ninth game-winning kick in 11 career attempts.

LEFT: Kevin Butler thrilled the fans in Chicago and on Channel Four TV as his late field goal took the Bears to victory.

RIGHT: Thurman Thomas broke for gains of 60, 39, 24, 15 and 15 yards as Buffalo overpowered the Jets.

The Road To Super Bowl XXV

Against the Jets, Thurman Thomas rushed for a career, single-game best 214 yards as the Bills rediscovered their touch, reversing the numbers of their loss the previous week.

The Giants took no chances against Miami, conquerors of Buffalo on Week Two, remorselessly controlling possession for a full 40 minutes and snuffing out the potential threat from Dolphins quarterback Dan Marino.

STANDINGS

AFC East	**W**	**L**	**T**	**PF**	**PA**	**Pct.**
Buffalo	2	1	0	63	47	.667
Miami	2	1	0	60	51	.667
New England	1	2	0	47	82	.333
N.Y. Jets	1	2	0	51	76	.333
Indianapolis	0	3	0	34	66	0.000

AFC Central	**W**	**L**	**T**	**PF**	**PA**	**Pct.**
Cincinnati	3	0	0	87	43	1.000
Cleveland	1	2	0	48	51	.333
Houston	1	2	0	60	77	.333
Pittsburgh	1	2	0	26	42	.333

AFC West	**W**	**L**	**T**	**PF**	**PA**	**Pct.**
L.A. Raiders	3	0	0	51	25	1.000
Denver	2	1	0	67	68	.667
Kansas City	2	1	0	64	48	.667
San Diego	1	2	0	54	52	.333
Seattle	0	3	0	44	68	0.000

NFC East	**W**	**L**	**T**	**PF**	**PA**	**Pct.**
N.Y. Giants	3	0	0	75	30	1.000
Washington	2	1	0	63	41	.667
Dallas	1	2	0	39	61	.333
Philadelphia	1	2	0	68	71	.333
Phoenix	1	2	0	30	80	.333

NFC Central	**W**	**L**	**T**	**PF**	**PA**	**Pct.**
Chicago	3	0	0	67	29	1.000
Tampa Bay	2	1	0	75	76	.667
Detroit	1	2	0	62	75	.333
Green Bay	1	2	0	52	72	.333
Minnesota	1	2	0	69	46	.333

NFC West	**W**	**L**	**T**	**PF**	**PA**	**Pct.**
San Francisco	3	0	0	58	38	1.000
Atlanta	1	2	0	74	67	.333
L.A. Rams	1	2	0	80	77	.333
New Orleans	1	2	0	43	52	.333

Week Four

American Football Conference

Cincinnati 16 at Seattle 31
Cleveland 0 at Kansas City 34
Denver 28 at Buffalo 29
Houston 17 at San Diego 7
Miami 28 at Pittsburgh 6
New York Jets 37 at New England 13

National Football Conference

Dallas 17 at New York Giants 31
Green Bay 24 at Detroit 21
Tampa Bay 23 at Minnesota 20 (OT)
Washington 38 at Phoenix 10

Interconference Games

Chicago 10 at Los Angeles Raiders 24
Indianapolis 24 at Philadelphia 23

Interconference Play

AFC 4 – NFC 4

Game of The Week
Green Bay 24 - Detroit 21

A quarter of a century has passed since Green Bay dominated the NFL with five league titles in a period of seven years, and it was in the decade before then that the Detroit Lions won the championship three times in six years. But ever since 1930 these two have been going at it, home and away, in one of the NFL's most fiercely contested rivalries. Even when both teams stand at 1–2 for the campaign, as was the case on Week Four, for nostalgia alone they're worth the price of the ticket. As usual, the multitude which gathered in Pontiac Stadium to witness their 120th meeting was not disappointed.

The home fans would be savouring the prospect of quarterback Rodney Peete scampering and spraying his passes around from the heart of the Lions' Silver Stretch offense. For Green Bay, quarterback Don Majkowski was feeling his way back cautiously after being involved in a preseason contractual dispute and he still had not rediscovered his best form. By the end, however, it was difficult to avoid the allusion with 'Majik', his nickname, for it had been with the deftness of an illusionist that he had pulled the game out of the fire.

Earlier, in response to Detroit's opening score, a Chris Jacke field goal and Majkowski's three-yard touchdown pass to tight end Ed West had given Green Bay a 10–7 advantage. However, with a few tricks of his own, Peete worked the Lions back into the lead, first engineering Barry Sanders' three-yard touchdown run and then rounding off a 33-yard drive with his seven-yard ramble. Enter the magician.

Completing four consecutive passes and subsequently rushing for a 15-yard gain, Majkowski drove the Packers down to the Detroit four-yard line. A few steps to the right opened up the defense just enough to confirm the certainty of his diagonal touchdown pass to running back Michael Haddix. But with only 3:09 remaining and Green Bay still adrift by four points, something special was needed. And that's what Majkowski produced. Despite being sacked twice, he held his nerve. Completing passes of four, 29 and eight yards, and mixing in runs of 11 and eight yards, he set up the final blow which came when wide receiver Jeff Query's diving grab on third-and-17 secured Majkowski's 26-yard touchdown pass with little under one minute to play.

LEFT: Quarterback Don Majkowski threw three touchdown passes and rushed for 88 yards in Green Bay's come-from-behind victory.

The Road To Super Bowl XXV

For the second time in the campaign, the Giants defeated Dallas. While they were never in serious danger, the margin of victory came with the help of a pair of errors, a fumble and a poorly thrown pass, by Cowboys quarterback Troy Aikman.

A devastating, fourth-quarter spell of one minute and 17 seconds, which saw touchdowns on an 80-yard blocked field goal return by Cornelius Bennett, a 39-yard interception return by Leonard Smith and a two-yard run by Kenneth Davis after a fumble, enabled Buffalo to turn probable defeat into a stunning, 29–28 victory over Denver.

LEFT: Bobby Humphrey's rushing helped Denver to a 21-9 lead before Buffalo staged a late rally for victory.

Outstanding Individual Performances

100 Yards Rushing

Bobby Humphrey (Denver) 34-177-18-1
Gary Anderson (Tampa Bay) 22-108-22-1
Blair Thomas (N.Y. Jets) 20-100-21-0

100 Yards Pass Receiving

Rob Moore (N.Y. Jets) 9-175-69t-1
Gary Clark (Washington) 8-162-42t-2
Keith Byars (Philadelphia) 12-133-25-0
Bruce Hill (Tampa Bay) 5-104-43-1
Albert Bentley (Indianapolis) 3-104-73-0
Willie Gault (L.A. Raiders) 4-103-59-0
Hassan Jones (Minnesota) 5-101-41t-1

Passing

Phil Simms (N.Y. Giants) 22-16-188-0-27t-3
Stan Humphries (Washington) 25-20-257-0-42t-2
Steve DeBerg (Kansas City) 21-12-189-0-47t-2
Dave Krieg (Seattle) 24-17-217-1-63t-2
Randall Cunningham (Philadelphia) 34-22-274-0-43-2
Troy Aikman (Dallas) 26-21-233-1-23-1
Vinny Testaverde (Tampa Bay) 19-11-162-0-43-1
Don Majkowski (Green Bay) 46-28-289-0-29-3

Standings

AFC East	W	L	T	PF	PA	Pct.
Buffalo	3	1	0	92	75	.750
Miami	3	1	0	88	57	.750
N.Y. Jets	2	2	0	88	89	.500
Indianapolis	1	3	0	58	89	.250
New England	1	3	0	60	119	.250
AFC Central	**W**	**L**	**T**	**PF**	**PA**	**Pct.**
Cincinnati	3	1	0	103	74	.750
Houston	2	2	0	77	84	.500
Cleveland	1	3	0	48	85	.250
Pittsburgh	1	3	0	32	70	.250
AFC West	**W**	**L**	**T**	**PF**	**PA**	**Pct.**
L.A. Raiders	4	0	0	75	35	1.000
Kansas City	3	1	0	98	48	.750
Denver	2	2	0	95	97	.500
San Diego	1	3	0	61	69	.250
Seattle	1	3	0	75	84	.250

NFC East	W	L	T	PF	PA	Pct.
N.Y. Giants	4	0	0	106	47	1.000
Washington	3	1	0	101	51	.750
Dallas	1	3	0	56	92	.250
Philadelphia	1	3	0	91	95	.250
Phoenix	1	3	0	40	118	.250
NFC Central	**W**	**L**	**T**	**PF**	**PA**	**Pct.**
Chicago	3	1	0	77	53	.750
Tampa Bay	3	1	0	98	96	.750
Green Bay	2	2	0	76	93	.500
Detroit	1	3	0	83	99	.250
Minnesota	1	3	0	89	69	.250
NFC West	**W**	**L**	**T**	**PF**	**PA**	**Pct.**
San Francisco**	3	0	0	58	38	1.000
Atlanta**	1	2	0	74	67	.333
L.A. Rams**	1	2	0	80	77	.333
New Orleans**	1	2	0	43	52	.333

**Did not play on Week Four

Week Five

American Football Conference

Cleveland 30 at Denver 29
Kansas City 19 at Indianapolis 23
Los Angeles Raiders 24 at Buffalo 38
New York Jets 16 at Miami 20
San Diego 14 at Pittsburgh 36
Seattle 33 at New England 20

National Football Conference

Detroit 34 at Minnesota 27
Green Bay 13 at Chicago 27
New Orleans 27 at Atlanta 28
Tampa Bay 10 at Dallas 14

Interconference Games

Cincinnati 34 at Los Angeles Rams 31 (OT)
San Francisco 24 at Houston 21

Interconference Play

AFC 5 – NFC 5

Game of The Week
Cincinnati 34 - Los Angeles Rams 31 (Overtime)

Cincinnati entered the 1990 season widely fancied to win the AFC Central division title, and the Bengals fans could reasonably live with a Week-Four loss to Seattle after seeing their team win its first three games. By contrast, the Rams had struggled. True, they had seen off a solid Tampa Bay club, but, either side of that win, reverses at the hands of Green Bay and Philadelphia had cast doubts upon their ability to challenge the mighty 49ers in the NFC West.

Under the new scheduling system, the Rams had been given Week Four off, and its debilitating effect on the coordination of teamwork, which is so vital in this most complex of pursuits, was evident as Cincinnati unleashed a fire-storm which threatened to asphyxiate the very life out of the home team. With quarterback Boomer Esiason delivering a fusillade of telling passes, touchdown receptions of 27 and nine yards by running back James Brooks, coupled with a one-yard touchdown run by fullback Eric Ball, saw the Bengals take a 21–0 lead after barely 5:29 of the second quarter. Was American Football ever this easy?

Even when the response came it was unimpressive, ponderous and pedestrian. But the result of a ten-play, 65-yard drive was a valuable seven points. And then someone lit a fuse. Slowly, inexorably, it burned until, in a burst of stars, wide receiver Flipper Anderson caught a 55-yard touchdown bomb from quarterback Jim Everett. The Bengals responded but it was brushed aside as Rams touchdowns by Damone Johnson and Cleveland Gary tied the scores at 28–28. Now let's think about this.

More cautiously now, with the game on the line, Cincinnati edged ahead with a field goal. But it was with equal care that the Rams used six plays to move 34 yards as they re-established the deadlock with 1:36 left in regulation time. Let's take a little more time to settle this one.

There was every indication that the game would produce the first tie of the 1990 season. However, after more than one nervous exchange, Esiason took charge. A 22-yard pass to Harold Green and a 27-yarder to Tim McGee left placekicker Jim Breech within field goal range. And with 3:04 left in overtime he did what is expected of a 12th-year pro, collecting the winning points from 44 yards out.

The Road To Super Bowl XXV

For the second week in a row, the Bills mounted a shocking rally, producing 24 unanswered, fourth-quarter points to hand the Raiders their first loss of the campaign. Touchdowns came on James Lofton's 42-yard pass reception, James Williams' 38-yard blocked punt return and a 49-yard fumble return by Nate Odomes, while a fumble recovery following a sack by Cornelius Bennett, set up Scott Norwood's 23-yard field goal.

New York was one of four NFC East teams for which no games were scheduled.

Quarterback Bubby Brister combined with rookie tight end Eric Green for Pittsburgh's first offensive touchdown of the season.

Cincinnati tight end Rodney Holman caught ten passes for 161 yards in the Bengals' overtime win against the Rams.

Outstanding Individual Performances

100 Yards Rushing
Neal Anderson (Chicago) 21-141-52-1
Emmitt Smith (Dallas) 23-121-16-1
Bobby Humphrey (Denver) 20-106-26-1

100 Yards Pass Receiving
Rodney Holman (Cincinnati) 10-161-27-0
Andre Rison (Atlanta) 10-154-45-2
Flipper Anderson (L.A. Rams) 7-144-55t-1
Tim McGee (Cincinnati) 8-142-32-0
Mervyn Fernandez (L.A. Raiders) 8-134-35-0
John Taylor (San Francisco) 4-132-78t-2
Sterling Sharpe (Green Bay) 5-129-76t-1
Mark Duper (Miami) 5-125-69t-2
Webster Slaughter (Cleveland) 7-123-43t-1
James Brooks (Cincinnati) 7-109-30-2
Hart Lee Dykes (New England) 5-103-35t-1
Henry Ellard (L.A. Rams) 7-100-29-0

Passing
Bubby Brister (Pittsburgh) 14-11-132-0-39-2
John Fourcade (New Orleans) 17-10-235-0-68t-2
Joe Montana (San Francisco) 28-20-318-1-78t-3
Boomer Esiason (Cincinnati) 44-30-471-0-32-3
Dave Krieg (Seattle) 25-17-254-1-45t-2
Vinny Testaverde (Tampa Bay) 21-13-194-0-58t-1

Standings

AFC East	W	L	T	PF	PA	Pct.
Buffalo	4	1	0	130	99	.800
Miami	4	1	0	108	73	.800
Indianapolis	2	3	0	81	108	.400
N.Y. Jets	2	3	0	104	109	.400
New England	1	4	0	80	152	.200

AFC Central	W	L	T	PF	PA	Pct.
Cincinnati	4	1	0	137	105	.800
Cleveland	2	3	0	78	114	.400
Houston	2	3	0	98	108	.400
Pittsburgh	2	3	0	68	84	.400

AFC West	W	L	T	PF	PA	Pct.
L.A. Raiders	4	1	0	99	73	.800
Kansas City	3	2	0	117	71	.600
Denver	2	3	0	124	127	.400
Seattle	2	3	0	108	104	.400
San Diego	1	4	0	75	105	.200

NFC East	W	L	T	PF	PA	Pct.
N.Y. Giants**	4	0	0	106	47	1.000
Washington**	3	1	0	101	51	.750
Dallas	2	3	0	70	102	.400
Philadelphia**	1	3	0	91	95	.250
Phoenix**	1	3	0	40	118	.250

**Did not play on Week Five

NFC Central	W	L	T	PF	PA	Pct.
Chicago	4	1	0	104	66	.800
Tampa Bay	3	2	0	108	110	.600
Detroit	2	3	0	117	126	.400
Green Bay	2	3	0	89	120	.400
Minnesota	1	4	0	116	103	.200

NFC West	W	L	T	PF	PA	Pct.
San Francisco	4	0	0	82	59	1.000
Atlanta	2	2	0	102	94	.500
L.A. Rams	1	3	0	111	111	.250
New Orleans	1	3	0	70	80	.250

WEEK SIX

American Football Conference
Cincinnati 17 at Houston 48
Pittsburgh 34 at Denver 17
San Diego 39 at New York Jets 3
Seattle 17 at Los Angeles Raiders 24

National Football Conference
Dallas 3 at Phoenix 20
Green Bay 14 at Tampa Bay 26
Los Angeles Rams 9 at Chicago 38
Minnesota 24 at Philadelphia 32
New York Giants 24 at Washington 20
San Francisco 45 at Atlanta 35

Interconference Games
Cleveland 20 at New Orleans 25
Detroit 24 at Kansas City 43

Interconference Play
AFC 6 – NFC 6

Wide receiver Ernest Givins was one of five players to catch a touchdown pass from Warren Moon as Houston drubbed Cincinnati.

Game of The Week
Pittsburgh 34 - Denver 17

In 1989, the Pittsburgh Steelers started slowly before mounting a charge, and their 1990 campaign had opened in similar fashion. In the first four outings their only success had been a Week-Two upset of Houston. Alarmingly, over that period, the Steelers, under new offensive coordinator Joe Walton, had been unable to produce an offensive touchdown. On Week Five against San Diego, the drought had broken, but they needed a follow-up win to keep pace in a divisional race which promised to go down to the wire.

With only two victories from five outings, the Broncos had disappointed. Furthermore, they entered this game without star running back Bobby Humphrey, cornerback Tyrone Braxton and defensive end Alphonso Carreker. Even so, urged on by the rabid faithful at Mile High Stadium, they offered a fearsome proposition to any visiting team. The Steelers, then, hardly could have chosen a more difficult proving ground on which to test the credibility of their challenge. They started badly.

Denver dominated the opening quarter, moving out to a ten-point lead and, subsequently, responding immediately after wide receiver Louis Lipps had opened Pittsburgh's account. The Broncos' 80-yard scoring drive had included John Elway's 59-yard pass to wide receiver Mark Jackson. 5:40 inside the second quarter, leading 17–7 and going well, hardly can they have imagined that they'd scored their final points of the game.

A week earlier against San Diego, Steelers rookie tight end Eric Green had caught his first three NFL passes, scoring two touchdowns. And it was to Green that Pittsburgh quarterback Bubby Brister looked for the finishing touch, a three-yard reception, on a 55-yard touchdown-scoring drive. It marked the beginning of a rally which would produce 27 unanswered points. Green caught two more touchdown passes which, though of modest dimensions, remarkably, took his total to five from only seven career receptions. Brister, meanwhile, amassed 353 yards including 141 to Lipps. With Cincinnati losing to Houston, Pittsburgh moved to within one game of the lead in the AFC Central.

The Road To Super Bowl XXV
With Buffalo enjoying the weekend off, the Giants were given all they could handle by traditional rival Washington, who drew to within one point at 20–21 in the final quarter. Critically, however, Redskins quarterback Stan Humphries was intercepted three times while, for the Giants, Phil Simms threw scoring passes of 80 and two yards, and set up another touchdown with his 61-yard pass completion to tight end Mark Bavaro.

Outstanding Individual Performances

100 Yards Rushing

Barry Word (Kansas City) 18-200-53t-2
Marion Butts (San Diego) 26-121-20-2
Johnny Johnson (Phoenix) 19-120-28-1

100 Yards Pass Receiving

Jerry Rice (San Francisco) 13-225-29-5
Andre Rison (Atlanta) 9-172-75t-2
Eric Martin (New Orleans) 8-153-58-1
Cris Carter (Minnesota) 6-151-78t-2
Louis Lipps (Pittsburgh) 9-141-33-1
Sterling Sharpe (Green Bay) 7-139-35-0
Barry Sanders (Detroit) 5-135-47t-1
Fred Barnett (Philadelphia) 4-114-40t-1
Stephen Baker (N.Y. Giants) 3-109-80t-1
Ernest Givins (Houston) 6-101-30-1
Anthony Miller (San Diego) 5-100-29t-1

Passing

Bubby Brister (Pittsburgh) 28-21-353-0-90-4
Warren Moon (Houston) 33-21-369-1-42t-5
Jay Schroeder (L.A. Raiders) 26-19-235-0-23-3
Phil Simms (N.Y. Giants) 22-13-283-0-80t-2
Jim Harbaugh (Chicago) 25-18-248-0-32-2
Chris Miller (Atlanta) 31-18-291-0-75t-3
Joe Montana (San Francisco) 49-32-476-2-43t-6
Billy Joe Tolliver (San Diego) 18-12-169-0-29t-1
Steve Walsh (New Orleans) 26-15-243-1-58-3
Dave Krieg (Seattle) 36-22-294-0-50-2
Vinny Testaverde (Tampa Bay) 29-17-292-0-74-1
Steve DeBerg (Kansas City) 26-15-256-0-60-1

Given a chance to re-establish his career by Kansas City, Barry Word, who had been working for a telephone company, unleashed his formidable power against Detroit, rushing for a Chiefs club-record 200 yards.

Standings

AFC East	W	L	T	PF	PA	Pct.
Buffalo**	4	1	0	130	99	.800
Miami**	4	1	0	108	73	.800
Indianapolis**	2	3	0	81	108	.400
N.Y. Jets	2	4	0	107	148	.333
New England**	1	4	0	80	152	.200

**Did not play on Week Six

AFC Central	W	L	T	PF	PA	Pct.
Cincinnati	4	2	0	154	153	.667
Houston	3	3	0	146	125	.500
Pittsburgh	3	3	0	102	101	.500
Cleveland	2	4	0	98	139	.333

AFC West	W	L	T	PF	PA	Pct.
L.A. Raiders	5	1	0	123	90	.833
Kansas City	4	2	0	160	95	.667
Denver	2	4	0	141	161	.333
San Diego	2	4	0	114	108	.333
Seattle	2	4	0	125	128	.333

NFC East	W	L	T	PF	PA	Pct.
N.Y. Giants	5	0	0	130	67	1.000
Washington	3	2	0	121	75	.600
Philadelphia	2	3	0	123	119	.400
Phoenix	2	3	0	60	121	.400
Dallas	2	4	0	73	122	.333

NFC Central	W	L	T	PF	PA	Pct.
Chicago	5	1	0	142	75	.833
Tampa Bay	4	2	0	134	124	.667
Detroit	2	4	0	141	169	.333
Green Bay	2	4	0	103	146	.333
Minnesota	1	5	0	140	135	.167

NFC West	W	L	T	PF	PA	Pct.
San Francisco	5	0	0	127	94	1.000
Atlanta	2	3	0	137	139	.400
New Orleans	2	3	0	95	100	.400
L.A. Rams	1	4	0	120	149	.200

Week Seven

American Football Conference

Cincinnati 34 at Cleveland 13
Denver 27 at Indianapolis 17
Kansas City 7 at Seattle 19
Los Angeles Raiders 24 at San Diego 9
New England 10 at Miami 17
New York Jets 27 at Buffalo 30

National Football Conference

Atlanta 24 at Los Angeles Rams 44
Dallas 17 at Tampa Bay 13
Philadelphia 7 at Washington 13
Phoenix 19 at New York Giants 20

Interconference Games

New Orleans 10 at Houston 23
Pittsburgh 7 at San Francisco 27

Interconference Play

AFC 7 – NFC 7

Game of The Week
Dallas 17 - Tampa Bay 13

It was one of the surprises of the season thus far that Tampa Bay, a team regarded by many observers as being two years away from making a title bid, lay second in the NFC Central, one game adrift of the 5–1 Chicago Bears. The previous weekend, six turnovers had helped the Buccaneers to an impressive victory over Green Bay. Dallas, meanwhile, were in the process of reconstruction and the going was tough. An opening-day win against San Diego had been followed by losses in a brutal three-week spell when, twice, they had faced the New York Giants either side of travelling to the Washington Redskins. They did manage to squeak a 14–10 decision over Tampa Bay, but any euphoria subsequently evaporated in the cauldron of Sun Devil Stadium where the Phoenix Cardinals had been easy, 20–3 victors.

Issiac Holt's 64-yard interception return gave Dallas a lead.

Outstanding Individual Performances

100 Yards Rushing
Johnny Johnson (Phoenix) 30-108-27-0
Cleveland Gary (L.A. Rams) 19-102-23t-2

100 Yards Pass Receiving
Andre Rison (Atlanta) 5-161-71t-2
Jessie Hester (Indianapolis) 8-152-33-1
Mark Jackson (Denver) 6-127-66-1
Andre Reed (Buffalo) 8-116-19t-2
Mark Carrier (Tampa Bay) 6-113-37-0
Henry Ellard (L.A. Rams) 6-109-35t-1

Passing
John Elway (Denver) 30-21-317-0-66-2
Jim Kelly (Buffalo) 32-19-297-1-60t-4
Jim Everett (L.A. Rams) 38-24-302-0-37t-3
Chris Miller (Atlanta) 24-14-170-0-71t-2

Not once in the seven-game series with Dallas had Tampa Bay secured a win but, in front of their home crowd, they overcame the early disappointment of Vinny Testaverde's first interception in five games, moving 57 yards to set up Steve Christie's 23-yard field goal. Towards the end of the first half, another 57-yard drive came to fruition when wide receiver Danny Peebles snared Testaverde's two-yard touchdown pass. Perhaps the Buccaneers were about to earn their first victory over Dallas.

Only 5:22 remained in the third quarter when the Cowboys made their first response, a Ken Willis field goal capitalizing on a fumble by Bucs running back John Harvey which had given Dallas possession 26 yards from the Tampa Bay end zone. With less than seven minutes to play, Cowboys cornerback Issiac Holt returned his second interception of the game 64 yards for a stunning touchdown. Yet it all seemed to have been for nought as, with just 1:56 left, Christie's 32-yard field goal took the Buccaneers three points clear. The stage was set.

Shouldering the responsibility, Cowboys quarterback Troy Aikman took charge. Passing on five consecutive downs, Aikman completed plays of 14 and 18 yards and then scrambled for 20, before hitting wide receiver Michael Irvin with a 28-yard strike for the game-winning points with a mere 23 seconds remaining.

RIGHT: Johnny Meads had 14 tackles, 1.5 sacks, forced three fumbles and returned an interception 32 yards in Houston's win.

The Road To Super Bowl XXV

For the third consecutive game, Buffalo had to rally for victory. After trailing the Jets 14–0, quarterback Jim Kelly gradually took control, passing for touchdowns on completions of 19, 14, 60 and 14 yards, the fourth giving Buffalo its first lead and clinching the win.

With Phil Simms going out with an ankle injury, little-used reserve quarterback Jeff Hostetler saved the day, throwing a 38-yard touchdown pass and setting up the Matt Bahr field goal which came as time expired.

Standings

AFC East	W	L	T	PF	PA	Pct.
Buffalo	5	1	0	160	126	.833
Miami	5	1	0	125	83	.833
Indianapolis	2	4	0	98	135	.333
N.Y. Jets	2	5	0	134	178	.286
New England	1	5	0	90	169	.167
AFC Central	**W**	**L**	**T**	**PF**	**PA**	**Pct.**
Cincinnati	5	2	0	188	166	.714
Houston	4	3	0	169	135	.571
Pittsburgh	3	4	0	109	128	.429
Cleveland	2	5	0	111	173	.286
AFC West	**W**	**L**	**T**	**PF**	**PA**	**Pct.**
L.A. Raiders	6	1	0	147	99	.857
Kansas City	4	3	0	167	114	.571
Denver	3	4	0	168	178	.429
Seattle	3	4	0	144	135	.429
San Diego	2	5	0	123	132	.286

NFC East	W	L	T	PF	PA	Pct.
N.Y. Giants	6	0	0	150	86	1.000
Washington	4	2	0	134	82	.667
Dallas	3	4	0	90	135	.429
Philadelphia	2	4	0	130	132	.333
Phoenix	2	4	0	79	141	.333
NFC Central	**W**	**L**	**T**	**PF**	**PA**	**Pct.**
Chicago**	5	1	0	142	75	.833
Tampa Bay	4	3	0	147	141	.571
Detroit**	2	4	0	141	169	.333
Green Bay**	2	4	0	103	146	.333
Minnesota**	1	5	0	140	135	.167

**Did not play on Week Seven

NFC West	W	L	T	PF	PA	Pct.
San Francisco	6	0	0	154	101	1.000
Atlanta	2	4	0	161	183	.333
L.A. Rams	2	4	0	164	173	.333
New Orleans	2	4	0	105	123	.333

Week Eight

American Football Conference

Buffalo 27 at New England 10
Miami 27 at Indianapolis 7
New York Jets 17 at Houston 12

National Football Conference

Chicago 31 at Phoenix 21
Detroit 27 at New Orleans 10
Minnesota 10 vs Green Bay 24 (at Milwaukee)
Philadelphia 21 at Dallas 20
Washington 10 at New York Giants 21

Interconference Games

Cincinnati 17 at Atlanta 38
Cleveland 17 at San Francisco 20
Los Angeles Rams 10 at Pittsburgh 41
Tampa Bay 10 at San Diego 41

Interconference Play

AFC 9 – NFC 9

Game of The Week
Cleveland 17 - San Francisco 20

For the San Francisco 49ers, it was all a matter of strolling through the regular season in preparation for the real thing in the playoffs. Though perhaps not with the unquestioned authority of a league champion, none the less they had won all six of their games. By contrast, the Browns were having difficulties. With only two wins from seven outings, they were coming off defeats to New Orleans and Cincinnati. Under those circumstances, a trip to San Francisco would not be the popular choice.

In the early going, much went as expected, with the Browns unable to generate any kind of momentum, although the 49ers could not take advantage. However, all that was to change early in the second quarter when the NFL's most dangerous partnership of quarterback Joe Montana and wide receiver Jerry Rice combined on a 14-yard scoring play. Three plays later, Browns wide receiver Webster Slaughter lost possession under the force of a tackle by 49ers cornerback Eric Davis and safety Ronnie Lott recovered possession. Within three minutes, fullback Tom Rathman's one-yard plunge took San Francisco into a 14–0 lead. Even when Cleveland did respond, on Jerry Kauric's 45-yard field goal, it was cancelled out by Mike Cofer's 40-yarder on the return drive.

Trailing by the score of 17–3, Browns starting quarterback Bernie Kosar was replaced by backup Mike Pagel and, although he too had a trying time, he was able to capitalize on a Felix Wright interception, using two plays to set up his 11-yard touchdown pass to Slaughter. Growing in confidence, he then marched the Browns 66 yards, rounding off with a four-yard touchdown pass to tight end Ozzie Newsome. With the scores level and only 1:10 remaining in the game, the unthinkable, victory over San Francisco, began to look possible.

But if there is one team in the entire NFL which is at its most dangerous when the chips are down, it is San Francisco. Lopping off 35 yards on one pass completion to wide receiver Mike Sherrard, Montana moved into field goal position with five seconds remaining, allowing Cofer to finish the job from 45 yards out.

The Road To Super Bowl XXV

Thurman Thomas rushed for 136 yards and a touchdown as Buffalo handed the modest New England Patriots their fifth straight defeat.

The Giants intercepted three passes by reserve quarterback Stan Humphries and it was one of these, returned 28 yards for a touchdown by cornerback Everson Walls, which put the issue beyond doubt as New York beat a tough Washington team for the second time in three weeks.

Cornerback Gill Byrd's two interceptions took his career total to a San Diego club-record 30.

Outstanding Individual Performances

100 Yards Rushing

Thurman Thomas (Buffalo) 22-136-26-1

100 Yards Pass Receiving

Anthony Carter (Minnesota) 9-141-49t-1
Robert Clark (Detroit) 6-127-42-1
Al Toon (N.Y. Jets) 7-119-42t-1
Jay Novacek (Dallas) 7-105-29t-1

Passing

Chris Miller (Atlanta) 18-13-124-0-17-2
Jim Kelly (Buffalo) 20-14-208-0-52-1
Bubby Brister (Pittsburgh) 24-15-161-1-40-4
Timm Rosenbach (Phoenix) 30-18-256-0-40t-2
Rodney Peete (Detroit) 25-16-246-0-42-1
Phil Simms (N.Y. Giants) 24-15-145-0-16-2
Warren Moon (Houston) 43-30-381-0-31-1

In making a key, 35-yard reception, 49ers wide receiver Mike Sherrard broke the same leg for the third time in his career.

Standings

AFC East	W	L	T	PF	PA	Pct.
Buffalo	6	1	0	187	136	.857
Miami	6	1	0	152	90	.857
N.Y. Jets	3	5	0	151	190	.375
Indianapolis	2	5	0	105	162	.286
New England	1	6	0	100	196	.143

AFC Central	W	L	T	PF	PA	Pct.
Cincinnati	5	3	0	205	204	.625
Houston	4	4	0	181	152	.500
Pittsburgh	4	4	0	150	138	.500
Cleveland	2	6	0	128	193	.250

AFC West	W	L	T	PF	PA	Pct.
L.A. Raiders**	6	1	0	147	99	.857
Kansas City**	4	3	0	167	114	.571
Denver**	3	4	0	168	178	.429
Seattle**	3	4	0	144	135	.429
San Diego	3	5	0	164	142	.375

**Did not play on Week Eight

NFC East	W	L	T	PF	PA	Pct.
N.Y. Giants	7	0	0	171	96	1.000
Washington	4	3	0	144	103	.571
Philadelphia	3	4	0	151	152	.429
Dallas	3	5	0	110	156	.375
Phoenix	2	5	0	100	172	.286

NFC Central	W	L	T	PF	PA	Pct.
Chicago	6	1	0	173	96	.857
Tampa Bay	4	4	0	157	182	.500
Detroit	3	4	0	168	179	.429
Green Bay	3	4	0	127	156	.429
Minnesota	1	6	0	150	159	.143

NFC West	W	L	T	PF	PA	Pct.
San Francisco	7	0	0	174	118	1.000
Atlanta	3	4	0	199	200	.429
L.A. Rams	2	5	0	174	214	.286
New Orleans	2	5	0	115	150	.286

Week Nine

American Football Conference

Buffalo 42 at Cleveland 0
Los Angeles Raiders 7 at Kansas City 9
San Diego 31 at Seattle 14

National Football Conference

Chicago 26 at Tampa Bay 6
San Francisco 24 at Green Bay 20
Washington 41 at Detroit 38 (OT)

Interconference Games

Atlanta 9 at Pittsburgh 21
Dallas 9 at New York Jets 24
Denver 22 at Minnesota 27
Houston 13 at Los Angeles Rams 17
New England 20 at Philadelphia 48
New Orleans 21 at Cincinnati 7
New York Giants 24 at Indianapolis 7
Phoenix 3 at Miami 23

Interconference Play

AFC 12 – NFC 14

Game of The Week
Washington 41 - Detroit 38 (Overtime)

Taking stock as they approached mid-term, both Detroit and Washington had grounds for optimism. Although standing at 3–4, the Lions might feel that they were untangling the complexities of their offensive system and could point to a Week-Eight, 27–10 win over a good New Orleans club. Washington were coming off a 21–10 loss to the division-leading Giants but, at 4–3, were the leaders of the chasing pack. For both teams, now was the time to raise the tempo. And that's what they did in a scoring spectacle which climaxed with just 5:50 remaining in overtime.

This game might have been renamed 'the tale of two quarterbacks', each one playing for the Redskins. First, there was Stan Humphries, the team's senior backup, called into action because of an injury to starter Mark Rypien. Humphries featured prominently in four touchdowns but, unfortunately, three of them were scored by the Lions. Two plays after an early interception of Humphries' pass, Detroit scored the opening touchdown. A second interception, returned directly into the end zone, helped the Lions towards a 28–14 halftime lead. And when, for the third time, an intercepted pass was converted into a touchdown, giving Detroit a 35–14 advantage, Redskins head coach Joe Gibbs felt that enough was enough. It was time to give third-stringer Jeff Rutledge a turn at the wheel.

But this veteran of 11 NFL seasons, who had been signed as a free agent in the preseason, would not settle for mere match practice. Instead, he unleashed a furious assault, both on his opponents and all sensible probability. With Rutledge the dominant force, the Redskins paused only to allow a Detroit field goal as they surged for 24 points, the crucial touchdown coming when Rutledge himself ran 12 yards to round off an 85-yard drive with just 18 seconds left, taking the game into overtime.

Playing with greater caution now, both teams punted before Rutledge again clicked into gear. Starting at his own ten-yard line, he passed for gains of four, 40, 11, six and eight yards, and ran twice to set up position for a field goal attempt. And wouldn't you know that he was the holder for Lohmiller's kick which split the uprights?

The Road To Super Bowl XXV

Ottis Anderson rushed for two touchdowns and quarterback Phil Simms returned from injury to complete 17 of 21 passes as the Giants dominated the Colts, for whom running back Eric Dickerson was held to 26 yards on nine carries.

Without needing to raise the pace, Buffalo dealt the Cleveland Browns their second shutout loss of the campaign, a defeat which would cost head coach Bud Carson his job. For the Bills, Thurman Thomas rushed for two touchdowns and caught an 11-yard pass for a third.

Art Monk was one of three Washington wide receivers to catch passes for more than 100 yards in the Redskins' overtime win.

Craig (Ironhead) Heyward eases behind a block on his way to 122 yards rushing in the Saints' victory over Cincinnati.

Outstanding Individual Performances

100 Yards Rushing

Randall Cunningham (Philadelphia) 8-124-52t-1
Craig Heyward (New Orleans) 19-122-39-1
Rueben Mayes (New Orleans) 30-115-14-1
Heath Sherman (Philadelphia) 24-113-17-0
Barry Sanders (Detroit) 10-100-45t-1

100 Yards Pass Receiving

Jerry Rice (San Francisco) 6-187-64t-1
Art Monk (Washington) 13-168-40-0
Anthony Carter (Minnesota) 5-146-56t-1
Ricky Sanders (Washington) 11-132-33-0
Gary Clark (Washington) 8-132-34t-1
Andre Reed (Buffalo) 7-122-43-0
Irving Fryar (New England) 4-115-38-1

Passing

Randall Cunningham (Philadelphia) 24-15-240-0-38-4
Bubby Brister (Pittsburgh) 17-11-216-0-66-2
John Elway (Denver) 10-8-88-0-37-1
Jim Kelly (Buffalo) 19-14-200-0-43-1
Dan Marino (Miami) 25-18-205-0-35-2
Joe Montana (San Francisco) 40-25-411-0-64t-3
Rodney Peete (Detroit) 17-8-135-0-33t-2
Don Majkowski (Green Bay) 33-22-274-0-37-2
Jim Harbaugh (Chicago) 23-14-213-0-38-1
Jeff Rutledge (Washington) 42-30-363-0-40-1

Standings

AFC East	W	L	T	PF	PA	Pct.
Buffalo	7	1	0	229	136	.875
Miami	7	1	0	175	93	.875
N.Y. Jets	4	5	0	175	199	.444
Indianapolis	2	6	0	112	186	.250
New England	1	7	0	120	244	.125
AFC Central	**W**	**L**	**T**	**PF**	**PA**	**Pct.**
Cincinnati	5	4	0	212	225	.556
Pittsburgh	5	4	0	171	147	.556
Houston	4	5	0	194	169	.444
Cleveland	2	7	0	128	235	.222
AFC West	**W**	**L**	**T**	**PF**	**PA**	**Pct.**
L.A. Raiders	6	2	0	154	108	.750
Kansas City	5	3	0	176	121	.625
San Diego	4	5	0	195	156	.444
Denver	3	5	0	190	205	.375
Seattle	3	5	0	158	166	.375

NFC East	W	L	T	PF	PA	Pct.
N.Y. Giants	8	0	0	195	103	1.000
Washington	5	3	0	185	141	.625
Philadelphia	4	4	0	199	172	.500
Dallas	3	6	0	119	180	.333
Phoenix	2	6	0	103	195	.250
NFC Central	**W**	**L**	**T**	**PF**	**PA**	**Pct.**
Chicago	7	1	0	199	102	.875
Tampa Bay	4	5	0	163	208	.444
Detroit	3	5	0	206	220	.375
Green Bay	3	5	0	147	180	.375
Minnesota	2	6	0	177	181	.250
NFC West	**W**	**L**	**T**	**PF**	**PA**	**Pct.**
San Francisco	8	0	0	198	138	1.000
Atlanta	3	5	0	208	221	.375
L.A. Rams	3	5	0	191	227	.375
New Orleans	3	5	0	136	157	.375

Week Ten

American Football Conference

Denver 7 at San Diego 19
Indianapolis 13 at New England 10
Miami 17 at New York Jets 3
Seattle 17 at Kansas City 16

National Football Conference

Atlanta 24 at Chicago 30
Minnesota 17 at Detroit 7
New York Giants 31 at Los Angeles Rams 7
San Francisco 24 at Dallas 6
Tampa Bay 7 at New Orleans 35
Washington 14 at Philadelphia 28

Interconference Games

Green Bay 29 at Los Angeles Raiders 16
Phoenix 14 at Buffalo 45

Interconference Play

AFC 13 – NFC 15

Game of The Week
Seattle 17 - Kansas City 16

Entering Week Ten, Kansas City had become a genuine force and, as evidence, could point to a Week-Nine victory over the division-leading Los Angeles Raiders whom the Chiefs now trailed by only one game. Seattle, on the other hand, were still seeking an identity. Having lost heavily the previous weekend to San Diego, the Seahawks shared last place in the division with the slumping Denver Broncos. Interestingly, though, three weeks earlier, they'd comfortably handled the Chiefs by the score of 19–7.

For Kansas City outside linebacker Derrick Thomas it was a career day as he set an NFL single-game record with seven sacks. The unlucky recipient of his attentions was Seattle quarterback Dave Krieg, an enigma, much maligned by Seahawks fans but who, year after year, always finds enough to fight off his challengers. The end-game came down to a personal battle between Krieg and Thomas.

Before the thrilling climax it was close all the way, with the Chiefs scoring first and leading 6–3 at half time. Seattle nosed ahead on wide receiver Jeff Chadwick's 54-yard touchdown reception from Krieg but Kansas City clawed back, drawing to within one point on Nick Lowery's third field goal, 12:14 into the third quarter. A little more than a minute later, the Chiefs regained the lead when a Krieg fumble, caused by Thomas's third sack of the day, was recovered in the end zone by nose tackle Dan Saleaumua. Approaching the end of a scoreless fourth quarter, the decision rested on the arm of Krieg.

Gaining possession on the Seattle 34-yard line with only 48 seconds remaining, he opened up, completing passes of 16 yards to running back John L. Williams and a 25-yarder to wide receiver Tommy Kane. On what had to be the final play of the contest, Krieg was forced to scramble but, ironically, this gave Paul Skansi, the intended receiver, the time he need to find space in the end zone. Barely evading the grasping arms of Thomas, Krieg delivered the ball 25 yards to Skansi for the touchdown which, with Norm Johnson's PAT, gave Seattle its one-point victory with no time showing on the clock.

The Road To Super Bowl XXV

In the Giants' most polished performance of the campaign thus far, quarterback Phil Simms was near the top of his form, calmly directing the offense for 31 points as the Rams were crushed. The Giants were now well into the best start to a season in their history.

Even though attempting just 16 passes, Jim Kelly completed four for touchdowns as the Bills cruised to a 45–14 win over Phoenix. But they still were locked in a tie with Miami in the AFC East.

Kansas City outside linebacker Derrick Thomas plots the next sack on his NFL record-breaking day.

Heath Sherman rushed a club-record 35 times and caught two touchdown passes as the Eagles won their third straight game.

Outstanding Individual Performances

100 Yards Rushing
Craig Heyward (New Orleans) 20-155-47t-2
Heath Sherman (Philadelphia) 35-124-22-0
Marion Butts (San Diego) 16-114-45-0
Thurman Thomas (Buffalo) 26-112-43-0

100 Yards Pass Receiving
Jerry Rice (San Francisco) 12-147-37-1
Wendell Davis (Chicago) 5-105-51-1

Passing
Jim Kelly (Buffalo) 16-11-165-1-49-4
Dave Krieg (Seattle) 23-16-306-0-54t-2
Phil Simms (N.Y. Giants) 26-19-213-0-35-1

Standings

AFC East	W	L	T	PF	PA	Pct.
Buffalo	8	1	0	274	150	.889
Miami	8	1	0	192	96	.889
N.Y. Jets	4	6	0	178	216	.400
Indianapolis	3	6	0	125	196	.333
New England	1	8	0	130	257	.111

AFC Central	W	L	T	PF	PA	Pct.
Cincinnati**	5	4	0	212	225	.556
Pittsburgh**	5	4	0	171	147	.556
Houston**	4	5	0	194	169	.444
Cleveland**	2	7	0	128	235	.222

**Did not play on Week Ten

AFC West	W	L	T	PF	PA	Pct.
L.A. Raiders	6	3	0	170	137	.667
Kansas City	5	4	0	192	138	.556
San Diego	5	5	0	214	163	.500
Seattle	4	5	0	175	182	.444
Denver	3	6	0	197	224	.333

NFC East	W	L	T	PF	PA	Pct.
N.Y. Giants	9	0	0	226	110	1.000
Philadelphia	5	4	0	227	186	.556
Washington	5	4	0	199	169	.556
Dallas	3	7	0	125	204	.300
Phoenix	2	7	0	117	240	.222

NFC Central	W	L	T	PF	PA	Pct.
Chicago	8	1	0	229	126	.889
Green Bay	4	5	0	176	196	.444
Tampa Bay	4	6	0	170	243	.400
Detroit	3	6	0	213	237	.333
Minnesota	3	6	0	194	188	.333

NFC West	W	L	T	PF	PA	Pct.
San Francisco	9	0	0	222	144	1.000
New Orleans	4	5	0	171	164	.444
Atlanta	3	6	0	232	251	.333
L.A. Rams	3	6	0	198	258	.333

Week Eleven

American Football Conference

Houston 35 at Cleveland 23
Los Angeles Raiders 13 at Miami 10
New England 0 at Buffalo 14
New York Jets 14 at Indianapolis 17
Pittsburgh 3 at Cincinnati 27
San Diego 10 at Kansas City 27

National Football Conference

Dallas 24 at Los Angeles Rams 21
Detroit 0 at New York Giants 20
Green Bay 24 at Phoenix 21
New Orleans 17 at Washington 31
Philadelphia 24 at Atlanta 23
Tampa Bay 7 at San Francisco 31

Interconference Games

Chicago 16 at Denver 13 (OT)
Minnesota 24 at Seattle 21

Interconference Play

AFC 13 – NFC 17

Middle linebacker Mike Singletary had 20 tackles and recovered a fumble in the Bears' overtime win against Denver.

Game of The Week
Philadelphia 24 - Atlanta 23

The Philadelphia Eagles were on a roll. Their third consecutive victory the previous weekend had been all the more sweet for having been at the expense of divisional rival Washington, bringing the two teams level. Atlanta's hopes of a playoff spot hung by a thread, and a thin one at that. In all common sense the Falcons weren't going to be in postseason competition. But they had achieved something under new head coach Jerry Glanville. They were now seen as fighters who'd battle to the end.

Atlanta began well, using their 'Red Gun' offense to drive 72 yards on the opening possession, only to turn the ball over on downs after being at second-and-three at the Philadelphia four-yard line. In the second quarter, however, the Falcons made no mistake on a 73-yard march culminating in Tracy Johnson's one-yard touchdown plunge. Turning to play-action passes in the attempt to solve the problems posed by the Atlanta defense, Eagles quarterback Randall Cunningham completed passes of 33 and 27 yards in a 79-yard dash for tight end Keith Jackson's short-yardage touchdown reception.

However, the Falcons did not fold. Rather, they were even more determined in setting up Greg Davis field goals of 53, 46 and 28 yards. Even when Cunningham at his best subsequently threw nerve-testing touchdown passes of 17 and 30 yards, Atlanta were still able to fight back, regaining the lead at 23–21 on wide receiver Andre Rison's 23-yard touchdown catch. However, on their next possession, the Falcons were forced to punt, with the Eagles taking over in decent field position at their own 47. Here was the key to the result.

Needing only to move into field goal range and with time not a critical factor, Cunningham used all his experience to advance the ball just 24 yards in eight plays, and, from 46 yards out, placekicker Roger Ruzek took Philadelphia into a one-point lead. It held up for the remaining one minute and 45 seconds, giving the Eagles the best possible tonic for their Week-Twelve confrontation with the undefeated New York Giants.

The Road To Super Bowl XXV

Phil Simms completed 13 of 18 passes for 170 yards and a pair of touchdowns as the Giants dominated the dangerous Detroit Lions. With their record for the campaign now 10–0 and with a four-game lead in the NFC East, the Giants were virtually assured of a playoff spot.

Against the 1–8 Patriots, Buffalo needed a pair of touchdowns from Thurman Thomas, the second coming on an 80-yard run, for a surprisingly hard-fought victory.

Dallas placekicker Ken Willis delivers the ball 23 yards, straight and true, to defeat the Rams.

Outstanding Individual Performances

100 Yards Rushing

Thurman Thomas (Buffalo) 22-165-80t-2
Earnest Byner (Washington) 26-116-22-0
Neal Anderson (Chicago) 28-111-11-0
James Brooks (Cincinnati) 20-105-21-0
Johnny Johnson (Phoenix) 15-103-41-0
Cleveland Gary (L.A. Rams) 24-103-48-3

100 Yards Pass Receiving

Sterling Sharpe (Green Bay) 10-157-54t-1
Gary Clark (Washington) 8-131-34-2
Eric Martin (New Orleans) 10-131-25-0
Curtis Duncan (Houston) 7-130-37t-1
Emmitt Smith (Dallas) 4-117-57-0
Ernie Jones (Phoenix) 7-117-25t-2
Webster Slaughter (Cleveland) 6-104-50-0
Roy Green (Phoenix) 4-102-54-1
Al Toon (N.Y. Jets) 7-100-28-0

Passing

Warren Moon (Houston) 32-24-322-0-46t-5
Phil Simms (N.Y. Giants) 18-13-170-0-57t-2
Mark Rypien (Washington) 38-26-311-0-35-4
Randall Cunningham (Philadelphia) 27-16-214-0-33-3
Jeff George (Indianapolis) 22-14-249-1-50-2
Steve DeBerg (Kansas City) 24-11-171-0-90t-3
Timm Rosenbach (Phoenix) 30-17-285-1-54-3
Troy Aikman (Dallas) 32-17-303-1-61t-3

Standings

AFC East	W	L	T	PF	PA	Pct.
Buffalo	9	1	0	288	150	.900
Miami	8	2	0	202	109	.800
Indianapolis	4	6	0	142	210	.400
N.Y. Jets	4	7	0	192	233	.364
New England	1	9	0	130	271	.100
AFC Central	**W**	**L**	**T**	**PF**	**PA**	**Pct.**
Cincinnati	6	4	0	239	228	.600
Houston	5	5	0	229	192	.500
Pittsburgh	5	5	0	174	174	.500
Cleveland	2	8	0	151	270	.200
AFC West	**W**	**L**	**T**	**PF**	**PA**	**Pct.**
L.A. Raiders	7	3	0	183	147	.700
Kansas City	6	4	0	219	148	.600
San Diego	5	6	0	224	190	.455
Seattle	4	6	0	196	206	.400
Denver	3	7	0	210	240	.300

NFC East	W	L	T	PF	PA	Pct.
N.Y. Giants	10	0	0	246	110	1.000
Philadelphia	6	4	0	251	209	.600
Washington	6	4	0	230	186	.600
Dallas	4	7	0	149	225	.364
Phoenix	2	8	0	138	264	.200
NFC Central	**W**	**L**	**T**	**PF**	**PA**	**Pct.**
Chicago	9	1	0	245	139	.900
Green Bay	5	5	0	200	217	.500
Minnesota	4	6	0	218	209	.400
Tampa Bay	4	7	0	177	274	.364
Detroit	3	7	0	213	257	.300
NFC West	**W**	**L**	**T**	**PF**	**PA**	**Pct.**
San Francisco	10	0	0	253	151	1.000
New Orleans	4	6	0	188	195	.400
Atlanta	3	7	0	255	275	.300
L.A. Rams	3	7	0	219	282	.300

Week Twelve

American Football Conference

Buffalo 24 at Houston 27
Indianapolis 34 at Cincinnati 20
Kansas City 27 at Los Angeles Raiders 24
Miami 30 at Cleveland 13
Pittsburgh 24 at New York Jets 7
Seattle 13 at San Diego 10 (OT)

National Football Conference

Atlanta 7 at New Orleans 10
Chicago 13 at Minnesota 41
Los Angeles Rams 28 at San Francisco 17
New York Giants 13 at Philadelphia 31
Tampa Bay 10 vs Green Bay 20 (at Milwaukee)
Washington 17 at Dallas 27 (Thanksgiving)

Interconference Games

Denver 27 at Detroit 40 (Thanksgiving)
New England 14 at Phoenix 34

Interconference Play

AFC 13 – NFC 19

Game of The Week
Kansas City 27 - Los Angeles Raiders 24

It was just like the old days, the 1960s, when Kansas City and the then-Oakland Raiders fought out their own private war twice each year. It is a series which since then has seen many bitterly fought confrontations but not often with both teams neck-and-neck in the race for the divisional title. On Week Nine, Kansas City had beaten the Raiders in a close game decided by a pair of Raiders errors. Now, the Chiefs travelled to the Los Angeles Coliseum knowing that a win, while moving them into equal-first place in the division, also would bring the priceless advantage in the event of an end-of-season tie breaker. A win for the Raiders would take them two games clear and leave them in excellent shape to free-wheel into the playoffs.

History didn't take long to repeat itself as, once again, two turnovers led to scores. The first error came early in the second half when a fumble by quarterback

Cleveland Gary scored three touchdowns as the Rams halted San Francisco's NFL-record-equalling string of victories at 18.

Outstanding Individual Performances

100 Yards Rushing
Barry Sanders (Detroit) 23-147-23-1
Eric Dickerson (Indianapolis) 22-143-43-1
Anthony Thompson (Phoenix) 28-136-27-1
Emmitt Smith (Dallas) 23-132-48t-2
Marion Butts (San Diego) 28-128-19-0
Lorenzo White (Houston) 18-125-22-1

100 Yards Pass Receiving
Flipper Anderson (L.A. Rams) 8-149-53-0
Keith Byars (Philadelphia) 8-128-54-0
John L. Williams (Seattle) 9-110-60-0
Drew Hill (Houston) 6-102-43-0

Passing
Warren Moon (Houston) 22-16-300-0-43-2
Rich Gannon (Minnesota) 19-12-146-0-22t-3
Steve DeBerg (Kansas City) 21-12-149-0-24-3
Jeff George (Indianapolis) 31-21-251-0-75-3
Anthony Dilweg (Green Bay) 22-13-199-0-46-2
Dan Marino (Miami) 29-16-245-0-35t-2
Bob Gagliano (Detroit) 30-18-248-1-43t-3
Randall Cunningham (Philadelphia) 31-17-229-0-54-2
Tommy Hodson (New England) 29-17-182-0-22t-2

Jay Schroeder was recovered by Kansas City linebacker Derrick Thomas. Two plays later, Bill Jones caught an 11-yard touchdown pass. In the first half, Schroeder's bombs had brought reward and he quickly set about repairing the damage, passing for 30 and 20 yards to set up the game-tying touchdown by running back Marcus Allen. Late in the third quarter, Kansas City nosed into a 20–17 lead, but it looked in jeopardy as Schroeder marched the Raiders down to the Kansas City 27-yard line. However, a second fumble by the luckless quarterback would turn out to be critical. Not only did it negate a possible score for the home team but, also, Chiefs quarterback Steve DeBerg counterpunched with a 73-yard drive culminating in Jones' second 11-yard scoring catch.

Under pressure now, Los Angeles responded with Allen running in smoothly for his third touchdown of the game. But the knockout blow never materialized as Kansas City were not troubled in holding firm the rest of the way. There could now be few who doubted that the Chiefs were truly back in business.

The Road To Super Bowl XXV

The Giants' dreams of a perfect season ended in defeat to a Philadelphia club for which quarterback Randall Cunningham was in peerless form. However, even in defeat, results elsewhere meant that the Giants became the first NFL club to qualify for the playoffs.

On Monday evening, the Bills were unable to solve the problems presented by the Oilers' run-and-shoot offense mixed in with the rushing of Lorenzo White. The loss dropped them back into a tie with Miami.

Unheralded fullback Bill Jones, originally a 1989 12th-round draft pick who had been waived and resigned as a 1990 free agent, had his day in the sun at the Los Angeles Coliseum, catching two 11-yard touchdown passes from Steve DeBerg as the Chiefs confirmed their superiority over the Raiders.

Standings

AFC East	W	L	T	PF	PA	Pct.
Buffalo	9	2	0	312	177	.818
Miami	9	2	0	232	122	.818
Indianapolis	5	6	0	176	230	.455
N.Y. Jets	4	8	0	199	257	.333
New England	1	10	0	144	305	.091
AFC Central	**W**	**L**	**T**	**PF**	**PA**	**Pct.**
Cincinnati	6	5	0	259	262	.545
Houston	6	5	0	256	216	.545
Pittsburgh	6	5	0	198	181	.545
Cleveland	2	9	0	164	300	.182
AFC West	**W**	**L**	**T**	**PF**	**PA**	**Pct.**
Kansas City	7	4	0	246	172	.636
L.A. Raiders	7	4	0	207	174	.636
Seattle	5	6	0	209	216	.455
San Diego	5	7	0	234	203	.417
Denver	3	8	0	237	280	.273

NFC East	W	L	T	PF	PA	Pct.
N.Y. Giants*	10	1	0	259	141	.909
Philadelphia	7	4	0	282	222	.636
Washington	6	5	0	247	213	.545
Dallas	5	7	0	176	242	.417
Phoenix	3	8	0	172	278	.273

*Clinched Playoff Spot

NFC Central	W	L	T	PF	PA	Pct.
Chicago	9	2	0	258	180	.818
Green Bay	6	5	0	220	227	.545
Minnesota	5	6	0	259	222	.455
Detroit	4	7	0	253	284	.364
Tampa Bay	4	8	0	187	294	.333
NFC West	**W**	**L**	**T**	**PF**	**PA**	**Pct.**
San Francisco	10	1	0	270	179	.909
New Orleans	5	6	0	198	202	.455
L.A. Rams	4	7	0	247	299	.364
Atlanta	3	8	0	262	285	.273

Week Thirteen

American Football Conference

Cincinnati 16 at Pittsburgh 12
Houston 10 at Seattle 13 (OT)
Kansas City 37 at New England 7
Los Angeles Raiders 23 at Denver 20
New York Jets 17 at San Diego 38

National Football Conference

Atlanta 17 at Tampa Bay 23
Detroit 17 at Chicago 23 (OT)
Green Bay 7 at Minnesota 23
New Orleans 13 at Dallas 17
New York Giants 3 at San Francisco 7

Interconference Games

Indianapolis 17 at Phoenix 20
Los Angeles Rams 38 at Cleveland 23
Miami 20 at Washington 42
Philadelphia 23 at Buffalo 30

Interconference Play

AFC 14 – NFC 22

Game of The Week
New Orleans 13 - Dallas 17

Dallas were 5–7 while New Orleans had the slide-rule advantage at 5–6. Ordinarily, this game would have been dismissed as a side show. Yet it had been a curious feature of the 1990 campaign, thus far, that while the destinations of the NFC divisional titles were all but established, the race for the three wild-card spots was very much alive. After a poor start to the season, back-to-back wins over the Rams and Washington had thrust the Cowboys into the picture. The Saints had won only two of their first seven games but they, too, were gathering momentum and, the previous week, had rallied for victory against Atlanta. Adding spice to the mixture, Cowboys quarterback Troy Aikman would be coming face to face with his erstwhile rival within the club, Steve Walsh, who had been traded to New Orleans earlier in the campaign.

In the opening exchanges, Aikman did not fare well, completing just four of ten passes for 29 yards in the

San Francisco defensive end Kevin Fagan sacks Giants quarterback Phil Simms to clinch the 49ers' victory.

Outstanding Individual Performances

100 Yards Rushing
Marion Butts (San Diego) 26-159-52-2
Earnest Byner (Washington) 32-157-21-3
Bo Jackson (L.A. Raiders) 13-117-62t-2
Mike Rozier (Atlanta) 23-115-13-1
Barry Word (Kansas City) 19-112-18-0

100 Yards Pass Receiving
James Lofton (Buffalo) 5-174-71-1
Stephone Paige (Kansas City) 7-151-86t-1
Willie Drewrey (Tampa Bay) 2-119-89t-1
Fred Barnett (Philadelphia) 2-112-95t-1

Passing
Steve DeBerg (Kansas City) 21-15-331-0-86t-2
Jim Everett (L.A. Rams) 29-22-261-0-24-4
Mark Rypien (Washington) 28-21-245-1-47-3
Randall Cunningham (Philadelphia) 25-15-231-1-95t-3
Jim Kelly (Buffalo) 32-19-334-1-71-3
Troy Aikman (Dallas) 21-15-177-0-45-1

entire first half. By contrast, Walsh was impressive, marching the Saints 89 yards in 13 plays, culminating in the Rueben Mayes 15-yard touchdown run which gave New Orleans a 10–0 halftime lead.

Perhaps it was head coach Jimmy Johnson's words of encouragement which did the trick but, after the break, Aikman went to the air in style, completing a 45-yard bomb in a drive climaxed by running back Emmitt Smith's one-yard plunge. Walsh answered in part, drilling a 22-yard pass before handing over to placekicker Morten Andersen, whose 50-yard field goal padded the Saints' lead to 13–7. Undaunted, Aikman once again cranked the Dallas machine into gear, combining with wide receiver Michael Irvin on a classy, 80-yard drive which came to fruition with Aikman's five-yard pass to Daryl Johnston.

It was by only one point but, for the first time, Dallas enjoyed the advantage. But with it came the pressure of defending against a team which could throw caution to the wind. The Cowboys' defense was up to the task, which was eased when placekicker Ken Willis landed a late, 47-yard field goal.

The Road To Super Bowl XXV

Jim Kelly touchdown passes of 63, 56 and four yards, all in the first quarter, threatened to blow the visiting Eagles out of the stadium. But in the end, the Bills needed a pair of Scott Norwood field goals to enhance the margin of comfort.

The much-anticipated clash between the NFL leaders was a disappointment, with the 49ers scoring the only touchdown in a narrow victory. Two late thrusts by the Giants were repelled by outstanding San Francisco defense.

LEFT: James Lofton moved up to third on the NFL's all-time list for receiving yardage with a big game against the Eagles.

Standings

AFC East	**W**	**L**	**T**	**PF**	**PA**	**Pct.**
Buffalo	10	2	0	342	200	.833
Miami	9	3	0	252	164	.750
Indianapolis	5	7	0	193	250	.417
N.Y. Jets	4	9	0	216	295	.308
New England	1	11	0	151	342	.083

AFC Central	**W**	**L**	**T**	**PF**	**PA**	**Pct.**
Cincinnati	7	5	0	275	274	.583
Houston	6	6	0	266	229	.500
Pittsburgh	6	6	0	210	197	.500
Cleveland	2	10	0	187	338	.167

AFC West	**W**	**L**	**T**	**PF**	**PA**	**Pct.**
Kansas City	8	4	0	283	179	.667
L.A. Raiders	8	4	0	230	194	.667
Seattle	6	6	0	222	226	.500
San Diego	6	7	0	272	220	.462
Denver	3	9	0	257	303	.250

NFC East	**W**	**L**	**T**	**PF**	**PA**	**Pct.**
N.Y. Giants**	10	2	0	262	148	.833
Philadelphia	7	5	0	305	252	.583
Washington	7	5	0	289	233	.583
Dallas	6	7	0	193	255	.462
Phoenix	4	8	0	192	295	.333

**Clinched Playoff Spot

NFC Central	**W**	**L**	**T**	**PF**	**PA**	**Pct.**
Chicago*	10	2	0	281	197	.833
Green Bay	6	6	0	227	250	.500
Minnesota	6	6	0	282	229	.500
Tampa Bay	5	8	0	210	311	.385
Detroit	4	8	0	270	307	.333

*Division Champion

NFC West	**W**	**L**	**T**	**PF**	**PA**	**Pct.**
San Francisco*	11	1	0	277	182	.917
L.A. Rams	5	7	0	285	322	.417
New Orleans	5	7	0	211	219	.417
Atlanta	3	9	0	279	308	.250

*Division Champion

Week Fourteen

American Football Conference
Buffalo 31 at Indianapolis 7
Cleveland 14 at Houston 58
Denver 20 at Kansas City 31
New England 3 at Pittsburgh 24

National Football Conference
Chicago 9 at Washington 10
Minnesota 15 at New York Giants 23
New Orleans 24 at Los Angeles Rams 20
Phoenix 24 at Atlanta 13

Interconference Games
Los Angeles Raiders 38 at Detroit 31
Philadelphia 20 at Miami 23 (OT)
San Francisco 20 at Cincinnati 17 (OT)
Seattle 20 vs Green Bay 14 (at Milwaukee)

Interconference Play
AFC 17 – NFC 23

Roger Craig led a potent 49ers' ground game which gained 202 yards against the Bengals.

Game of The Week
Chicago 9 - Washington 10

By Week Fourteen the Chicago Bears had clinched the title in the NFC Central division but there remained work to do. Their next task was to ensure qualification for the playoffs as one of the NFC's two senior division winners, thus earning home-field advantage for part or all of their postseason involvement. Trailing the Giants by three games, for Washington hopes of a division title were unrealistic, but, as equal front runners in the race for a wild-card spot, they couldn't afford a slip. And with the pressure on, who fancies playing the Chicago Bears?

The game was close throughout and, while the defenses did not dominate, they surfaced at key moments. For Washington quarterback Mark Rypien there were five such moments, all resulting in pass interceptions, three of them by Chicago rookie free safety Mark Carrier. Carrier's first steal foiled a potential touchdown pass and, with that possession, the Bears marched 69 yards for a Kevin Butler 29-yard field goal. In the second quarter, Carrier's interception and return started Chicago on a 61-yard march for Butler's 23-yard field goal. Would you believe that, on the next Washington possession, Donnell Woolford intercepted to set up yet another field goal?

A less-composed head coach might have benched Rypien, but the former Washington State star was at the controls in the second half when the Redskins offered their response. Midway through the third quarter, after Rypien had completed a critical third-and-15 pass to Art Monk, wide receiver Gary Clark held on to an eight-yarder for a touchdown. With the Bears still leading by two points, in possession at their own 36-yard line and the clock winding down in the final quarter, tragically for Chicago, a Brad Muster fumble was recovered by Redskins free safety Todd Bowles. Little over two minutes remained in the game when Washington placekicker Chip Lohmiller slotted a 35-yard field goal to seal the victory. It had been a triumph for faith and perseverance.

The Road To Super Bowl XXV
The Colts were held to just 12 first-downs while Thurman Thomas gained 167 dual-purpose yards and scored two touchdowns as Buffalo dominated throughout to earn at least a wild-card spot in the playoffs.

Against Minnesota, the Giants took time to find their rhythm and trailed 15–10 with one quarter remaining. However, two Matt Bahr field goals, each set up by Giants interceptions, either side of Ottis Anderson's two-yard touchdown run, brought New York victory and, with it, the NFC Eastern division title.

Outstanding Individual Performances

00 Yards Rushing
- Barry Sanders (Detroit) 25-176-35t-2
- Bo Jackson (L.A. Raiders) 18-129-55t-1
- Earnest Byner (Washington) 28-121-18-0
- Merril Hoge (Pittsburgh) 19-117-41t-2
- Lorenzo White (Houston) 18-116-12-4
- Derrick Fenner (Seattle) 20-112-36-1
- Gill Fenerty (New Orleans) 10-104-60t-1

100 Yards Pass Receiving
- Flipper Anderson (L.A. Rams) 5-123-44-0
- Henry Ellard (L.A. Rams) 5-107-42t-1
- Ricky Proehl (Phoenix) 6-102-45t-1
- Jerry Rice (San Francisco) 8-101-29-0
- Willie Gault (L.A. Raiders) 3-101-68t-1

Passing
- Steve DeBerg (Kansas City) 27-18-254-0-49t-3
- Cody Carlson (Houston) 13-11-92-0-13-1
- Jim Kelly (Buffalo) 26-18-261-0-63-2
- Warren Moon (Houston) 25-17-190-0-24-2
- Blair Kiel (Green Bay) 31-23-198-0-17-2
- Jay Schroeder (L.A. Raiders)19-12-195-2-68t-3
- John Elway (Denver) 36-24-328-1-27-2

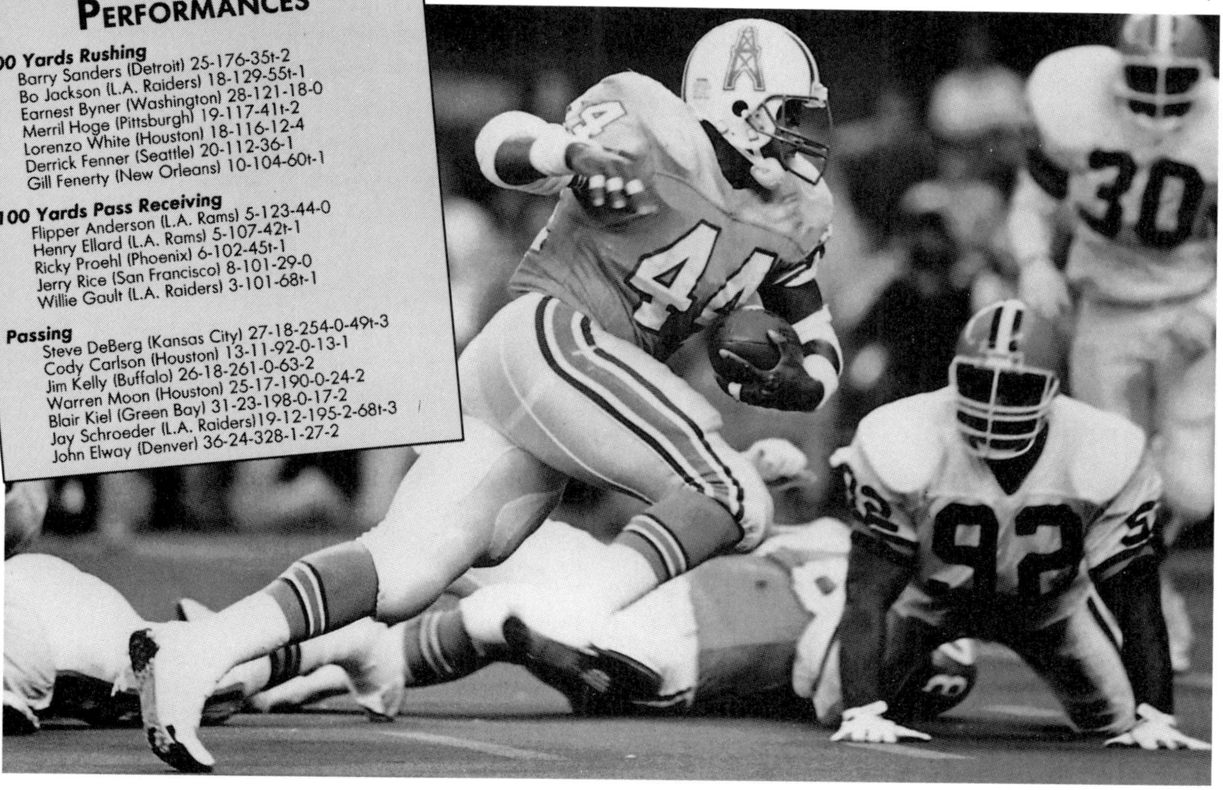

Running back Lorenzo White led the Oilers' rout of Cleveland.

Standings

AFC East	W	L	T	PF	PA	Pct.
Buffalo**	11	2	0	373	207	.846
Miami**	10	3	0	275	184	.769
Indianapolis	5	8	0	200	281	.385
N.Y. Jets***	4	9	0	216	295	.308
New England	1	12	0	154	366	.077

**Clinched Playoff Spot
***Did not play on Week Fourteen

AFC Central	W	L	T	PF	PA	Pct.
Cincinnati	7	6	0	292	294	.538
Houston	7	6	0	324	243	.538
Pittsburgh	7	6	0	234	200	.538
Cleveland	2	11	0	201	396	.154

AFC West	W	L	T	PF	PA	Pct.
Kansas City	9	4	0	314	199	.692
L.A. Raiders	9	4	0	268	225	.692
Seattle	7	6	0	242	240	.538
San Diego***	6	7	0	272	220	.462
Denver	3	10	0	277	334	.231

***Did not play on Week Fourteen

NFC East	W	L	T	PF	PA	Pct.
N.Y. Giants*	11	2	0	285	163	.846
Washington	8	5	0	299	242	.615
Philadelphia	7	6	0	325	275	.538
Dallas***	6	7	0	193	255	.462
Phoenix	5	8	0	216	308	.385

*Division Champion
***Did not play on Week Fourteen

NFC Central	W	L	T	PF	PA	Pct.
Chicago*	10	3	0	290	207	.769
Green Bay	6	7	0	241	270	.462
Minnesota	6	7	0	297	252	.462
Tampa Bay***	5	8	0	210	311	.385
Detroit	4	9	0	301	345	.308

*Division Champion
***Did not play on Week Fourteen

NFC West	W	L	T	PF	PA	Pct.
San Francisco*	12	1	0	297	199	.923
New Orleans	6	7	0	235	239	.462
L.A. Rams	5	8	0	305	346	.385
Atlanta	3	10	0	292	332	.231

*Division Champion

Week Fifteen

American Football Conference

Cincinnati 7 at Los Angeles Raiders 24
Houston 27 at Kansas City 10
Indianapolis 29 at New York Jets 21
San Diego 10 at Denver 20
Seattle 17 at Miami 24

National Football Conference

Chicago 21 at Detroit 38
Green Bay 0 at Philadelphia 31
Minnesota 13 at Tampa Bay 26
Phoenix 10 at Dallas 41
San Francisco 26 at Los Angeles Rams 10

Interconference Games

Atlanta 10 at Cleveland 13
Buffalo 17 at New York Giants 13
Pittsburgh 9 at New Orleans 6
Washington 25 at New England 10

Interconference Play

AFC 20 – NFC 24

The Road To Super Bowl XXV - Game of The Week
Buffalo 17 - New York Giants 13

Entering Week Fifteen, both the Giants and Buffalo were assured of playoff spots but there was still a great deal at stake. The Bills had an eye on the Miami Dolphins, their Week Sixteen opponents in a game which almost certainly would decide the destiny of the title in the AFC East. The Giants, who had clinched the NFC Eastern division title, were looking for the icing on the cake, namely, one of the NFC's top two qualifying spots and the playoff advantages which would come with it.

In one of their most inspired performances of the campaign, the Bills came away with the taste of victory, bitter-sweet in that starting quarterback Jim Kelly suffered knee ligament and cartilage damage which was certain to keep him out until the playoffs. For the Giants, defeat was all the more disheartening for the loss of their starting quarterback, Phil Simms, whose third-quarter foot injury gave every sign of ending his season. For both clubs, then, backup strength was put to the test.

It had become a feature of the 1990 New York Giants that their style of play almost certainly meant that they would dominate the time of possession. And this was the case against Buffalo, when they were in control of the ball for one second short of 38 minutes. In addition, they registered 20 first-downs to Buffalo's 13 and outgained the Bills by 313 net yards to 264. However, just four times were the Giants able to penetrate the Bills 20-yard line, coming away with the opening touchdown on Ottis Anderson's fourth-down one-yard run and a pair of Matt Bahr field goals, the second of which came with Jeff Hostetler in at quarterback.

For Buffalo, reserve quarterback Frank Reich came on towards the end of the first half with the Bills holding a 14–10 lead. He was still not attuned when Bahr's second field goal trimmed the margin to one point, and the omens were not good when he was sacked on the

Warren Moon carved up the Chiefs with the second-highest passing yardage total (527) in NFL history.

very first play of the answering drive. Defiantly he responded with a 43-yard completion to wide receiver Don Beebe, and he would complete four more passes in the drive to set up Scott Norwood's 29-yard field goal. The Buffalo defense did the rest, keeping the Giants at bay and, finally, slamming the door when Hostetler's fourth-and-ten pass from the Buffalo 26-yard line went to ground.

Buffalo's Jim Kelly (#12) was one of five quarterbacks to be sidelined with injury on this fateful weekend.

Outstanding Individual Performances

100 Yards Rushing
Earnest Byner (Washington) 39-149-20-1
Dexter Carter (San Francisco) 13-124-74t-1
Eric Dickerson (Indianapolis) 28-117-15-2
Bo Jackson (L.A. Raiders) 8-117-88-0
Vinny Testaverde (Tampa Bay) 7-105-48t-1
Rodney Hampton (N.Y. Giants) 21-105-41-0
Emmitt Smith (Dallas) 24-103-11t-4
Neal Anderson (Chicago) 22-100-14-0

100 Yards Pass Receiving
Haywood Jeffires (Houston) 9-245-87t-1
Tommy Kane (Seattle) 10-162-25-0
Hassan Jones (Minnesota) 7-162-75t-1
Ronnie Harmon (San Diego) 8-116-30-0
Fred Barnett (Philadelphia) 5-108-47-0
Anthony Carter (Minnesota) 8-106-23-0
Jerry Rice (San Francisco) 5-104-60t-1
Andre Rison (Atlanta) 6-100-40-0

Passing
Jim Kelly (Buffalo) 11-7-115-0-48-1
Jay Schroeder (L.A. Raiders) 20-10-163-0-44t-3
Rodney Peete (Detroit) 27-18-316-2-68t-4
Warren Moon (Houston) 45-27-527-0-87t-3
John Elway (Denver) 29-18-248-0-63-2

Standings

AFC East	W	L	T	PF	PA	Pct.
Buffalo**	12	2	0	390	220	.857
Miami**	11	3	0	299	201	.786
Indianapolis	6	8	0	229	302	.429
N.Y. Jets	4	10	0	237	324	.286
New England	1	13	0	164	391	.071

**Clinched Playoff Spot

AFC Central	W	L	T	PF	PA	Pct.
Houston	8	6	0	351	253	.571
Pittsburgh	8	6	0	243	206	.571
Cincinnati	7	7	0	299	318	.500
Cleveland	3	11	0	214	406	.214

AFC West	W	L	T	PF	PA	Pct.
L.A. Raiders**	10	4	0	292	232	.714
Kansas City	9	5	0	324	226	.643
Seattle	7	7	0	259	264	.500
San Diego	6	8	0	282	240	.429
Denver	4	10	0	297	344	.286

**Clinched Playoff Spot

NFC East	W	L	T	PF	PA	Pct.
N.Y. Giants*	11	3	0	298	180	.786
Washington**	9	5	0	324	252	.643
Philadelphia**	8	6	0	356	275	.571
Dallas	7	7	0	234	265	.500
Phoenix	5	9	0	226	349	.357

*Division Champion
**Clinched Playoff Spot

NFC Central	W	L	T	PF	PA	Pct.
Chicago*	10	4	0	311	245	.714
Green Bay	6	8	0	241	301	.429
Minnesota	6	8	0	310	278	.429
Tampa Bay	6	8	0	236	324	.429
Detroit	5	9	0	339	366	.357

*Division Champion

NFC West	W	L	T	PF	PA	Pct.
San Francisco*	13	1	0	323	209	.929
New Orleans	6	8	0	241	248	.429
L.A. Rams	5	9	0	315	372	.357
Atlanta	3	11	0	302	345	.214

*Division Champion

Week Sixteen

American Football Conference

Cleveland 0 at Pittsburgh 35
Denver 12 at Seattle 17
Houston 20 at Cincinnati 40
Kansas City 24 at San Diego 21
Miami 14 at Buffalo 24
New England 7 at New York Jets 42

National Football Conference

Dallas 3 at Philadelphia 17
Detroit 24 at Green Bay 17
Los Angeles Rams 13 at Atlanta 20
New Orleans 13 at San Francisco 10
New York Giants 24 at Phoenix 21
Tampa Bay 14 at Chicago 27

Interconference Games

Los Angeles Raiders 28 at Minnesota 24
Washington 28 at Indianapolis 35

Interconference Play

AFC 22 – NFC 24

Game of The Week
Houston 20 - Cincinnati 40

Just two games remained and the Houston Oilers were locked in a tie with Pittsburgh for first place in the AFC Central division. But they were coming to the boil. Their only loss since the division's compulsory weekend off had been to Seattle and, in that five-game sequence, their victims had included Buffalo and Kansas City. Over the same period, Cincinnati had won only twice. Losses to San Francisco and the Raiders had dropped them into third place in the division. Another defeat could have put an end to their playoff hopes.

In the chill of Riverfront Stadium, both teams started slowly, but a 49-yard Houston drive brought a three-point lead on the opening play of the second quarter. Three-and-a-half minutes later, Houston went ahead 10–0 on Warren Moon's 21-yard touchdown pass to wide receiver Haywood Jeffires. The Bengals hit back with James Brooks scampering for a 45-yard gain to set up Ickey Woods' one-yard touchdown run, but the PAT was missed. And just under two minutes from half time, after the Oilers had moved out to a 13–6 lead, Brooks sped 56 yards for the game-tying touchdown.

Sparked by Gerald McNeil's 64-yard return of the second-half kickoff, Houston quickly reasserted their authority, with Moon sneaking the final one yard into the end zone. Encouragingly for the Oilers, Cincinnati's response faltered on third-and-two at its own 39-yard line, forcing a punt. Another Houston score might have settled the issue.

With the season on the line, for their next possession the Bengals reverted to Brooks and the outstanding veteran responded yet again, surging 40 yards to help establish position for Stanford Jennings' one-yard scoring run which came on a fourth-down play.

The front door was wide open and the Oilers could do little to prevent the waves of Bengals flooding through. Woods crashed into the end zone from one yard out, giving Cincinnati its first lead at 27–20. Two plays after the recovery of a Houston fumble, quarterback Boomer Esiason combined with tight end Eric Kattus on a 16-yard touchdown play and, with 4:44 left in the game, Esiason delivered the coup de grâce, again in partnership with Kattus, from 22 yards out. Cincinnati were back in the hunt.

The Road To Super Bowl XXV

Chasing the victory which would gain one of the two senior divisional title spots, the Giants had difficulty shaking off the resilient Cardinals, whose flame expired only late in the game when the New York defense, led by Lawrence Taylor, finally held firm on four downs.

Even with Frank Reich standing in for the injured Jim Kelly, still the Bills had too many weapons for Miami. In avenging their loss of Week Two, Buffalo were assured of the AFC's senior playoff spot.

James Brooks rushed for a Bengals club-record 201 yards to set up an emphatic win over Houston.

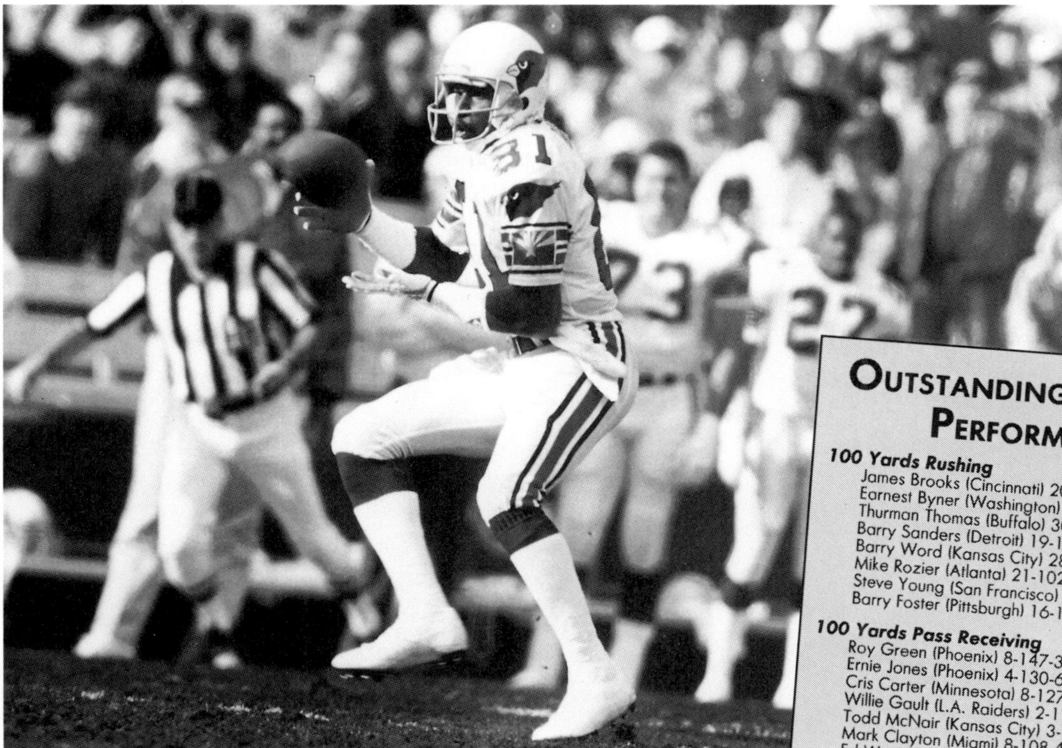

Cardinals wide receiver Roy Green terrorized the Giants defense with eight catches for 147 yards.

Outstanding Individual Performances

100 Yards Rushing
James Brooks (Cincinnati) 20-201-56t-1
Earnest Byner (Washington) 31-154-19-0
Thurman Thomas (Buffalo) 30-154-13t-1
Barry Sanders (Detroit) 19-133-37-1
Barry Word (Kansas City) 28-106-14-1
Mike Rozier (Atlanta) 21-102-14-1
Steve Young (San Francisco) 8-102-31-0
Barry Foster (Pittsburgh) 16-100-18-0

100 Yards Pass Receiving
Roy Green (Phoenix) 8-147-31-0
Ernie Jones (Phoenix) 4-130-68t-1
Cris Carter (Minnesota) 8-127-36-1
Willie Gault (L.A. Raiders) 2-117-61-0
Todd McNair (Kansas City) 3-111-65-1
Mark Clayton (Miami) 8-108-43-1
Ed West (Green Bay) 7-103-22-0

Passing
Jay Schroeder (L.A. Raiders) 15-10-234-0-61-4
Ken O'Brien (N.Y. Jets) 12-11-210-0-46-2
Bubby Brister (Pittsburgh) 19-10-139-0-21-4
Frank Reich (Buffalo) 21-15-234-0-43-2
Steve DeBerg (Kansas City) 27-19-251-0-65-2
Rich Gannon (Minnesota) 21-12-186-0-36-2
Boomer Esiason (Cincinnati) 21-11-184-0-28-2
Jeff George (Indianapolis) 33-18-252-0-42t-3

Standings

AFC East	**W**	**L**	**T**	**PF**	**PA**	**Pct.**
Buffalo*	13	2	0	414	234	.867
Miami**	11	4	0	313	225	.733
Indianapolis	7	8	0	264	330	.467
N.Y. Jets	5	10	0	279	331	.333
New England	1	14	0	171	433	.067

*Division Champion
**Clinched Playoff Spot

AFC Central	**W**	**L**	**T**	**PF**	**PA**	**Pct.**
Pittsburgh	9	6	0	278	206	.600
Cincinnati	8	7	0	339	338	.533
Houston	8	7	0	371	293	.533
Cleveland	3	12	0	214	441	.200

AFC West	**W**	**L**	**T**	**PF**	**PA**	**Pct.**
L.A. Raiders**	11	4	0	320	256	.733
Kansas City**	10	5	0	348	247	.667
Seattle	8	7	0	276	276	.533
San Diego	6	9	0	303	264	.400
Denver	4	11	0	309	361	.267

**Clinched Playoff Spot

NFC East	**W**	**L**	**T**	**PF**	**PA**	**Pct.**
N.Y. Giants*	12	3	0	322	201	.800
Philadelphia**	9	6	0	373	278	.600
Washington**	9	6	0	352	287	.600
Dallas	7	8	0	237	282	.467
Phoenix	5	10	0	247	373	.333

*Division Champion
**Clinched Playoff Spot

NFC Central	**W**	**L**	**T**	**PF**	**PA**	**Pct.**
Chicago*	11	4	0	338	259	.733
Detroit	6	9	0	363	383	.400
Green Bay	6	9	0	258	325	.400
Minnesota	6	9	0	334	306	.400
Tampa Bay	6	9	0	250	351	.400

*Division Champion

NFC West	**W**	**L**	**T**	**PF**	**PA**	**Pct.**
San Francisco*	13	2	0	333	222	.867
New Orleans	7	8	0	254	258	.467
L.A. Rams	5	10	0	328	392	.333
Atlanta	4	11	0	322	358	.267

*Division Champion

Week Seventeen

American Football Conference

Cleveland 14 at Cincinnati 21
Indianapolis 17 at Miami 23
Pittsburgh 14 at Houston 34
San Diego 12 at Los Angeles Raiders 17

National Football Conference

Dallas 7 at Atlanta 26
Los Angeles Rams 17 at New Orleans 20
Philadelphia 23 at Phoenix 21
San Francisco 20 at Minnesota 17

Interconference Games

Buffalo 14 at Washington 29
Detroit 10 at Seattle 30
Green Bay 13 at Denver 22
Kansas City 21 at Chicago 10
New York Giants 13 at New England 10
New York Jets 16 at Tampa Bay 14

Interconference Play

AFC 26 – NFC 26

Game of The Week
Los Angeles Rams 17 - New Orleans 20

With two weeks of the regular season to play, six teams were in contention for the sole remaining NFC wild-card spot but, on Week Sixteen, only New Orleans could manage a win. And what a win it was over the reigning Super Bowl Champion 49ers, coming from the boot of Morten Andersen with under five minutes left. Entering the final weekend, only Dallas and New Orleans were alive and Dallas held the advantage for, should the two teams end up with identical records, the Cowboys would advance, thanks to their Week Thirteen win over the Saints. However, the Cowboys went into the final game without starting quarterback Troy Aikman and it was a factor in their loss to Atlanta. None the less, it meant that, in the 224th and final game of the 1990 regular season, for New Orleans only a win would do. Appropriately, the contest would be viewed by the nationwide audience which assembled for ABC's Monday Night Game.

For much of the game, the Saints did not find the task too difficult. Wide receiver Floyd Turner's 26-yard touchdown reception and Craig (Ironhead) Heyward's one-yard scoring run gave them a 14–3 lead entering the final quarter. But the Rams came back, drawing to within four points on Willie (Flipper) Anderson's 47-yard touchdown catch. New Orleans placekicker Morten Andersen responded with a 41-yard field goal but, with 1:19 left in regulation time, Robert Delpino took a one-yard reception to level the scores. For Saints quarterback Steve Walsh, thoughts went back to earlier in the campaign, when he had been traded to New Orleans by Dallas. Ironically, it was on a play used by Dallas and which had been introduced to the Saints' repertoire only two weeks before this game that he found wide receiver Eric Martin for a 34-yard completion. With time running out, everything rested yet again on the composure of Andersen. Tragically, it seemed, his 29-yard field goal attempt was blocked by Rams nose tackle Alvin Wright. But wait. Wright had been adjudged to be offside. With the retaken kick, now from 24 yards out and only five seconds remaining, Andersen put New Orleans into the playoffs.

A superb effort by the little-used Cody Carlson, subbing for the injured Warren Moon, clinched a wild-card berth for the Oilers.

The Road To Super Bowl XXV

With nothing resting on the outcome, the Giants were tentative against New England and escaped with a three-point win when, for the Patriots, Jason Staurovsky's late, 42-yard field goal attempt was off-target.

Having achieved their objective the previous weekend, the Bills opted to keep some key players on the sideline, even bringing on third-string quarterback Gale Gilbert, in a loss which had no bearing on their preparation for the playoffs.

Not even Johnny Bailey's touchdown on a club-record 95-yard punt return could inspire the Bears against the dominant Chiefs.

Outstanding Individual Performances

100 Yards Rushing

Mike Rozier (Atlanta) 21-155-67-0
Rod Bernstine (San Diego) 27-114-14-0
Eric Dickerson (Indianapolis) 20-110-16-0
Sammie Smith (Miami) 29-108-13-1

100 Yards Pass Receiving

Ricky Proehl (Phoenix) 7-132-38t-1
Henry Ellard (L.A. Rams) 5-130-43-0
Jerry Rice (San Francisco) 9-118-22-1
Webster Slaughter (Cleveland) 6-115-32-0
Eric Green (Pittsburgh) 7-105-46-0

Passing

Randall Cunningham (Philadelphia) 19-13-172-1-27t-3
Cody Carlson (Houston) 29-22-247-1-53t-3
Steve Young (San Francisco) 24-15-205-0-34t-2
Timm Rosenbach (Phoenix) 31-19-301-1-45t-3
Jim Everett (L.A. Rams) 36-22-290-0-47t-2
Steve DeBerg (Kansas City) 32-25-276-0-41-0

Standings

AFC East	W	L	T	PF	PA	Pct.
Buffalo*	13	3	0	428	263	.813
Miami**	12	4	0	336	242	.750
Indianapolis	7	9	0	281	353	.438
N.Y. Jets	6	10	0	295	345	.375
New England	1	15	0	181	446	.063
AFC Central	**W**	**L**	**T**	**PF**	**PA**	**Pct.**
Cincinnati*	9	7	0	360	352	.563
Houston**	9	7	0	405	307	.563
Pittsburgh	9	7	0	292	240	.563
Cleveland	3	13	0	228	462	.188
AFC West	**W**	**L**	**T**	**PF**	**PA**	**Pct.**
L.A. Raiders*	12	4	0	337	268	.750
Kansas City**	11	5	0	369	257	.688
Seattle	9	7	0	306	286	.563
San Diego	6	10	0	315	281	.375
Denver	5	11	0	331	374	.313

NFC East	W	L	T	PF	PA	Pct.
N.Y. Giants*	13	3	0	335	211	.813
Philadelphia**	10	6	0	396	299	.625
Washington**	10	6	0	381	301	.625
Dallas	7	9	0	244	308	.438
Phoenix	5	11	0	268	396	.313
NFC Central	**W**	**L**	**T**	**PF**	**PA**	**Pct.**
Chicago*	11	5	0	348	280	.688
Tampa Bay	6	10	0	264	367	.375
Detroit	6	10	0	373	413	.375
Green Bay	6	10	0	271	347	.375
Minnesota	6	10	0	351	326	.375
NFC West	**W**	**L**	**T**	**PF**	**PA**	**Pct.**
San Francisco*	14	2	0	353	239	.875
New Orleans**	8	8	0	274	275	.500
L.A. Rams	5	11	0	345	412	.313
Atlanta	5	11	0	348	365	.313

*Division Champion
**Wild Card

Week Eighteen

First-Round Playoffs

AFC Kansas City 16 - Miami 17

A Dan Marino-led rally, producing two fourth-quarter touchdowns, brought Miami a thrilling one-point victory. Kansas City, who opened the scoring on Nick Lowery's 27-yard field goal, did not trail until 3:28 left to play when Marino found wide receiver Mark Clayton with a 12-yard touchdown pass. Earlier in that quarter, Marino's one-yard scoring pass to fullback Tony Paige had climaxed a 66-yard drive and brought the Dolphins back into a game which seemed beyond recall. Before then, Miami's only points had come on an astonishing playoff-record-setting 58-yard field goal by Pete Stoyanovich, as Kansas City drove steadily for a 10–3, halftime lead topped up by Lowery's third-quarter field goals of 25 and 38 yards. But the Chiefs could not quite deliver a knockout blow. Gathering for one final effort, Kansas City suffered a critical penalty which left Lowery 52 yards out for what would be a last-gasp field goal attempt. Sadly for the Chiefs, his effort was short by just a couple of feet.

AFC Houston 14 - Cincinnati 41

In a performance of ruthless power and efficiency, Cincinnati overwhelmed Houston, leading by the score of 20–0 at half time and racing to 34 points before allowing the Oilers to make their first statement. From the opening kickoff, Cincinnati set the tone, moving 70 yards with 46 of them coming on Boomer Esiason's pass to tight end Rodney Holman. Other scores followed with disheartening regularity and variety, two after errors, an interception and a fumble, by Houston quarterback Cody Carlson who started in replacement of the injured Warren Moon. By contrast, Houston's complex run-and-shoot offense was not a factor and only 28 seconds remained in the second quarter when the Oilers registered their initial first-down. Their second began a ten-play drive ending in Carlson's 16-yard touchdown pass to wide receiver Ernest Givins. But the Bengals replied immediately, tight end Eric Kattus restoring the margin with his nine-yard touchdown reception. Reflected Carlson, "We started off so slow and it just snowballed."

Earnest Byner (#21) rushed for 49 yards and caught seven passes for a further 77 yards as the Redskins rallied to defeat the Eagles.

Boomer Esiason connected on 14 of 20 passes and threw for two touchdowns as the Bengals dominated the Oilers.

NFC Washington 20 - Philadelphia 6

The Redskins withstood early Philadelphia pressure before responding with 20 unanswered points as they advanced to meet the reigning Super Bowl Champion 49ers. Twice, midway through the opening quarter and early in the second, Philadelphia had to settle for Roger Ruzek field goals of 37 and 28 yards after having been in touchdown-scoring position. On both occasions, they were halted on third-down sacks by outside linebacker Monte Coleman and defensive end Charles Mann. Washington's response came six minutes before half time when wide receiver Art Monk caught a 16-yard touchdown pass. But perhaps the major play came shortly before the interval when, following an apparent fumble by Washington running back Earnest Byner, Eagles rookie cornerback Ben Smith returned the ball 94 yards for what would have been a Philadelphia touchdown. However, the instant replay official over-ruled the on-field call, allowing Washington to retain possession. It was a blow from which the Eagles could not recover as, gradually, they slipped out of contention.

NFC New Orleans 6 - Chicago 16

A multi-purpose performance by running back Neal Anderson, who rushed for 102 yards on a Bears playoff-record 27 carries, ably supported by co-running back Brad Muster, established the platform for a Chicago victory which was duly clinched when quarterback Mike Tomczak engineered a 76-yard drive for Kevin Butler's 21-yard field goal with 2:47 remaining. Anderson even completed a 22-yard pass, building on an interception by cornerback John Mangum, as the Bears went 32 yards for the opening field goal. Again, he caught a 31-yard pass in the drive culminating in the touchdown which gave Chicago a 10–0 lead, 1:51 into the second quarter. The Saints, whose tenacity had never been in doubt, battled bravely and appeared to have drawn level in the third quarter when cornerback Vince Buck returned a blocked field goal 61 yards for an apparent touchdown. However, that play was nullified by an offside penalty and Butler pressed home the advantage for Chicago with a 22-yard field goal.

Week Nineteen
Second-Round Playoffs

NFC Washington 10 - San Francisco 28

With San Francisco protecting a tenuous, 21–10 lead, outstanding end zone defense halted serious Washington threats on three consecutive possessions before, on the fourth in the sequence, an unlikely pass interception and even less likely 61-yard touchdown return by 49ers nose tackle Michael Carter settled the issue. San Francisco had taken the initiative in the second quarter on Joe Montana touchdown passes of ten and eight yards to wide receivers Jerry Rice and Mike Sherrard respectively. Earlier, however, the Redskins had offered the prospect of an upset as they established a 10–7 advantage. And in the second half they would carve out three major opportunities as the 49ers offense stalled. But in turn, from the San Francisco seven- and 15-yard lines, Rypien's passes were intercepted in the end zone. Yet another pass from the 14-yard line was batted down inside the 49ers end zone and, finally, gleefully pulling in a tipped ball, Carter wrote a story to tell his grandchildren.

Marcus Allen rushed for 140 yards to pace the Raiders' victory over a plucky Cincinnati.

NFC Chicago 3 - New York Giants 31

If there was one question remaining unanswered about the 1990 New York Giants, it concerned the ability of reserve quarterback Jeff Hostetler to operate in the cauldron of the playoffs. But he was a key figure in a team performance which brushed the Bears aside with surprising ease. Chicago attempted five fourth-down plays but converted only one. By contrast, the Giants were successful on all four similar attempts with Hostetler a factor in three. His six-yard pass completion and ten-yard run converted two fourth-and-one downs while his third-quarter, nine-yard scramble dealt with the problem of fourth-and-six. All three conversions led to touchdowns, the third of which came when Hostetler ran the final three yards of a 49-yard drive. For good measure, his eight-yard run on third-and-one helped to set up the last Giants score. With the defense closing down on the Bears' powerful rushing game, there was every reason for the men from New Jersey to anticipate with confidence their impending confrontation with San Francisco.

AFC Cincinnati 10 - Los Angeles Raiders 20

Without injured All-Pro tackle Anthony Munoz and guard Bruce Reimers, and with running back James Brooks hampered by a dislocated thumb, Cincinnati gave the Raiders more than a few moments of worry before finally succumbing to superior power and efficiency. The Bengals even took the lead, slicing through the 'Silver and Black' defense for 87 yards with the opening possession before settling for Jim Breech's 27-yard field goal. However, the home team was quick to respond, as running backs Bo Jackson and Marcus Allen found gaps in the return march climaxing in a 13-yard touchdown reception by Mervyn Fernandez. Trailing 10–3, the Bengals clawed back to tie, 3:11

Nose tackle Michael Carter (#95) was the unlikely hero for San Francisco.

inside the final quarter, on Stanford Jennings' eight-yard scoring catch. But that only served to spark the Raiders to their best, quarterback Jay Schroeder responding quickly with a 41-yard touchdown pass to tight end Ethan Horton. Subsequently, a time-consuming, ten-play drive produced Jeff Jaeger's 25-yard field goal, leaving Cincinnati in a hopeless position, ten points adrift with only 19 seconds remaining.

AFC Miami 34 - Buffalo 44

A year earlier, the Bills had been eliminated at the divisional playoff stage, by the score of 34–30, in a hectic encounter settled by an end zone interception which thwarted a potential game-winning touchdown pass. And for much of the way, this game was not dissimilar, with both teams confounding the wintry conditions in a scoring spectacular. Quarterback Jim Kelly returned from injury showing impeccable touch, guiding the Bills to leads of 20–3 and 27–10 before Miami, with Dan Marino also rising to the occasion, drew inexorably closer to trail by only three points at 30–27, just inside the final quarter. But this time there would be no mistake as Kelly rekindled his game, once more unleashing his wide receivers Andre Reed and James Lofton. First, passing 23 yards to Lofton, Kelly set up a five-yard touchdown run by Thurman Thomas and then, barely more than half a minute later, he capitalized on a fumble recovery by passing 26 yards for a touchdown to Reed.

WEEK TWENTY

CONFERENCE CHAMPIONSHIPS

NFC New York Giants 15 - San Francisco 13

The 49ers were just two victories away from a unique place in history as the only team to win three straight Super Bowl Championships. Even on a bad day, they were expected to plot a route to victory. And this especially was the case if it all rested on a last-minute drive, in which special variety of nerve-testing technique quarterback Joe Montana had no peer. The outstanding wide receiver of modern times, Jerry Rice, was coming off a season in which he had led the entire NFL in every category of receiving except average yardage. Perhaps more important than the array of individual stars, the vast majority of the squad wasn't just playoff hardened, it was Super Bowl tempered.

By contrast, of all the championship contenders, the Giants had the poorest late-season record with only three wins from the final six games. But had they needed to pass any kind of credibility test, they'd done so with flying colours the previous week against Chicago when the NFC's best rushing offense was stopped cold. In their 7–3 loss to San Francisco on Week Thirteen, they had been in contention to the last, finally going down when quarterback Phil Simms was sacked while attempting to pass from the 49ers 27-yard line with three seconds left.

Not many people felt that the championship game would follow a similar course but, as the game developed, it became apparent that a close finish was in prospect. However, after careful play by both teams had sent them into half time tied at 6–6 on field goals, Montana opened up, passing 61 yards for a touchdown to wide receiver John Taylor. Undeterred, the Giants cut the deficit to four points on Matt Bahr's 46-yard field goal and, with 5:47 left to play in the game, Bahr repeated from 38 yards to complete a drive in which linebacker Gary Reasons had rambled for 30 yards on a fake punt. Yet when the 49ers took over possession, the outcome seemed inevitable. Steve Young was on in place of the injured Montana but, in only four plays, San Francisco had swept down to the New York 40-yard line. But on the ensuing play, running back Roger Craig fumbled on contact with Giants nose tackle Erik Howard and Lawrence Taylor recovered for the Giants. Six plays later, with only four seconds remaining, Bahr was in position, 42 yards out, for the most important kick of his career. With no time showing on the clock his kick was good and true.

Joe Montana suffered broken ribs, a broken finger and concussion from Leonard Marshall's crunching sack.

James Lofton caught five passes for 113 yards and two touchdowns.

AFC Los Angeles Raiders 3 - Buffalo 51

If regular-season record meant anything, Buffalo truly deserved to contest the AFC Championship Game. The only losses in the AFC's best profile had been to Miami, Houston and Washington. On Week Sixteen, revenge against the Dolphins also had secured the Eastern division title. A year on from the Bills' playoff exit at the hands of Cleveland, there was undeniable evidence of maturity in that, whereas the 1989 squad was expected to be competitive, their successors assumed that they would win. However, while their superiority over Miami had been confirmed in the divisional playoffs and though bolstered by the memory of victory over their championship game opponents back on Week Five, the Bills would be aware that it was a much-improved Los Angeles club which made the trip to Rich Stadium.

Into town strode the Raiders with almost, if not all, the polish of old restored to a defiant gloss. Boasting the AFC's equal-second-best regular-season record, Al Davis's lads were back in the big time with a vengeance. Even though the incomparable Bo Jackson would not be available because of a hip injury, they were ready to play alright. In their campaign loss to Buffalo, they had dominated before going down after what might be described as a series of errors in execution, Buffalo's outstanding special teams play notwithstanding. The general feeling was that the game would be a montage of pyrotechnics; an explosive expression of talent; a close encounter with the extraordinary.

The real thing was all of that, except that the fireworks came from Buffalo alone in one of the most one-sided playoff games in league history. From the start, when Bills quarterback Jim Kelly fumbled the ball only to see it return obediently to his waiting hands, thence to be delivered to a wide-open James Lofton streaming into the end zone, the gods clearly had cast their votes. In a first half of shattering brilliance, Kelly passed for 247 yards, Thurman Thomas ran for 109 and the Bills helped themselves to an NFL postseason-record 41 points. The gameplan called for a unusual mix of run and pass out of a no-huddle offense and it worked to perfection – or perhaps better than that. Anything like this form in the Super Bowl would make Buffalo a formidable opponent.

SUPER BOWL XXV

Buffalo 19 – New York Giants 20

Tampa Stadium, Tampa, Florida, January 27th, 1991

It was debatable just which of several aspects of the Buffalo offense might provide the Giants with their biggest headache. Showing no traces of a knee injury on his return after missing the final two regular-season games, quarterback Jim Kelly, the NFL leading passer, had presided over the destruction of both Miami and the Raiders in the most authoritative manner. In the playoffs, Kelly's effectiveness had been unquestionably amplified by former All-Pro wide receiver James Lofton, a 13th-year veteran who had averaged a frightening 20.3 yards on 35 catches over the campaign but then turned back the clock with seven catches for 149 yards and five for 113. Lofton's senior partner, Andre Reed, was regarded as a model of reliability. Some might argue that the main danger lay at Kelly's shoulder in the backfield, where AFC-leading running back Thurman Thomas was a dual-purpose threat, also having led the league in total yards from scrimmage with 1,829 while scoring 13 touchdowns. A much underrated offensive line built around Pro Bowl center Kent Hull was sure to give Kelly all the protection he needed.

Jim Kelly

Jeff Hostetler

On defense, the Bills would be coming from every angle, posing a variety of problems ranging from the overwhelming force of its pass rushing to a numbing resistance against the run. Featuring defensive end Bruce Smith, linebackers Shane Conlan, Cornelius Bennett and Darryl Talley, and a secondary reinforced by the return of free safety Mark Kelso and cornerback Kirby Jackson, the unit offered few, if any, easy options.

Having eliminated the 49ers, the Giants had passed the most severe test possible. Reserve quarterback Jeff Hostetler had been a revelation, playing in replacement of the injured Phil Simms since late in the Week Fifteen loss to Buffalo. No ordinary passer himself, he brought elusiveness and daring to the rôle. And though not prolific, starting wide receivers Stephen Baker and Mark Ingram were of the 'see you later' variety, averaging 20.8 and 19.2 yards respectively. The Giants favoured the run over the pass and herein lay a potential problem for them. Rookie Rodney Hampton, the player in form, was injured, meaning that much

Super Bowl MVP Ottis Anderson (#24) takes on Bills defenders Darryl Talley (#56) and Bruce Smith (#78).

Thurman Thomas scoots 31 yards for a touchdown.

would be required of Ottis Anderson. A former superstar, Anderson no longer was the beautiful, fluid runner who swept the ends. Usually, he spent the preseason wondering if he'd survive the cut. But he was tough. The joker in the pack was the multi-purpose Dave Meggett, a bobby-dazzler, whose responsibilities as a third-down or safety-valve receiver had brought him a club-leading 39 catches.

Defensively, the Giants represented the NFC's best. Led by outside linebacker Lawrence Taylor, in 12 of 18 games opponents had been restricted to no more than one touchdown. If Taylor had slowed a little since the Giants' crushing victory in Super Bowl XXI, inside linebacker Pepper Johnson had taken up any slack, earning his first Pro Bowl selection. Strong man Erik Howard was the foundation of the front wall at nose tackle, with defensive end Leonard Marshall exerting a predatory influence. A reconstructed secondary of Mark Collins, Everson Walls, Myron Guyton and Greg Jackson would take care of the back door.

In so far as any game is predictable, the first half of this one contained few surprises, with each club following its published recipe. The Giants ground away steadily, dominating the time of possession by almost 18 minutes to Buffalo's 12. Kelly used Lofton on a 61-yard play to set up a field goal, while passes to Thomas and Reed led to Don Smith's one-yard run. Even Bruce Smith's safety tackle of Hostetler was not wholly unexpected. Apart from a couple of receptions by little-used tight end Howard Cross, the Giants, too, used their known approach. Interestingly, Anderson looked particularly sprightly, rushing for 39 yards on seven carries, while Meggett's average of 7.4 yards on five rushes mirrored his regular-season form. Baker's late-first-half touchdown reception sent the Giants into the locker room trailing by only two points and primed for the resumption.

With the initial second-half possession, New York used up nine minutes and 29 seconds in moving 75 yards on 14 plays for Anderson's one-yard touchdown run. Towards the end of the third quarter and into the fourth, however, the Bills opened up, taking only one and a half minutes to drive 63 yards, the final 31 coming on Thomas's scoring run. Leading 19–17, the suggestion was that the Bills could go on to victory. But the Giants responded, this time draining the clock of a valuable seven minutes and 32 seconds in a 14-play drive for Matt Bahr's 21-yard field goal. The stage was set for the finale.

Each team would punt before Kelly gathered for one march. Beginning at the Buffalo ten with 2:16 remaining, he moved the offense down to the Giants 29, before stepping aside in favour of placekicker Scott Norwood with eight seconds showing on the game clock. It is never quite as exciting when the game is decided by failure, but the Giants did not complain when Norwood's brave effort slid to the right side of the post, the wrong side for Buffalo.

The Game

Scoring By Quarters

1st Quarter
New York: Bahr, 28-yard field goal (7:46)
Buffalo 0 - New York 3
Buffalo: Norwood, 23-yard field goal (9:09)
Buffalo 3 - New York 3

2nd Quarter
Buffalo: D. Smith, 1-yard run; Norwood kick (2:30)
Buffalo 10 - New York 3
Buffalo: B. Smith safety (6:33)
Buffalo 12 - New York 3
New York: Baker, 14-yard pass from Hostetler; Bahr kick (14:35)
Buffalo 12 - New York 10

3rd Quarter
New York: Anderson, 1-yard run; Bahr kick (9:29)
Buffalo 12 - New York 17

4th Quarter
Buffalo: Thomas, 31-yard run; Norwood kick (0:08)
Buffalo 19 - New York 17
New York: Bahr, 21-yard field goal (7:40)
Buffalo 19 - New York 20

Giants All-Pro linebacker Lawrence Taylor.

A regal Bill Parcells celebrates the pinnacle of a coach's career.

Bills head coach Marv Levy came so close.

ANATOMY OF SUPER BOWL XXV

1st Quarter

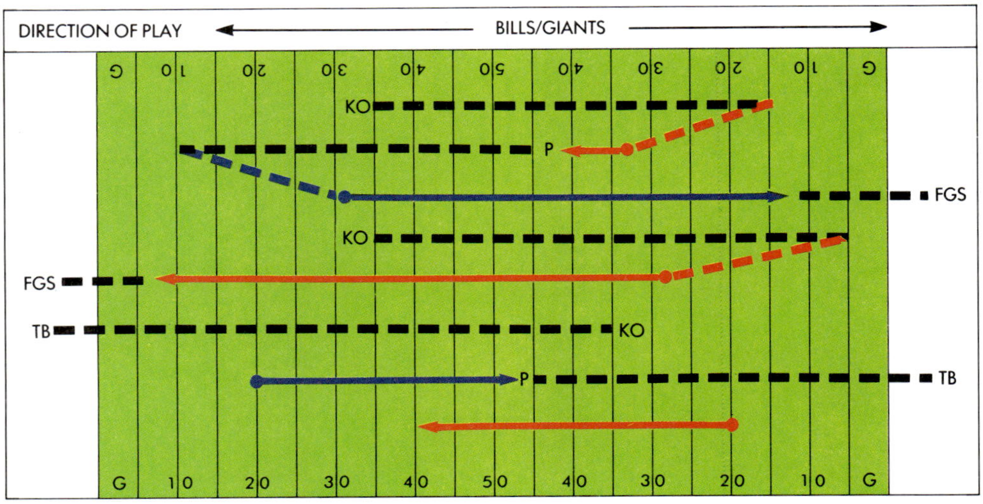

FIRST DOWNS

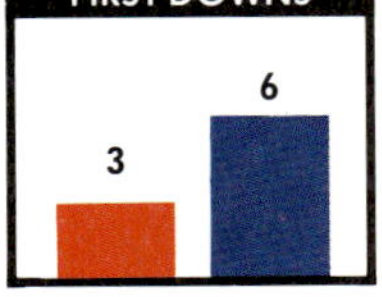

YARDS RUSHING

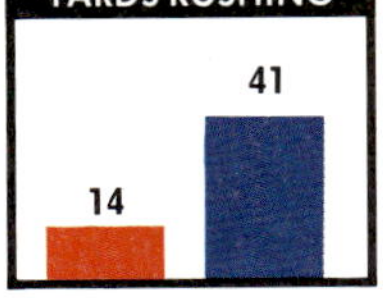

YARDS PASSING

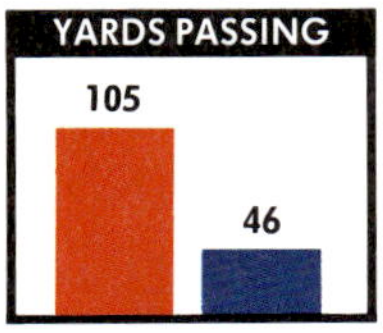

THIRD DOWN CONVERSIONS

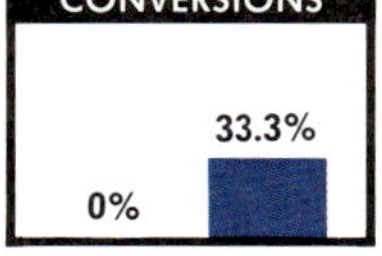

TIME OF POSSESSION

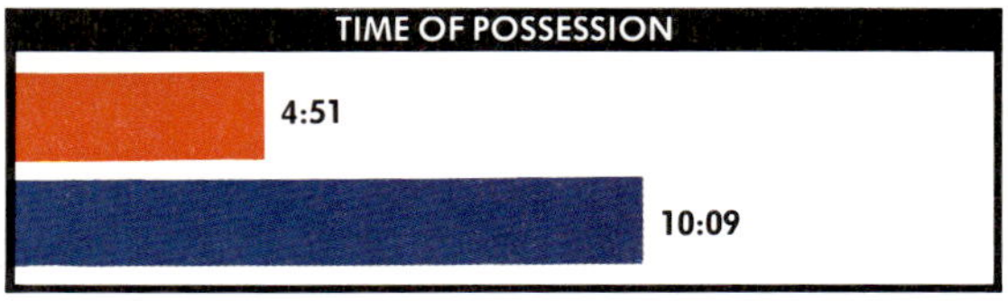

SCORE AFTER FIRST QUARTER

Bills	3
Giants	3

2nd Quarter

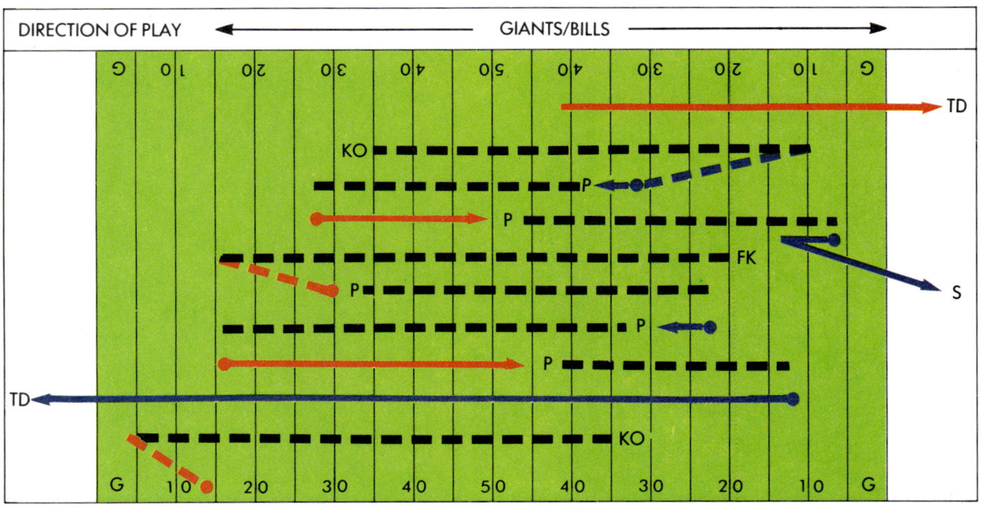

FIRST DOWNS

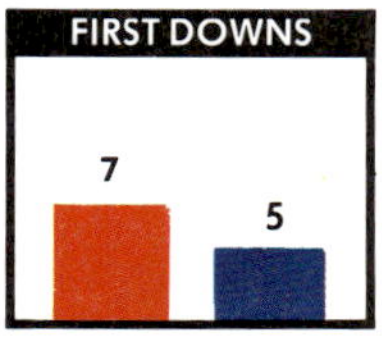

YARDS RUSHING

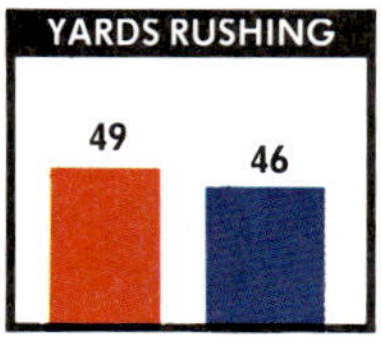

YARDS PASSING

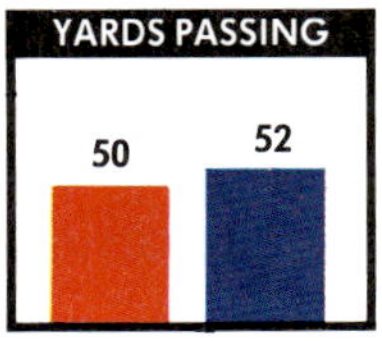

THIRD DOWN CONVERSIONS

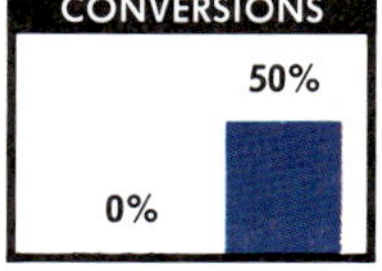

TIME OF POSSESSION

SCORE AFTER SECOND QUARTER

Bills	12
Giants	10

KEY

Bills	(orange)
Giants	(blue)
Kickoff/Punt Return	dashed lines
Start of Drives	dots
Kickoff/Punt/Field Goal	black dashed line

KO – Kickoff
P – Punt
FGS – Field Goal Scored
FGM – Field Goal Missed
TB – Touchback
TD – Touchdown
S – Safety
FK – Free Kick

3rd Quarter

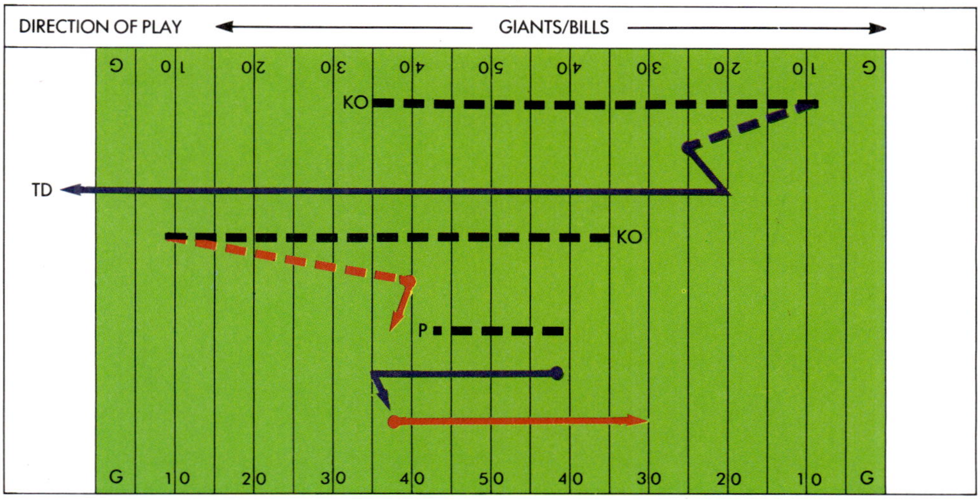

FIRST DOWNS	
Bills	3
Giants	7

YARDS RUSHING	
Bills	15
Giants	46

YARDS PASSING	
Bills	25
Giants	60

THIRD DOWN CONVERSIONS	
Bills	0%
Giants	80%

TIME OF POSSESSION	
Bills	3:08
Giants	11:52

SCORE AFTER THIRD QUARTER	
Bills	12
Giants	17

4th Quarter

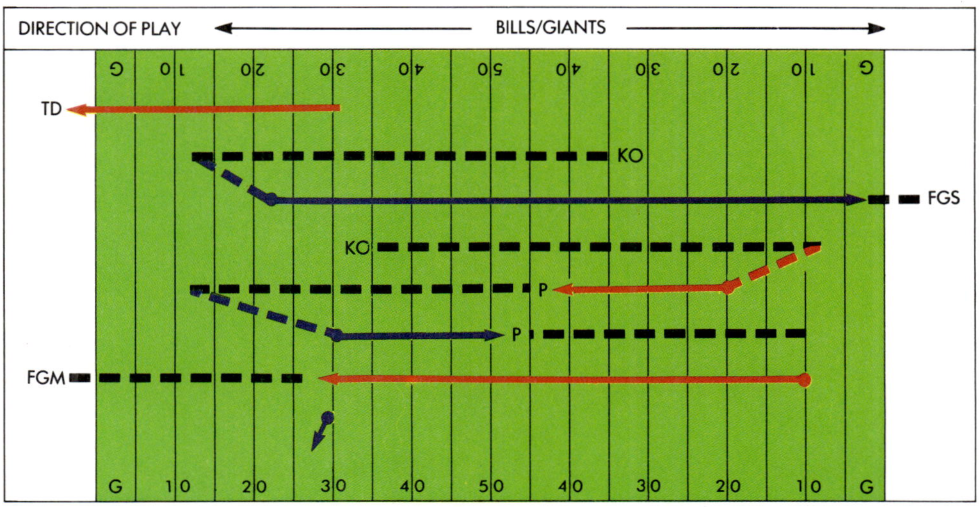

FIRST DOWNS	
Bills	5
Giants	6

YARDS RUSHING	
Bills	88
Giants	39

YARDS PASSING	
Bills	25
Giants	57

THIRD DOWN CONVERSIONS	
Bills	50%
Giants	50%

TIME OF POSSESSION	
Bills	4:15
Giants	10:45

SCORE AFTER FOURTH QUARTER	
Bills	19
Giants	20

THE PRO BOWL

At the end of each season, the best players from each conference fly off to Hawaii to give the fans out there a treat. The teams are selected by a ballot of head coaches and players in each conference. Each team has two equal votes, those being the head coach's and a consensus of the players' selections. Coaches and players may vote only for players in their own conference and may not vote for players from their own teams. In the most recent AFC-NFC Pro Bowl, a pair of fourth-quarter touchdown passes from Buffalo quarterback Jim Kelly, either side of a Nick Lowery field goal, rallied the AFC for the 23–21 victory which trimmed the NFC's lead in the series to 12–9.

ABOVE: Enthusiasm brought Reyna Thompson his Pro Bowl selection.
LEFT: 12.5 sacks earned Greg Townsend a first Pro Bowl trip.

AFC-NFC Pro Bowl Results – NFC leads series 12–9

YEAR	DATE	WINNER	LOSER	SITE	ATTENDANCE
1991	Feb. 3	AFC 23	NFC 21	Honolulu	50,345
1990	Feb. 4	NFC 27	AFC 21	Honolulu	50,445
1989	Jan. 29	NFC 34	AFC 3	Honolulu	50,113
1988	Feb. 7	AFC 15	NFC 6	Honolulu	50,113
1987	Feb. 1	AFC 10	NFC 6	Honolulu	50,101
1986	Feb. 2	NFC 28	AFC 24	Honolulu	50,101
1985	Jan. 27	AFC 22	NFC 14	Honolulu	50,385
1984	Jan. 29	NFC 45	AFC 3	Honolulu	50,445
1983	Feb. 6	NFC 20	AFC 19	Honolulu	49,883
1982	Jan. 31	AFC 16	NFC 13	Honolulu	50,402
1981	Feb. 1	NFC 13	AFC 7	Honolulu	50,360
1980	Jan. 27	NFC 37	AFC 27	Honolulu	49,800
1979	Jan. 29	NFC 13	AFC 7	Los Angeles	46,281
1978	Jan. 23	NFC 14	AFC 13	Tampa	51,337
1977	Jan. 17	AFC 24	NFC 14	Seattle	64,752
1976	Jan. 26	NFC 23	AFC 20	New Orleans	30,546
1975	Jan. 20	NFC 17	AFC 10	Miami	26,484
1974	Jan. 20	AFC 15	NFC 13	Kansas City	66,918
1973	Jan. 21	AFC 33	NFC 28	Dallas	37,091
1972	Jan. 23	AFC 26	NFC 13	Los Angeles	53,647
1971	Jan. 24	NFC 24	AFC 6	Los Angeles	48,222

Pro Bowl Rosters
(Original selections - starters in capitals)

OFFENSE	**AMERICAN FOOTBALL CONFERENCE**		**NATIONAL FOOTBALL CONFERENCE**	
Wide Receivers	ANDRE REED	Buffalo	JERRY RICE	San Francisco
	ANTHONY MILLER	San Diego	ANDRE RISON	Atlanta
	Drew Hill	Houston	Sterling Sharpe	Green Bay
	Ernest Givins	Houston	Gary Clark	Washington
Tight Ends	RODNEY HOLMAN	Cincinnati	KEITH JACKSON	Philadelphia
	Ferrell Edmunds	Miami	Steve Jordan	Minnesota
Tackles	ANTHONY MUNOZ	Cincinnati	JIM LACHEY	Washington
	BRUCE ARMSTRONG	New England	JACKIE SLATER	L.A. Rams
	Richmond Webb	Miami	Lomas Brown	Detroit
Guards	BRUCE MATTHEWS	Houston	RANDALL McDANIEL	Minnesota
	MIKE MUNCHAK	Houston	MARK BORTZ	Chicago
	Steve Wisniewski	L.A. Raiders	Guy McIntyre	San Francisco
Centers	KENT HULL	Buffalo	JAY HILGENBERG	Chicago
	Don Mosebar	L.A. Raiders	Bart Oates	N.Y. Giants
Quarterbacks	WARREN MOON	Houston	JOE MONTANA	San Francisco
	Jim Kelly	Buffalo	Randall Cunningham	Philadelphia
Running Backs	THURMAN THOMAS	Buffalo	BARRY SANDERS	Detroit
	MARION BUTTS	San Diego	NEAL ANDERSON	Chicago
	Bobby Humphrey	Denver	Earnest Byner	Washington
	Bo Jackson	L.A. Raiders	Johnny Johnson	Phoenix
DEFENSE				
Defensive Ends	BRUCE SMITH	Buffalo	REGGIE WHITE	Philadelphia
	GREG TOWNSEND	L.A. Raiders	CHRIS DOLEMAN	Minnesota
	Jeff Cross	Miami	Richard Dent	Chicago
Interior Linemen	MICHAEL DEAN PERRY	Cleveland	JEROME BROWN	Philadelphia
	Ray Childress	Houston	Jerry Ball	Detroit
Outside Linebackers	DERRICK THOMAS	Kansas City	CHARLES HALEY	San Francisco
	LESLIE O'NEAL	San Diego	LAWRENCE TAYLOR	N.Y. Giants
	Cornelius Bennett	Buffalo	Pat Swilling	New Orleans
	Darryl Talley*	Buffalo		
Inside Linebackers	JOHN OFFERDAHL	Miami	PEPPER JOHNSON	N.Y. Giants
	SHANE CONLAN	Buffalo	MIKE SINGLETARY	Chicago
	David Little	Pittsburgh	Vaughan Johnson	New Orleans
			Chris Spielman*	Detroit
Cornerbacks	ROD WOODSON	Pittsburgh	DARRELL GREEN	Washington
	ALBERT LEWIS	Kansas City	CARL LEE	Minnesota
	Kevin Ross	Kansas City	Wayne Haddix	Tampa Bay
Safeties	STEVE ATWATER	Denver	JOEY BROWNER	Minnesota
	DAVID FULCHER	Cincinnati	RONNIE LOTT	San Francisco
	Dennis Smith	Denver	Mark Carrier	Chicago
SPECIAL TEAMS				
Placekicker	NICK LOWERY	Kansas City	MORTEN ANDERSEN	New Orleans
Punter	ROHN STARK	Indianapolis	SEAN LANDETA	N.Y. Giants
Kick Returner	CLARENCE VERDIN	Indianapolis	MEL GRAY	Detroit
Specialist	STEVE TASKER	Buffalo	REYNA THOMPSON	N.Y. Giants
HEAD COACH	ART SHELL	L.A. Raiders	GEORGE SEIFERT	San Francisco

*Special selection made by head coach

AN ALL-PRO TEAM

Anyone can pick his or her own All-Pro team and just about everyone does. Here's my dream team.

Wide Receivers	Jerry Rice	San Francisco
	Andre Rison	Atlanta
Tight End	Rodney Holman	Cincinnati
Tackles	Anthony Munoz	Cincinnati
	Jim Lachey	Washington
Guards	Mike Munchak	Houston
	Randall McDaniel	Minnesota
Center	Jay Hilgenberg	Chicago
Quarterback	Joe Montana	San Francisco
Running Backs	Bo Jackson	L.A. Raiders
	Barry Sanders	Detroit
Defensive Ends	Bruce Smith	Buffalo
	Reggie White	Philadelphia
Defensive Tackles	Ray Childress	Houston
	Michael Dean Perry	Cleveland
Outside Linebackers	Derrick Thomas	Kansas City
	Lawrence Taylor	N.Y. Giants
Inside Linebackers	Mike Singletary	Chicago
	Pepper Johnson	N.Y. Giants
Safeties	Joey Browner	Minnesota
	Steve Atwater	Denver
Cornerbacks	Albert Lewis	Kansas City
	Rod Woodson	Pittsburgh
Placekicker	Kevin Butler	Chicago
Punter	Rohn Stark	Indianapolis
Punt Returner	Clarence Verdin	Indianapolis
Kickoff Returner	Dave Meggett	N.Y. Giants
Special-team Specialist	Steve Tasker	Buffalo
Head Coach	Bill Parcells	N.Y. Giants

ABOVE RIGHT: An injury may have ended the short career of Bo Jackson, one of the NFL's best-ever running backs.

BELOW RIGHT: Joe Montana has earned his place among the gods.

Chapter Two

All-Time Records

Champions 1920-1990

National Football League 1920-1969
(Until 1933 based solely on regular-season play)

1920 Akron Pros
1921 Chicago Staleys
1922 Canton Bulldogs
1923 Canton Bulldogs
1924 Cleveland Bulldogs
1925 Chicago Cardinals
1926 Frankford Yellow Jackets
1927 New York Giants
1928 Providence Steam Roller
1929 Green Bay Packers
1930 Green Bay Packers
1931 Green Bay Packers
1932 Chicago Bears 9 – Portsmouth Spartans 0 (Championship Playoff)

NFL Championship Games 1933-69
1933 Chicago Bears 23 – New York Giants 21
1934 New York Giants 30 – Chicago Bears 13
1935 Detroit Lions 26 – New York Giants 7
1936 Green Bay Packers 21 – Boston Redskins 6
1937 Washington Redskins 28 – Chicago Bears 21
1938 New York Giants 23 – Green Bay Packers 17
1939 Green Bay Packers 27 – New York Giants 0
1940 Chicago Bears 73 – Washington Redskins 0
1941 Chicago Bears 37 – New York Giants 9
1942 Washington Redskins 14 – Chicago Bears 6
1943 Chicago Bears 41 – Washington Redskins 21
1944 Green Bay Packers 14 – New York Giants 7
1945 Cleveland Rams 15 – Washington Redskins 14
1946 Chicago Bears 24 – New York Giants 14
1947 Chicago Cardinals 28 – Philadelphia Eagles 21
1948 Philadelphia Eagles 7 – Chicago Cardinals 0
1949 Philadelphia Eagles 14 – Los Angeles Rams 0
1950 Cleveland Browns 30 – Los Angeles Rams 28
1951 Los Angeles Rams 24 – Cleveland Browns 17
1952 Detroit Lions 17 – Cleveland Browns 7
1953 Detroit Lions 17 – Cleveland Browns 16
1954 Cleveland Browns 56 – Detroit Lions 10
1955 Cleveland Browns 38 – Los Angeles Rams 14
1956 New York Giants 47 – Chicago Bears 7
1957 Detroit Lions 59 – Cleveland Browns 14
1958 Baltimore Colts 23 – New York Giants 17 (OT)
1959 Baltimore Colts 31 – New York Giants 16
1960 Philadelphia Eagles 17 – Green Bay Packers 13
1961 Green Bay Packers 37 – New York Giants 0
1962 Green Bay Packers 16 – New York Giants 7
1963 Chicago Bears 14 – New York Giants 10
1964 Cleveland Browns 27 – Baltimore Colts 0
1965 Green Bay Packers 23 – Cleveland Browns 12
1966 Green Bay Packers 34 – Dallas Cowboys 27
1967 Green Bay Packers 21 – Dallas Cowboys 17
1968 Baltimore Colts 34 – Cleveland Browns 0
1969 Minnesota Vikings 27 – Cleveland Browns 7

AFL Championship Games 1960-1969
1960 Houston Oilers 24 – Los Angeles Chargers 16
1961 Houston Oilers 10 – San Diego Chargers 3
1962 Dallas Texans 20 – Houston Oilers 17 (OT)
1963 San Diego Chargers 51 – Boston Patriots 10
1964 Buffalo Bills 20 – San Diego Chargers 7
1965 Buffalo Bills 23 – San Diego Chargers 0
1966 Kansas City Chiefs 31 – Buffalo Bills 7
1967 Oakland Raiders 40 – Houston Oilers 7
1968 New York Jets 27 – Oakland Raiders 23
1969 Kansas City Chiefs 17 – Oakland Raiders 7

Conference Championship Games 1970-1990

NFC
1970 Dallas Cowboys 17 – San Francisco 49ers 10
1971 Dallas Cowboys 14 – San Francisco 49ers 3
1972 Washington Redskins 26 – Dallas Cowboys 3
1973 Minnesota Vikings 27 – Dallas Cowboys 10
1974 Minnesota Vikings 14 – Los Angeles Rams 10
1975 Dallas Cowboys 37 – Los Angeles Rams 7
1976 Minnesota Vikings 24 – Los Angeles Rams 13
1977 Dallas Cowboys 23 – Minnesota Vikings 6
1978 Dallas Cowboys 28 – Los Angeles Rams 0
1979 Los Angeles Rams 9 – Tampa Bay Buccaneers 0
1980 Philadelphia Eagles 20 – Dallas Cowboys 7
1981 San Francisco 49ers 28 – Dallas Cowboys 27
1982 Washington Redskins 31 – Dallas Cowboys 17
1983 Washington Redskins 24 – San Francisco 49ers 21

1984 San Francisco 49ers 23 – Chicago Bears 0
1985 Chicago Bears 24 – Los Angeles Rams 0
1986 New York Giants 17 – Washington Redskins 0
1987 Washington Redskins 17 – Minnesota Vikings 10
1988 San Francisco 49ers 28 – Chicago Bears 3
1989 San Francisco 49ers 30 – Los Angeles Rams 3
1990 New York Giants 15 – San Francisco 49ers 13

AFC
1970 Baltimore Colts 27 – Oakland Raiders 17
1971 Miami Dolphins 21 – Baltimore Colts 0
1972 Miami Dolphins 21 – Pittsburgh Steelers 17
1973 Miami Dolphins 27 – Oakland Raiders 10
1974 Pittsburgh Steelers 24 – Oakland Raiders 13
1975 Pittsburgh Steelers 16 – Oakland Raiders 10
1976 Oakland Raiders 24 – Pittsburgh Steelers 7
1977 Denver Broncos 20 – Oakland Raiders 17
1978 Pittsburgh Steelers 34 – Houston Oilers 5
1979 Pittsburgh Steelers 27 – Houston Oilers 13
1980 Oakland Raiders 34 – San Diego Chargers 27
1981 Cincinnati Bengals 27 – San Diego Chargers 7
1982 Miami Dolphins 14 – New York Jets 0
1983 Los Angeles Raiders 30 – Seattle Seahawks 14
1984 Miami Dolphins 45 – Pittsburgh Steelers 28
1985 New England Patriots 31 – Miami Dolphins 14
1986 Denver Broncos 23 – Cleveland Browns 20 (OT)
1987 Denver Broncos 38 – Cleveland Browns 33
1988 Cincinnati Bengals 21 – Buffalo Bills 10
1989 Denver Broncos 37 – Cleveland Browns 21
1990 Buffalo Bills 51 – Los Angeles Raiders 3

Walter Payton reigns supreme as the most prolific running back in NFL history.

SUPER BOWL 1966-1990

Season	SB	Winner		Loser		Stadium	Attendance
1966	I	Green Bay	35	Kansas City	10	Los Angeles Coliseum	61,946
1967	II	Green Bay	33	Oakland	14	Miami Orange Bowl	75,546
1968	III	N.Y. Jets	16	Baltimore	7	Miami Orange Bowl	75,389
1969	IV	Kansas City	23	Minnesota	7	New Orleans Tulane Stadium	80,562
1970	V	Baltimore	16	Dallas	13	Miami Orange Bowl	79,204
1971	VI	Dallas	24	Miami	3	New Orleans Tulane Stadium	81,023
1972	VII	Miami	14	Washington	7	Los Angeles Coliseum	90,182
1973	VIII	Miami	24	Minnesota	7	Houston Rice Stadium	71,882
1974	IX	Pittsburgh	16	Minnesota	6	New Orleans Tulane Stadium	80,997
1975	X	Pittsburgh	21	Dallas	17	Miami Orange Bowl	80,187
1976	XI	Oakland	32	Minnesota	14	Pasadena Rose Bowl	103,438
1977	XII	Dallas	27	Denver	10	New Orleans Superdome	75,583
1978	XIII	Pittsburgh	35	Dallas	31	Miami Orange Bowl	79,484
1979	XIV	Pittsburgh	31	L.A. Rams	19	Pasadena Rose Bowl	103,985
1980	XV	Oakland	27	Philadelphia	10	New Orleans Superdome	76,135
1981	XVI	San Francisco	26	Cincinnati	21	Pontiac Silverdome	81,270
1982	XVII	Washington	27	Miami	17	Pasadena Rose Bowl	103,667
1983	XVIII	L.A. Raiders	38	Washington	9	Tampa Stadium	72,920
1984	XIX	San Francisco	38	Miami	16	Stanford Stadium	84,059
1985	XX	Chicago	46	New England	10	New Orleans Superdome	73,818
1986	XXI	N.Y. Giants	39	Denver	20	Pasadena Rose Bowl	101,063
1987	XXII	Washington	42	Denver	10	San Diego Jack Murphy Stadium	73,302
1988	XXIII	San Francisco	20	Cincinnati	16	Miami Joe Robbie Stadium	75,179
1989	XXIV	San Francisco	55	Denver	10	New Orleans Superdome	72,919
1990	XXV	N.Y. Giants	20	Buffalo Bills	19	Tampa Stadium	73,813

All-Time Individual Records

(Regular Season only – New Records and Records tied are in bold type)

Career Best

SEASONS PLAYED	26	George Blanda
GAMES PLAYED	340	George Blanda
POINTS	2,002	George Blanda (9-TD, 943-EP, 335-FG)
EXTRA POINTS	943	George Blanda
FIELD GOALS	373	Jan Stenerud
TOUCHDOWNS		
Rushing and Pass Receiving	126	Jim Brown (106-R, 20-P)
Rushing	110	Walter Payton
Pass Receiving	100	Steve Largent
Passes Thrown	342	Fran Tarkenton
By Interception Return	9	Ken Houston
By Punt Return	8	Jack Christiansen
		Rick Upchurch
By Kickoff Return	6	Ollie Matson
		Gale Sayers
		Travis Williams
By Fumble Recovery Return	4	Billy Thompson
YARDAGE		
Rushing	16,726	Walter Payton
Pass Receiving	13,089	Steve Largent
Passing	47,003	Fran Tarkenton
HOW MANY TIMES		
Pass Receptions	819	Steve Largent
Passes Completed	3,686	Fran Tarkenton
Interceptions	81	Paul Krause
100-Yard Rushing Games	77	Walter Payton
100-Yard Pass Receiving Games	50	Don Maynard
1,000-Yard Rushing Seasons	10	Walter Payton
1,000-Yard Pass Receiving Seasons	8	Steve Largent
MOST SEASONS LEADING LEAGUE		
Points	5	Don Hutson, Green Bay 1940-44
		Gino Cappelletti, Boston 1961, 1963-66
Extra Points	8	George Blanda, Chicago Bears 1956, Houston 1961-62, Oakland 1967-69, 1972, 1974
Field Goals	5	Lou Groza, Cleveland Browns 1950, 1952-54, 1957
Touchdowns	8	Don Hutson, Green Bay 1935-38, 1941-44
Touchdowns, Rushing	5	Jim Brown, Cleveland Browns 1957-59, 1963, 1965
Touchdowns, Pass Receiving	9	Don Hutson, Green Bay 1935-38, 1940-44
Touchdowns, Passes Thrown	4	Johnny Unitas, Baltimore 1957-60
		Len Dawson, Dallas Texans 1962, Kansas City 1963, 1965-66
Yards, Rushing	8	Jim Brown, Cleveland Browns 1957-61, 1963-65
Yards, Pass Receiving	7	Don Hutson, Green Bay 1936, 1938-39, 1941-44
Yards, Passing	5	Sonny Jurgensen, Philadelphia 1961-62, Washington 1966-67, 1969
Pass Receptions	8	Don Hutson, Green Bay 1936-37, 1939, 1941-45
Passes Completed	5	Sammy Baugh, Washington 1937, 1943, 1945, 1947-48
Pass Interceptions	3	Everson Walls, Dallas 1981-82, 1985

Season Best

POINTS	176	Paul Hornung, Green Bay 1960 (15-TD, 41-EP, 15-FG)
EXTRA POINTS	66	Uwe von Schamann, Miami 1984
FIELD GOALS	35	Ali Haji-Sheikh, N.Y. Giants 1983

TOUCHDOWNS		
Rushing and Pass Receiving	24	John Riggins, Washington 1983 (24-R)
Rushing	24	John Riggins, Washington 1983
Pass Receiving	22	Jerry Rice, San Francisco 1987
Passes Thrown	48	Dan Marino, Miami 1984
By Interception Return	4	Ken Houston, Houston 1971
		Jim Kearney, Kansas City 1972
By Punt Return	4	Jack Christiansen, Detroit 1951
		Rick Upchurch, Denver 1976
By Kickoff Return	4	Travis Williams, Green Bay 1967
		Cecil Turner, Chicago 1970
By Fumble Recovery Return	2	By many players
YARDAGE		
Rushing	2,105	Eric Dickerson, L.A. Rams 1984
Pass Receiving	1,746	Charley Hennigan, Houston 1961
Passing	5,084	Dan Marino, Miami 1984
HOW MANY TIMES		
Pass Receptions	106	Art Monk, Washington 1984
Passes Completed	378	Dan Marino, Miami 1986
Interceptions	14	Dick (Night Train) Lane, L.A. Rams 1952

Game Best

POINTS	40	Ernie Nevers (6-TD, 4-EP), Chicago Cardinals v Chicago Bears 1929
EXTRA POINTS	9	Pat Harder, Chicago Cardinals v N.Y. Giants 1948
		Bob Waterfield, L.A. Rams v Baltimore 1950
		Charlie Gogolak, Washington v N.Y. Giants 1966
FIELD GOALS	7	Jim Bakken, St Louis v Pittsburgh 1967
		Rich Karlis, Minnesota v L.A. Rams 1989
TOUCHDOWNS		
All methods of scoring	6	Ernie Nevers (6-R), Chicago Cardinals v Chicago Bears 1929
		Dub Jones (4-R, 2-P), Cleveland v Chicago Bears 1951
		Gale Sayers (4-R, 1-P, 1-Ret), Chicago Bears v San Francisco 1965
Rushing	6	Ernie Nevers, Chicago Cardinals v Chicago Bears 1929
Pass Receiving	5	Bob Shaw, Chicago Cardinals v Baltimore 1950
		Kellen Winslow, San Diego v Oakland 1981
		Jerry Rice, San Francisco v Atlanta 1990
Passes Thrown	7	Sid Luckman, Chicago Bears v N.Y. Giants 1943
		Adrian Burk, Philadelphia v Washington 1954
		George Blanda, Houston v N.Y. Titans 1961
		Y.A. Tittle, N.Y. Giants v Washington 1962
		Joe Kapp, Minnesota v Baltimore 1969
YARDAGE		
Rushing	275	Walter Payton, Chicago v Minnesota 1977
Pass Receiving	336	Willie (Flipper) Anderson, L.A. Rams v New Orleans 1989
Passing	554	Norm Van Brocklin, L.A. Rams v N.Y. Yanks 1951
HOW MANY TIMES		
Rushing Attempts	45	Jamie Morris, Washington v Cincinnati 1988
Pass Receptions	18	Tom Fears, L.A. Rams v Green Bay 1950
Passes Completed	42	Richard Todd, N.Y. Jets v San Francisco 1980
Interceptions	4	By many players
LONGEST		
Touchdown Rushing	99 yds	Tony Dorsett, Dallas v Minnesota 1983
Touchdown Pass Receiving	99 yds	Andy Farkas (from Filchock), Washington v Pittsburgh 1939
		Bobby Mitchell (from Izo), Washington v Cleveland 1963
		Pat Studstill (from Sweetan), Detroit v Baltimore 1966
		Gerry Allen (from Jurgensen), Washington v Chicago 1968
		Cliff Branch (from Plunkett), L.A. Raiders v Washington 1983
		Mike Quick (from Jaworski), Philadelphia v Atlanta 1985
Field Goal	63 yds	Tom Dempsey, New Orleans v Detroit 1970
Punt Return (All TDs)	98 yds	Gil LeFebvre, Cincinnati v Brooklyn 1933

		Charlie West, Minnesota v Washington 1968
		Dennis Morgan, Dallas v St Louis 1974
		Terance Mathis, N.Y. Jets v Dallas 1990
Kickoff Return (All TDs)	106 yds	Al Carmichael, Green Bay v Chicago Bears 1956
		Noland Smith, Kansas City v Denver 1967
		Roy Green, St Louis v Dallas 1979
Interception Return (TD)	103 yds	Vencie Glenn, San Diego v Denver 1987
Fumble Recovery Return (TD)	104 yds	Jack Tatum, Oakland v Green Bay 1972

TEAM RECORDS

Most Championships	11	Green Bay, 1929-31, 1936, 1939, 1944, 1961-62, 1965-67
	9	Chicago Staleys/Bears, 1921, 1932-33, 1940-41, 1943, 1946, 1963, 1985
	6	**N.Y. Giants, 1927, 1934, 1938, 1956, 1986, 1990**
	4	Baltimore, 1958-59, 1968, 1970
		Cleveland Browns, 1950, 1954-55, 1964
		Detroit, 1935, 1952-53, 1957
		Oakland/L.A. Raiders, 1967, 1976, 1980, 1983
		Pittsburgh, 1974-75, 1978-79
		San Francisco, 1981, 1984, 1988-89
		Washington, 1937, 1942, 1982, 1987
Most Consecutive Games Won (inc. playoffs)	18	Chicago Bears, 1933-34 and 1941-42
		Miami, 1972-73
		San Francisco, 1989-90
Most Consecutive Games Won	17	Chicago Bears, 1933-34 (exc. playoffs)
Most Consecutive Games Lost	26	Tampa Bay, 1976-77
Most Points in a Season	541	Washington, 1983
Fewest Points in a Season (Since 1932)	37	Cincinnati-St Louis, 1934
Most Points in a Game	72	Washington v N.Y. Giants, 1966
Most Points (Both Teams) in a Game	113	Washington v N.Y. Giants, 1966
Fewest Points (Both Teams) in a Game	0	Many teams; last time N.Y. Giants v Detroit, 1943

ALL-TIME TOP TWENTY

(1990 Active players in capitals)

All-Time Leading Rushers

		Yrs.	Att.	Yards	Ave.	TDs
1.	Walter Payton	13	3,838	16,726	4.4	110
2.	Tony Dorsett	12	2,936	12,739	4.3	77
3.	Jim Brown	9	2,359	12,312	5.2	106
4.	Franco Harris	13	2,949	12,120	4.1	91
5.	ERIC DICKERSON	8	2,616	11,903	4.6	86
6.	John Riggins	14	2,916	11,352	3.9	104
7.	O.J. Simpson	11	2,404	11,236	4.7	61
8.	OTTIS ANDERSON	12	2,499	10,101	4.0	80
9.	Earl Campbell	8	2,187	9,407	4.3	74
10.	Jim Taylor	10	1,941	8,597	4.4	83
11.	Joe Perry	14	1,737	8,378	4.8	53
12.	Larry Csonka	11	1,891	8,081	4.3	64
13.	MARCUS ALLEN	9	1,960	7,957	4.1	75
14.	GERALD RIGGS	9	1,911	7,940	4.2	58
15.	FREEMAN McNEIL	10	1,704	7,604	4.5	36
16.	Mike Pruitt	11	1,844	7,378	4.0	51
17.	JAMES BROOKS	10	1,515	7,347	4.8	47
18.	Leroy Kelly	10	1,727	7,274	4.2	74
19.	George Rogers	7	1,692	7,176	4.2	54
20.	ROGER CRAIG	8	1,686	7,064	4.2	50

All-Time Leading Receivers

		Yrs.	No.	Yards	Ave.	TDs
1.	Steve Largent	14	819	13,089	16.0	100
2.	Charlie Joiner	18	750	12,146	16.2	65
3.	ART MONK	11	730	9,935	13.6	52
4.	OZZIE NEWSOME	13	662	7,980	12.1	47
5.	Charley Taylor	13	649	9,110	14.0	79
6.	JAMES LOFTON	13	642	11,963	18.6	61
7.	Don Maynard	15	633	11,834	18.7	88
8.	Raymond Berry	13	631	9,275	14.7	68
9.	Harold Carmichael	14	590	8,985	15.2	79
10.	Fred Biletnikoff	14	589	8,974	15.2	76
11.	Harold Jackson	16	579	10,372	17.9	76
12.	Lionel Taylor	10	567	7,195	12.7	45
13.	Wes Chandler	11	559	8,966	16.0	56
14.	STANLEY MORGAN	14	557	10,716	19.2	72
15.	J.T. SMITH	13	544	6,974	12.8	35
16.	Lance Alworth	11	542	10,266	18.9	85
17.	Kellen Winslow	9	541	6,741	12.5	45
18.	John Stallworth	14	537	8,723	16.2	63
19.	ROY GREEN	12	522	8,496	16.3	66
20.	Bobby Mitchell	11	521	7,954	15.3	65

All-Time Passer Ratings

		Yrs.	Att.	Comp.	Yards	TDs	Int.	Rating
1.	JOE MONTANA	12	4,579	2,914	34,998	242	123	93.4
2.	DAN MARINO	8	4,181	2,480	31,416	241	136	88.5
3.	BOOMER ESIASON	7	2,687	1,520	21,381	150	98	85.8
	JIM KELLY	5	2,088	1,251	15,730	105	72	85.8
5.	Roger Staubach	11	2,958	1,685	22,700	153	109	83.4
6.	Neil Lomax	8	3,153	1,817	22,771	136	90	82.7
7.	Len Dawson	19	3,741	2,136	28,711	239	183	82.6
	Sonny Jurgensen	18	4,262	2,433	32,224	255	189	82.6
9.	DAVE KRIEG	11	3,291	1,909	24,052	184	136	82.3
10.	JIM EVERETT	5	2,038	1,154	15,345	101	73	82.2
	KEN O'BRIEN	9	2,878	1,697	20,444	109	78	82.2
12.	Ken Anderson	16	4,475	2,654	32,838	197	160	81.9
13.	Danny White	13	2,950	1,761	21,959	155	132	81.7
14.	Bart Starr	16	3,149	1,808	24,718	152	138	80.5
15.	Fran Tarkenton	18	6,467	3,686	47,003	342	266	80.4
16.	BERNIE KOSAR	6	2,363	1,364	16,450	85	62	80.3
17.	Dan Fouts	15	5,604	3,297	43,040	254	242	80.2
18.	WARREN MOON	7	3,025	1,701	22,989	134	112	79.9
19.	TONY EASON	8	1,564	911	11,142	61	51	79.7
20.	JIM McMAHON	9	1,840	1,056	13,398	77	66	79.3

Tight end Ozzie Newsome, veteran of 13 great seasons with the Cleveland Browns, retired as the fourth-leading pass receiver in NFL history.

Johnny Unitas established the standards against which others are mentioned. The rules governing the forward pass were less generous to quarterbacks in Unitas's era.

All-Time Leading Scorers

	Yrs.	TDs	EPs	FGs	Total
1. George Blanda	26	9	943	335	2,002
2. Jan Stenerud	19	0	580	373	1,699
3. Jim Turner	16	1	521	304	1,439
4. Mark Moseley	16	0	482	300	1,382
5. Jim Bakken	17	0	534	282	1,380
6. Fred Cox	15	0	519	282	1,365
7. PAT LEAHY	17	0	528	278	1,362
8. Lou Groza	17	1	641	234	1,349
9. Chris Bahr	14	0	490	241	1,213
10. NICK LOWERY	12	0	375	259	1,152
11. Gino Cappelletti*	11	42	350	176	1,130
12. Ray Wersching	15	0	456	222	1,122
13. Don Cockroft	13	0	432	216	1,080
14. Garo Yepremian	14	0	444	210	1,074
15. JIM BREECH	12	0	459	201	1,062
16. Bruce Gossett	11	0	374	219	1,031
17. EDDIE MURRAY	11	0	341	225	1,016
18. Sam Baker	15	2	428	179	977
19. MATT BAHR	12	0	378	199	975
20. Rafael Septien	10	0	420	180	960

* Includes four two-point conversions

Passes Completed	No.
1. Fran Tarkenton	3,686
2. Dan Fouts	3,297
3. JOE MONTANA	2,914
4. Johnny Unitas	2,830
5. Ken Anderson	2,654
6. Jim Hart	2,593
7. DAN MARINO	2,480
8. John Brodie	2,469
9. Sonny Jurgensen	2,433
10. STEVE DeBERG	2,376
11. JOE FERGUSON	2,369
12. Roman Gabriel	2,366
13. John Hadl	2,363
14. Norm Snead	2,276
15. Ken Stabler	2,270
16. Ron Jaworski	2,187
17. PHIL SIMMS	2,164
18. Len Dawson	2,136
19. Y.A. Tittle	2,118
20. Craig Morton	2,053

Yards Passing	Yards
1. Fran Tarkenton	47,003
2. Dan Fouts	43,040
3. Johnny Unitas	40,239
4. JOE MONTANA	34,998
5. Jim Hart	34,665
6. John Hadl	33,503
7. Ken Anderson	32,838
8. Sonny Jurgensen	32,224
9. John Brodie	31,548
10. DAN MARINO	31,416
11. Norm Snead	30,797
12. JOE FERGUSON	29,817
13. Roman Gabriel	29,444
14. Len Dawson	28,711
15. PHIL SIMMS	28,519
16. STEVE DeBERG	28,490
17. Y.A. Tittle	28,339
18. Ron Jaworski	28,190
19. Terry Bradshaw	27,989
20. Ken Stabler	27,938

Touchdown Passes	No.
1. Fran Tarkenton	342
2. Johnny Unitas	290
3. Sonny Jurgensen	255
4. Dan Fouts	254
5. John Hadl	244
6. JOE MONTANA	242
7. DAN MARINO	241
8. Len Dawson	239
9. George Blanda	236
10. John Brodie	214
11. Terry Bradshaw	212
Y.A. Tittle	212
13. Jim Hart	209
14. Roman Gabriel	201
15. Ken Anderson	197
16. JOE FERGUSON	196
Bobby Layne	196
Norm Snead	196
19. Ken Stabler	194
20. Bob Griese	192

INDEX OF RETIRED PLAYERS LISTED IN THE ALL-TIME STATISTICS

ALLEN Gerry, Baltimore (1966), Washington (1967-69)
ALWORTH Lance, San Diego (1962-70), Dallas (1971-72)
ANDERSON Ken, Cincinnati (1971-86)
BAHR Chris, Cincinnati (1976-79), Oakland/L.A. Raiders (1980-88), San Diego (1989)
BAKER Sam, Washington (1953 and 1956-59), Cleveland (1960-61), Dallas Cowboys (1962-63), Philadelphia (1964-69)
BAKKEN Jim, St Louis (1962-78)
BAUGH Sammy, Washington (1937-52)
BERRY Raymond, Baltimore (1955-67)
BILETNIKOFF Fred, Oakland (1965-78)
BLANDA George, Chicago Bears (1949 and 1950-58), Baltimore (1950), Houston (1960-66), Oakland (1967-75)
BRADSHAW Terry, Pittsburgh (1970-83)
BRANCH Cliff, Oakland/L.A. Raiders (1972-85)
BRODIE John, San Francisco (1957-73)
BROWN Jim, Cleveland (1957-65)
BURK Adrian, Baltimore (1950), Philadelphia (1951-56)
CAMPBELL Earl, Houston (1978-84), New Orleans (1984-85)
CAPPELLETTI Gino, Boston Patriots (1960-70)
CARMICHAEL Al, Green Bay (1953-58), Denver (1960-61)
CARMICHAEL Harold, Philadelphia (1971-83), Dallas (1984)
CHANDLER Wes, New Orleans (1978-81), San Diego (1981-87), San Francisco (1988)
CHRISTIANSEN Jack, Detroit (1951-58)
COCKROFT Don, Cleveland (1968-80)
COX Fred, Minnesota (1963-77)
CSONKA Larry, Miami (1968-74 and 1979), N.Y. Giants (1976-78)
DAWSON Len, Pittsburgh (1957-59), Cleveland (1960-61), Dallas Texans/Kansas City (1962-75)
DEMPSEY Tom, New Orleans (1969-70), Philadelphia (1971-74), L.A. Rams (1975-76), Houston (1977), Buffalo (1978-79)
DORSETT Tony, Dallas (1977-87), Denver (1988)
FARKAS Andy, Washington (1938-44), Detroit (1945)
FEARS Tom, L.A. Rams (1948-56)
FILCHOCK Frank, Pittsburgh (1938), Washington (1938-41 and 1944-45), N.Y. Giants (1946), Baltimore (1950)
FOUTS Dan, San Diego (1973-87)
GABRIEL Roman, L.A. Rams (1962-72), Philadelphia (1973-77)
GOGOLAK Charlie, Washington (1966-68), Boston/New England (1970-72)
GOSSETT Bruce, L.A. Rams (1964-69), San Francisco (1970-74)
GRIESE Bob, Miami (1967-80)
GROZA Lou, Cleveland Browns (1946-59 and 1961-67)
HADL John, San Diego (1962-72), L.A. Rams (1973-74), Green Bay (1974-75), Houston (1976-77)
HAJI-SHEIKH Ali, N.Y. Giants (1983-85), Atlanta (1986), Washington (1987)
HARDER Pat, Chicago Cardinals (1946-50), Detroit (1951-53)
HARRIS Franco, Pittsburgh (1972-83), Seattle (1984)
HART Jim, St Louis (1966-83), Washington (1984)
HENNIGAN Charley, Houston (1960-66)
HORNUNG Paul, Green Bay (1957-62 and 1964-66)
HOUSTON Ken, Houston (1967-72), Washington (1973-80)
HUTSON Don, Green Bay (1935-45)
IZO George, St Louis (1960), Washington (1961-64), Detroit (1965), Pittsburgh (1966)
JACKSON Harold, L.A. Rams (1968 and 1973-77), Philadelphia (1969-72), New England (1978-81), Minnesota (1982), Seattle (1983)
JAWORSKI Ron, L.A. Rams (1973-76), Philadelphia (1977-86), Miami (1987-88), Kansas City (1989)
JOINER Charlie, Houston (1969-72), Cincinnati (1972-75), San Diego (1976-86)
JONES Dub, Miami (AAFC) (1946), Brooklyn (AAFC) (1946-48), Cleveland (1948-55)
JURGENSEN Sonny, Philadelphia (1957-63), Washington (1964-74)
KAPP Joe, Minnesota (1967-69), Boston Patriots (1970)
KEARNEY Jim, Detroit (1965-66), Kansas City (1967-75), New Orleans (1976)

KELLY Leroy, Cleveland (1964-73)
KRAUSE Paul, Washington (1964-67), Minnesota (1968-79)
LANE Dick (Night Train), L.A. Rams (1952-53), Chicago Cardinals (1954-59), Detroit (1960-65)
LARGENT Steve, Seattle (1976–89)
LAYNE Bobby, Chicago Bears (1948), N.Y. Bulldogs (1949), Detroit (1950-58), Pittsburgh (1958-62)
LeFEBVRE Gil, Cincinnati Reds (1933-34), Detroit (1935)
LOMAX Neil, St. Louis/Phoenix (1981-88)
LUCKMAN Sid, Chicago Bears (1939-50)
MATSON Ollie, Chicago Cardinals (1952 and 1954-58), L.A. Rams (1959-62), Detroit (1963), Philadelphia (1964-66)
MAYNARD Don, N.Y. Giants (1958), N.Y. Titans/Jets (1960-72), St Louis (1973)
MITCHELL Bobby, Cleveland (1958-61), Washington (1962-68)
MORGAN Dennis, Dallas (1974), Philadelphia (1975)
MORTON Craig, Dallas (1965-74), N.Y. Giants (1974-76), Denver (1977-82)
MOSELEY Mark, Philadelphia (1970), Houston (1971-72), Washington (1974-86), Cleveland (1986)
NEVERS Ernie, Duluth Eskimos (1926-27), Chicago Cardinals (1929-31)
PAYTON Walter, Chicago (1975-87)
PERRY Joe, San Francisco (1948-60 and 1963), Baltimore (1961-62)
PLUNKETT Jim, New England (1971-75), San Francisco (1976-77), Oakland/L.A. Raiders (1978-85)
PRUITT Mike, Cleveland (1976-84), Buffalo (1985), Kansas City (1985-86)
RIGGINS John, N.Y. Jets (1971-75), Washington (1976-79 and 1981-85)
ROGERS George, New Orleans (1981-84), Washington (1985-87)
SAYERS Gale, Chicago (1965-71)
SEPTIEN Rafael, L.A. Rams (1977), Dallas (1978-86)
SHAW Bob, Cleveland/L.A. Rams (1945-49), Chicago Cardinals (1950)
SIMPSON O.J., Buffalo (1969-77), San Francisco (1978-79)
SMITH Noland, Kansas City (1967-69), San Francisco (1969)
SNEAD Norm, Washington (1961-63), Philadelphia (1964-70), Minnesota (1971), N.Y. Giants (1972-74 and 1976), San Francisco (1974-75)
STABLER Ken, Oakland (1970-79), Houston (1980-81), New Orleans (1982-84)
STARR Bart, Green Bay (1956-71)
STAUBACH Roger, Dallas (1969-79)
STENERUD Jan, Kansas City (1967-79), Green Bay (1980-83), Minnesota (1984-85)
STUDSTILL Pat, Detroit (1961-62 and 1964-67), L.A. Rams (1968-71), New England (1972)
SWEETAN Karl, Detroit (1966-67), New Orleans (1968), L.A. Rams (1969-70)
TARKENTON Fran, Minnesota (1961-66 and 1972-78), N.Y. Giants (1967-71)
TATUM Jack, Oakland (1971-79), Houston (1980)
TAYLOR Charley, Washington (1964-75 and 1977)
TAYLOR Jim, Green Bay (1958-66), New Orleans (1967)
TAYLOR Lionel, Chicago Bears (1959), Denver (1960-66), Houston (1967-68)
THOMPSON Billy, Denver (1969-81)
TITTLE Y.A., Baltimore (1948-50), San Francisco (1951-60), N.Y. Giants (1961-64)
TODD Richard, N.Y. Jets (1976-83), New Orleans (1984-85)
TURNER Cecil, Chicago (1968-73)
TURNER Jim, N.Y. Jets (1964-70), Denver (1971-79)
UNITAS Johnny, Baltimore (1956-72), San Diego (1973)
UPCHURCH Rick, Denver (1975-83)
VAN BROCKLIN Norm, L.A. Rams (1949-57), Philadelphia (1958-60)
von SCHAMANN Uwe, Miami (1979-84)
WATERFIELD Bob, Cleveland/L.A. Rams (1945-52)
WERSCHING Ray, San Diego (1973-76), San Francisco (1977-87)
WEST Charlie, Minnesota (1968-73), Detroit (1974-77), Denver (1978-79)
WHITE Danny, Dallas (1976-88)
WILLIAMS Travis, Green Bay (1967-70), L.A. Rams (1971)
WINSLOW Kellen, San Diego (1979-87)
YEPREMIAN Garo, Detroit (1966-67), Miami (1970-78), New Orleans (1979), Tampa Bay (1980-81)

CHAPTER THREE

SUPER BOWL SILVER ANNIVERSARY TEAM

To mark the 25th staging of the Super Bowl, fans were given the opportunity to select the best team drawn from participating head coaches and players. The San Francisco 49ers, winners of the title four times, were honoured by the selection of that number of players. But fans recognized the enduring greatness of the only other four-time winners, the Pittsburgh Steelers, by voting in the largest contingent, nine. The Oakland/Los Angeles Raiders, champions three times, were granted five berths on the dreamboat.

Franco Harris was the great 'money back'. Harris led the rushing offense in the Steelers' four Super Bowl Championships.

OFFENSE

Position	Name	Votes	Pct. of Votes
Head Coach	Vince Lombardi	397,923	35.7
Quarterback	Joe Montana	747,801	67.5
Running Back	Franco Harris	620,931	29.2
Running Back	Larry Csonka	518,690	24.4
Wide Receiver	Lynn Swann	775,447	36.6
Wide Receiver	Jerry Rice	622,849	29.4
Tight End	Dave Casper	712,096	66.2
Tackle	Art Shell	686,645	32.5
Tackle	Forrest Gregg	447,473	21.2
Guard	Gene Upshaw	612,571	29.3
Guard	Jerry Kramer	424,104	20.3
Center	Mike Webster	641,163	59.9
Placekicker	Jan Stenerud	422,654	43.2
Kick Returner	John Taylor	349,826	32.3

As the potential head coach, Pittsburgh's Chuck Noll, San Francisco's Bill Walsh, Miami's Don Shula and Tom Landry of the Cowboys might consider themselves unfortunate to be up against the popular choice. But the lingering vision of Vince Lombardi carried the day. Committed to basics delivered with ruthless efficiency, to Lombardi, whose Green Bay Packers won the NFL title five times in a seven-year span, went the responsibility of establishing the authority of the senior league in the face of the upstart AFL challengers in Super Bowl I. On that day in the Los Angeles Memorial Coliseum, the Kansas City Chiefs were dominated by the score of 35-10 and, for good measure, a year later the Oakland Raiders were defeated 33-14. It is a fitting tribute to Lombardi the man and Lombardi the head coach that the Super Bowl trophy now bears his name.

Lombardi liked big running backs. He would have loved Franco Harris and Larry Csonka. Unassuming, thoughtful, explosive, a high-voltage discharge – all are descriptions of Harris, who delivered his 6-2, 225-pound frame with unexpected speed. As a 1972 rookie

One hand on one ankle never had much hope of stopping Larry Csonka.

in his first pro start, Harris rushed for only 35 yards and fumbled twice in a loss to the Bengals but, by the end of that season, Pittsburgh had won its first AFC Central division title. "It was no coincidence," defensive leader Joe Greene was quick to reflect. That year also saw Harris make 'The Immaculate Reception', a shoestring catch of a last-minute deflected pass, before racing 42 yards for the game-winning touchdown against Oakland in the AFC divisional playoffs. In his 12 years with the club, Pittsburgh never had a losing season. Setting single-game records with 34 carries for 158 yards, Harris was a significant factor in Pittsburgh's first Super Bowl victory, a 16-6 decision over Minnesota. His Super Bowl career records of 101 attempts for 354 yards and four touchdowns, as a member of four NFL Champion teams, still stand.

Csonka has been described as a primeval force, seismic in application. Wearing a helmet looking more like a relic from the Peloponnesian Wars than standard issue, if he had a move, it was not much more than an almost involuntary swerve, as much the inevitable consequence of an uncontrollable momentum as it was intent. Essentially, he had only one direction, north-south, seeking to draw opponents into a collision out of which only one man, Csonka, was likely to emerge, steam-valves holding firm, pistons pumping. He gave Miami a degree of ball control on which to hang an entire offensive philosophy, relegating the future Hall of Fame axis of quarterback Bob Griese and wide receiver Paul Warfield to a supporting rôle. Csonka had three 1,000-yard rushing seasons, each one culminating in a Super Bowl appearance for Miami. In Game VII, he bruised his way for 112 yards on just 15 carries, setting up both touchdowns in the Dolphins' 14-7 win against Washington. The following year, he set Super Bowl records with 145 yards on 33 carries and scored a pair of touchdowns as Miami subdued Minnesota by the score of 24-7.

It may have been predictable that fans would vote San Francisco's Joe Montana as the quarterback of the anniversary team, but few could have estimated his popularity to be better than five times that of the other four-time Super Bowl winner, Pittsburgh's Terry Bradshaw, and that Montana would receive more than twice as many votes as all the rest combined! The only man ever to be the Super Bowl MVP three times, twice his individual greatness was partially obscured by an avalanche of points as Miami were beaten 38-16 and the Broncos were overwhelmed 55-10. In recalling his most exciting series in Super Bowl play, the game-winning drive against Cincinnati in Super Bowl XXIII when he took the 49ers 92 yards in 12 plays culminating in his ten-yard touchdown pass to John Taylor, doubtless the voters took account of the fact that, only the previous year, against strong medical advice, he had made an astonishing comeback from a spinal injury. The Super Bowl career-leading passer, he has thrown for 11 touchdowns without an interception. Maybe the most telling statement came from former teammate Randy Cross, who offered, "If every game were a Super Bowl, Joe would be undefeated."

Their greatness belonged to different decades but Lynn Swann and Jerry Rice are joined by the common bond of being the outstanding wide receivers to grace the Super Bowl arena. If Swann raised the position to an art form, a demonstration of serenity and beauty, Rice's contributions have been those of fluid, surging power and ruthless execution.

Swann was a rookie when the Steelers won their first Super Bowl title. In that tense game with Minnesota he didn't catch a pass. But the following year against Dallas, his 32-yard reception set up Pittsburgh's opening touchdown. His gravity-defying, leaping 53-yard catch shortly before half time was all for nought as placekicker Roy Gerela missed a 36-yard field goal attempt. But, with 3:02 remaining in the game, he homed in underneath a Terry Bradshaw pass which flew a full 59 yards through the air and glided the final five yards for the touchdown which gave Pittsburgh an 11-point cushion, in what turned out to be a 21-17 victory. Three years later in a rematch with Dallas, Swann's partner, John Stallworth, was the big-play exponent, but Swann was the leading receiver with seven catches for 124 yards and a touchdown as Pittsburgh won a shootout, 35-31. His 47-yard touchdown catch against the Rams helped Pittsburgh to a fourth NFL Championship in six seasons.

"Lynn Swann was an idol....It would amaze me how he could fly through the air....I'll never forget that catch against Dallas...." said Rice after being voted MVP in Super Bowl XXIII. He had tied the single-game record with 11 catches and set the new single-game mark for receiving yards with 215. All this after a week in which a severely sprained ankle had kept him off the practice field. The following year, in Game XXIV, he caught seven passes for 148 yards and touchdowns covering 20, 38 and 28 yards. "Rice brings a great deal more than you'd think to the position," said one scout. "Faster than people realized when the 49ers drafted him, he has an extra gear and excellent sense of what's going on around him. And with those big, strong hands of his..." he went on. It's no secret that many defensive backs will attempt to intimidate a wide receiver with

LEFT: Wide receiver Lynn Swann brought a special kind of grace and beauty to the game.

RIGHT: Wide receiver Jerry Rice has assaulted the NFL records for pass receiving and threatens to leave them in tatters.

80

Dave Casper, who made the over-the-shoulder catch appear routine, was the voters' choice by a wide margin.

verbal abuse. It didn't affect Swann's play but, occasionally, he'd register his contempt for that kind of behaviour. Rice has come under similar pressure, notably in the days leading up to Super Bowl XXIV when Denver safety Steve Atwater promised to make every collision tell. Rice's response was to use Atwater as a springboard, bouncing off the free safety and into an open space to make his first touchdown catch.

The position of tight end is not the most glamorous. Some tight ends are pure blockers while others are almost exclusively receivers. Cincinnati's Dan Ross enjoyed his day in the sun, setting the record with 11 passes in Super Bowl XVI, while the Giants' Mark Bavaro has been a force in two New York title wins. But to those who remember the Raiders' victory over Minnesota in Super Bowl XI there was no other choice than Dave Casper. That day, Casper caught four passes for 70 yards and the opening touchdown. He played in only the one game but it was enough to make his indelible mark.

One game also might have sufficed for the Raiders' pairing of guard Gene Upshaw and tackle Art Shell but, as a left-side combination, they helped the team to victory in two NFL title games (XI and XV), Upshaw being the only player to participate in Super Bowls in three decades. Imagine the matchup, Oakland versus Minnesota, Shell and Upshaw coming nose to nose with the Vikings' Jim Marshall and Alan Page. The result was total dominance for the men in silver helmets as, repeatedly, half of the famed 'Purple Gang' defensive line was left prostrate in a wasteland exploited for most of a 137-yard individual rushing total by Raiders running back Clarence Davis. The former USC flier never had a better day in the pros. As Upshaw said, "Art and I played together for so long that we looked at ourselves as one guy. Art was the left hand and I was the right hand. We worked together."

Custodianship of the right side went to another club pairing, Green Bay guard Jerry Kramer and tackle Forrest Gregg. By the time of Super Bowl I, Kramer and Gregg were word-perfect in delivery of Lombardi's script. In turn, Kansas City and Oakland were forced to accept the message. "The finest player I have ever coached," offered Lombardi about Gregg, who went on to help Dallas to victory in Super Bowl VI. If Kramer was a touch behind Gregg in terms of straight-ahead power, he more than compensated when it came to range and expression, classically when blocking on the Packers' bread-and-butter play, the power sweep.

For the pivotal position, no one came close to the combination of quickness, timing, strength and field awareness of Pittsburgh's Mike Webster. He played backup center and guard on the Steelers' first two victorious squads before finding a home at center. Webster, who may be the only NFL player recognizable for his muscled arms, was an iron man, playing in 220 regular-season games for Pittsburgh before extending his career as part-time player-coach with Kansas City.

DEFENSE

Position	Name	Votes	Pct. of Votes
Defensive End	L.C. Greenwood	590,672	26.5
Defensive End	Ed (Too Tall) Jones	499,279	22.4
Defensive Tackle	Joe Greene	813,591	37.5
Defensive Tackle	Randy White	402,707	18.5
Outside Linebacker	Jack Ham	764,904	36.4
Outside Linebacker	Ted Hendricks	599,836	28.5
Inside Linebacker	Jack Lambert	672,149	30.9
Inside Linebacker	Mike Singletary	526,410	24.2
Cornerback	Ronnie Lott	697,335	34.6
Cornerback	Mel Blount	383,752	19.0
Safety	Donnie Shell	524,180	24.8
Safety	Willie Wood	369,468	17.4
Punter	Ray Guy	858,825	79.2

Appropriately, the man who was the first draft pick of Chuck Noll, when he became head coach of the Steelers in 1969, was the most popular scrimmage player selected by the fans. That player, Joe Greene, was the foundation upon which the Pittsburgh dynasty was constructed. Widely known as 'Mean Joe', a nickname he did not readily accept, Greene could take on offensive linemen in bunches, creating mayhem and freeing teammates to rampage. Much as several 49ers clubs of the 1980s could embark on a drive just knowing that they would score, the Steelers defenses of a decade earlier were equally certain of stopping opponents. At times, with Greene supercharged, they even felt confident of forcing a turnover.

Playing alongside Greene, at left defensive end, L.C. Greenwood was the perfect partner. Towering somewhere in the region of six feet six-or-seven, he'd been a lowly tenth-round pick in the same year as Greene but he would become the perfect foil, complementing Greene's strength with his stealth, subtle shifts of pace and the instinctive capacity for timing his leap to swat down a pass.

While Greene and Greenwood offered opponents their first taste of what came to be known as the Steel Curtain, Ed (Too Tall) Jones and Randy White formed a part of the outer crust of the Doomsday Defense which helped to make the Dallas Cowboys a perennial contender. Renowned for his natural strength, White was nicknamed 'Manster', half-man, half-monster, by teammate Charlie Waters. It was a tag that White didn't particularly like but, as was his nature, he wasn't going to make a fuss about it. A man not given to overt displays of emotion and never seeking personal publicity, White preferred to enjoy the warmth of achievement in private. Jones was another who did his talking on the gridiron. At six feet nine inches tall, he also carried a 275-pound load which was unusual for his

The ferocious Joe Greene was the most inspirational defensive leader of the 1970s.

era. Renowned for batting down passes at the line of scrimmage, less obvious was his major contribution, that of controlling the run which mostly went to his side of the field. Teammate Harvey Martin, a much-feared exponent of the pass rush who, together with White, was voted co-MVP in Super Bowl XII, credits Jones for much of his personal success. Teak-tough, Jones never taped his hands or ankles and shunned the use of outer medication that some players apply as a necessary ritual. The only games he missed for Dallas came in 1979, when he tried out as a professional boxer. He won all six of his contests.

The voters clearly had a leaning towards height, for, in addition to Greenwood and Jones, they liked the 6-7 Ted Hendricks at outside linebacker. One of several misfits to be gathered together in the way only Raiders owner Al Davis can, 'The Mad Stork', as he was nicknamed, had enjoyed Super Bowl success with the Baltimore Colts. It wasn't just physically that Hendricks towered over his opponents. Also, he had a superior intellect and, with it, a sense of humour that was both wry and irreverent. Once, commenting on the popular view of the Raiders' attitude towards the rules of the game, Hendricks quipped, "The Raiders are responsible for many rule changes. There's the no-clothesline rule; the no-spearing rule; the no-hitting out-of-bounds rule; no throwing helmets; the no-stickum rule. So you see, we're not all bad."

At 6-1, the other outside linebacker, Jack Ham, hardly could have been more different physically, but his capacity to read a game, adjust to circumstances,

was unsurpassed. It was this quality which made him turn what otherwise might have been seen as big plays into routine operations. Not least for his modesty, Ham was one of the most popular Pittsburgh players. In the book, 'The Professionals', respected writer Ray Didinger tells the story of the Pittsburgh rooters who established a Jack Ham fan club – The Dobre Shunka Society. Dobre Shunka is 'Great Ham' in Polish.

The late George Allen, head coach of the Rams and Washington, once said, "What Ham does on intelligence, Lambert does on instinct. I'm not saying Lambert isn't smart, but that he's a natural, who obviously loves to play, who loves to hit, who takes pride in playing hurt." Allen might have mentioned the man's charisma. Once he stepped onto a football field, Lambert shifted immediately into leadership mode. If the boys needed enthusing, he'd vent his anger in the huddle and then would go out and set the example. 'World of Sport' viewers may remember Lambert in Super Bowl XIV. It wasn't obvious to anyone, except Lambert, that Rams quarterback Vince Ferragamo was going to throw a screen pass. But long before Ferragamo turned to deliver, Lambert's arm was raised, frantically directing teammates to his right, where Cullen Bryant had filtered into the clear. A few Steelers defenders were closer to

ABOVE: Jack Lambert directed operations from his pivotal position at middle linebacker.

LEFT: Cat-quick, fearless and with an unrivalled sense of position and timing, Jack Ham was the complete outside linebacker.

Though undersized, Randy White had immense strength and was always a dangerous pass rusher.

the action, but guess who eventually brought Bryant down for only a two-yard gain?

"If he's good enough, he's big enough," might be one comment of Mike Singletary, a six-foot, 230-pound linebacker who controlled the middle and directed operations at the heart of the Bears' '46' defensive system which dismantled opponents on the way to victory in Super Bowl XX. The ultimate perfectionist, Singletary wasn't content to be the Bears' leading tackler every year. It became a matter of pride to work on pass coverage until he earned a place in the nickel defense, an area normally off-limits to a middle linebacker. "Mike is the glue that holds this defense together," said former Chicago outside linebacker Otis Wilson.

The steel thread continued into the defensive secondary, with Mel Blount at cornerback and Donnie Shell at strong safety. The third member of the Steelers' defense to be elected to the Pro Football Hall of Fame following Greene and Ham, at 6-3, 205 pounds, Blount was unusually big for the position in the 1970s but it was not at the expense of speed. His form of intimidation was to lope alongside an opponent, looking him in the eye and matching him stride for stride. And he had supreme confidence. "If the scales were balanced,

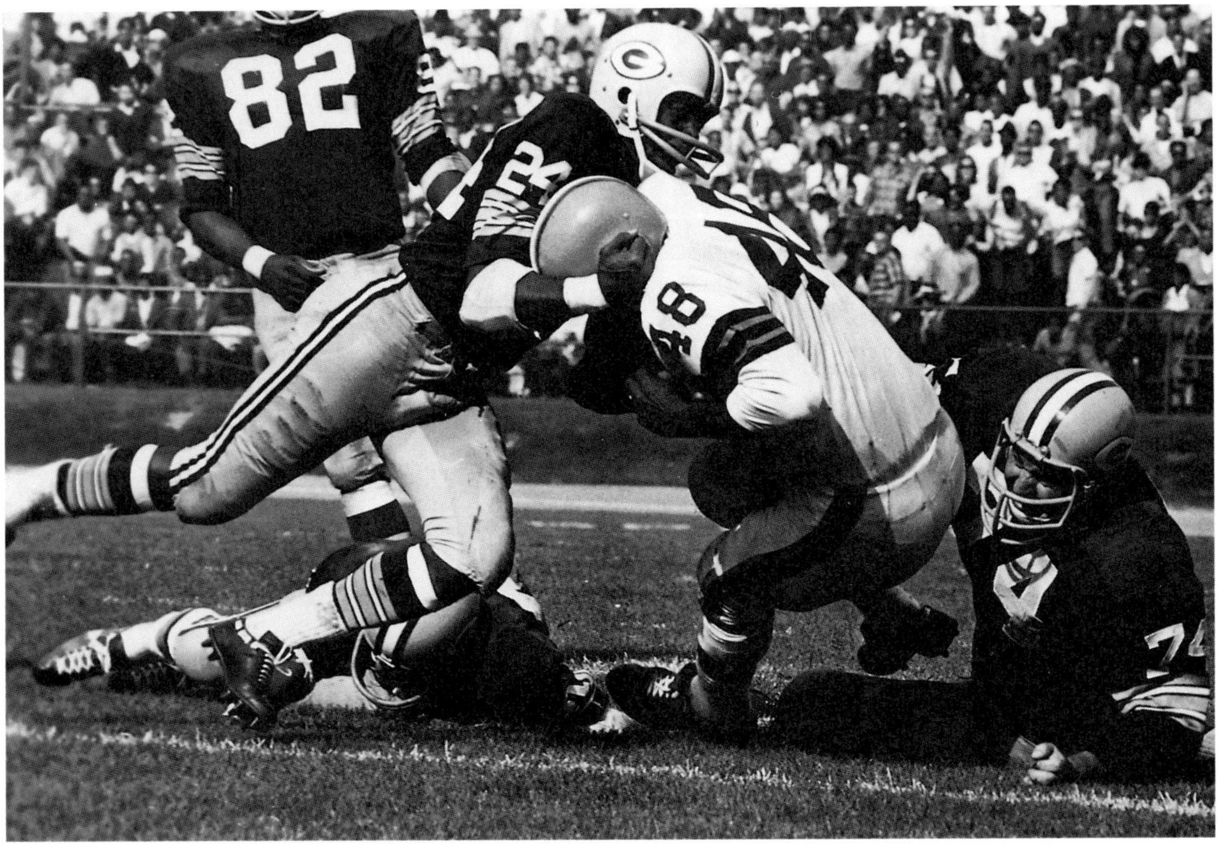

Cornerback Willie Wood, an outstanding pass defender, advances to tackle Cleveland running back Ernie Green.

there was nobody I couldn't cover," says Blount, and he backed that up even after the rules changes of the late 1970s gave advantages to wide receivers. Starting for Pittsburgh in all four of their Super Bowl appearances, Blount intercepted a Fran Tarkenton pass and recovered a Minnesota fumble in Super Bowl IX, while his interception of a Roger Staubach pass in Super Bowl XIII ended a Dallas threat and sparked a quick-fire drive culminating in the touchdown which gave Pittsburgh a 21-14 halftime lead.

Shell came up the hard way, going to the Steelers training camp as a free agent, making the roster as a backup and first captain of the Pittsburgh special teams, and serving his apprenticeship before moving up to start on the Steelers third and fourth Super Bowl title squads. A college linebacker, at 5-11 and 190 pounds Shell didn't have the size to play that position in the pros but his instincts made him a superior strong safety. Nobody ever described him as being particularly athletic or fast but he had the will to succeed.

Many still regard it as the key play in Super Bowl I, when Willie Wood intercepted Len Dawson's pass and returned the ball 50 yards to set up the Elijah Pitts touchdown which gave Green Bay a 21-10 lead. Wood also played his part the following season, with seven tackles and a 31-yard punt return as the Packers retained their title. He went undrafted in 1960 and, despite letters to every NFL club, only the Packers were interested. Lombardi saw great potential, using him sparingly, nurturing him as a rookie. In his third year, Wood topped the NFL with nine interceptions. Lombardi, known for the attention to detail and rigid discipline he expected of his players, gave Wood the freedom of the gridiron. "He has the ability to make plays, so we let him," explained Lombardi.

The only point of argument over Ronnie Lott is his playing position, for he has starred on Super Bowl Champion teams twice at left cornerback and twice at free safety. Few secondary players in league history have possessed the combination of speed, hard-hitting, subtle awareness and field generalship which has made Lott the premier defensive back of the last decade. One of three rookie defensive backs who started for the 49ers in Super Bowl XVI, only Lott was still starting in the reconstructed unit which again held off the Cincinnati Bengals seven years later. Modestly, he described himself as the old guy trying to keep everybody together.

It was a major surprise in the 1973 draft when the Raiders made Ray Guy the only pure punter ever to be selected in the first round (Russell Erxleben, drafted by New Orleans in 1979, was a dual-purpose kicker). But over the next 14 years, Guy more than repaid the compliment, establishing himself as the best at his craft in league history and, in context, outdistancing his NFC counterpart in all three of Super Bowls XI, XV and XVIII. The first punter to hit the giant television screen in the Louisiana Superdome (it was in the 1977 Pro Bowl), Guy also was a solid special teams tackler and could stand in at quarterback. But he may be remembered best for one astonishing play in Super Bowl XVIII, when his one-handed, leaping catch of a badly snapped ball and 42-yard punt turned possible disaster into excellent field position.

Jan Stenerud, too, established a notable precedent in August, 1991, when he became the first pure

Punter Ray Guy was the most popular selection overall for the Anniversary Team.

San Francisco free safety Ronnie Lott takes off with his 48th career interception – a 49ers record.

placekicker to be elected to the Pro Football Hall of Fame. Ice-cool with howitzer strength, Stenerud was a threat from any distance, remarkably setting a single-season record for percentage field goal accuracy (91.6) at the age of 40 in 1981 and still able to land three 50-yards-plus field goals out of four attempts in the penultimate campaign of his 19-year career. Widely credited as being the placekicker who gave credibility to the soccer style, Stenerud's most important kick may the 48-yard field goal with which he set the Super Bowl record and launched the Kansas City Chiefs on their way to victory against Minnesota in Game IV. Said Chiefs head coach Hank Stram, "The Vikings were staring in disbelief. They couldn't believe we didn't punt."

San Francisco's John Taylor was preferred to several classy returners, including Miami's Fulton Walker who averaged 35.4 yards on eight kickoff returns in two games and scored on a Super Bowl-record 98-yard run. But in terms of style alone, Taylor deserves his spot. His best return was his first, against Cincinnati in Super Bowl XXIII, when, after his misjudgement in allowing a punt to clear his position by some way, he was able to adjust quickly, gather in the bouncing ball and return it 45 yards for a series record.

CHAPTER FOUR

OUTSTANDING ROOKIES OF 1990

Towards the end of April each year, in a process called the Selection Meeting but known, more commonly, as the Draft, some 330 or so players, most of whom have completed their four-year period of eligibility to play collegiate football (they are known as seniors), are selected by NFL teams. An innovation in 1936, when there were only nine NFL clubs, these days the system absorbs two days at a New York hotel, with hordes of wildly enthusiastic fans in attendance. To the cheers and the groans, one by one the teams make their selections. Here are a few who attracted the cheers.

Most scouts felt that **Jeff George**, who was a junior, would have benefited from an extra year in college. But all that changed in the pre-draft workouts, when prospects are assessed by the clubs and scouting combines. After seeing George go through his paces, the Colts wasted little time dealing with the Atlanta Falcons, who held the rights to the first pick overall, to make certain they got their man. And the price was high, as they traded Pro Bowl offensive lineman Chris Hinton and a probable future Pro Bowler in wide receiver Andre Rison to Atlanta, together with their fifth-round option in 1990 and their first in 1991, in exchange for Atlanta's first- and fourth-round options in 1990. At that price, George would need to be good and he was. He had revealed his siege-gun arm in the trials but he was soon to show instinctive accuracy in his passes, an exceptionally quick release, toughness under pressure and leadership in the huddle. Even in a season hampered by an early injury, he joined the select group of Fran Tarkenton, Joe Namath, Greg Cook, Jim Plunkett, Jim McMahon, Dan Marino and Bernie Kosar, becoming only the eighth NFL rookie quarterback since 1961 to pass for more touchdowns than interceptions.

When the Cardinals drafted **Anthony Thompson** in the second round, they could feel well satisfied. The runner-up in the voting for the 1989 Heisman Trophy and NCAA record holder for both career touchdowns (68) and single-game rushing yardage (377), Thompson bore the hallmark of class. But it was seventh-round

The progress of Indianapolis quarterback Jeff George is well ahead of schedule.

pick **Johnny Johnson** who stole the honours. As a junior at San Jose State, he had been the first player in NCAA history to rush for more than 1,200 yards and catch 60 passes in the same season, but his senior year was marred by a dispute which resulted in his leaving the team. Even the Cardinals weren't sure how he would fit in and, tentatively, they saw him as an H-back. However, halfway through his first pro campaign, he was the NFC leading rusher and it was only after suffering an ankle injury against Green Bay on Week Eleven that his form fell away. Even so, he became the first Cardinals rookie running back since Ottis Anderson to be selected for the Pro Bowl. A powerful, smooth runner, Johnson also proved to be a solid blocker. It was when Johnson was injured that Thompson stepped in and promptly rushed for 136 yards, the team's highest individual total of the season.

The rapid emergence of Johnny Johnson gives the Cardinals the luxury of top-class choice at running back.

Ricky Proehl was the Cardinals' leading receiver despite not having one start.

If Johnson was a major surprise, the play of third-round pick **Ricky Proehl** was only marginally less so. With veterans Roy Green, Ernie Jones and J.T. Smith on hand, Proehl was not expected to be a factor immediately, yet he made his mark in Cardinals history by becoming the first rookie to lead the team in receiving since Bob Shaw in 1950. A scrappy competitor not blessed with burning speed but with sure hands and ice-cool composure, Proehl also was the NFL-leading rookie, catching 56 passes at a decent 14.3-yard average.

It says a great deal for the Steelers' new offensive philosophy that the 1990 yield of 67 receptions shared among three players was a record for the position of tight end. Historically, the emphasis has been on blocking as distinct from pass receiving. And in the

Rob Moore gives the Jets a second wide receiver of great presence.

enormous **Eric Green** they certainly found a player who knew how to throw his 274 pounds around the gridiron. But the rookie also showed a deft touch, slipping into the open for 34 receptions, steamrollering into the end zone a club position-record seven times. Physically, he could develop into the most dominating tight end in the NFL and, with a clutch of consensus all-rookie team selections in the bag, he is well on his way.

"He just had a field day on me. After what he did to me, I can't do anything but praise him. He's going to be one of the top wide receivers in this game," said disappointed but respectful New England cornerback Ronnie Lippett, after Jets rookie **Rob Moore** had caught nine passes for 175 yards and a touchdown on Week Four. Only the great Wesley Walker, who caught four passes for 178 yards against Oakland in 1977, has had a better rookie day for the Jets. Big, fast, fearless and able to make the circus catch, inevitably the comparisons with Mike Quick and Art Monk were made. But perhaps the best point in context was established by Moore when he matched the touchdown total of New York top receiver Al Toon with six, the most ever by a Jets rookie wide receiver. With 44 receptions over the season, Moore led all AFC rookies and came second in the NFL behind the Cardinals' Ricky Proehl.

If Moore completes the set at wide receiver for the Jets, **Blair Thomas** may well have taken the first steps on the road to giving the club franchise quality at running back. A player who doggedly fought his way back following a junior-season knee injury which required reconstructive surgery, Thomas was described by Penn State head coach Joe Paterno as "the best all-around back I have ever coached". Jets general manager Dick Steinberg saw him as "the complete package" and had no hesitation in making Thomas the

Blair Thomas showed flashes of the kind of class which could underpin the Jets' rushing game well into the 1990s.

Cornerback Tony Stargell survived his early-season difficulties and figures to develop as a force for the Jets.

second player drafted overall. Despite signing only late in the preseason following contractual negotiations, and being hampered by a succession of injuries, Thomas still led the Jets and all AFC rookies with 620 yards rushing, while a classy five-yard average is testimony to his breathtaking speed and devastating moves.

Not often have the Jets had three impact players arrive in one year but **Tony Stargell** rightly makes up the trio. Isolated one-on-one against wily veterans, tormented and exploited ruthlessly by offensive co-ordinators, for many rookie cornerbacks life in the NFL can be a disheartening experience. Stargell was no different from most. Left stranded by San Diego's Anthony Miller on Week Six and given the runaround by Buffalo's Andre Reed during the first half of the following game, Stargell was kept out after the interval. "I just didn't want him to get attacked all day long. He was under the gun," explained Jets defensive co-ordinator Pete Carroll. But the rookie didn't yield. He started the next game, bristling with confidence and,

22
53

over the last half of the season, hardly missed a tackle. Here's a player who may just settle a few scores in double-quick time.

Philadelphia defensive back **Ben Smith** was another who felt the draught as opposing receivers paid their compliments on the way to touchdown receptions. But in his case, the problem, and the solution, may be in establishing his true playing position. Without question, Smith has the instincts of a defensive back, but he may just lack the instant turn of foot to make the split-second adjustment necessary of a NFL cornerback. However, in terms of pure speed he is not found wanting; no one questions his ability to sense a play as the quarterback drops back and, when it comes to delivering the tackle, the result is certain. He could well settle into the Eagles' free safety spot for a decade.

The possibility of failure never was up for consideration when the Bears selected **Mark Carrier**. One of the first draftees to sign up for any club, Carrier, who is known for his discipline and work ethic, immediately set about becoming a pro free safety though, at just 180 pounds, some felt him to be undersized. Come opening day he was ready. His first interception came on Week Two and there would follow nine more, propelling Carrier to a new Chicago club single-season record and the outright leadership in the NFL. In the manner of those blessed with greatness, his achievements came in clutches, with two interceptions, 11 tackles, a forced fumble and a pass deflection as he earned NFC Defensive Player of the Week honours in November against Tampa Bay. Later, he picked off three passes against Washington. Not surprisingly, he was selected to the Pro Bowl.

It is one of the most prestigious opportunities in pro football to be the feature back for the Dallas Cowboys and, even as a rookie, **Emmitt Smith** assumed that responsibility with style and class. Following lengthy contractual negotiations, Smith made a slow start as he explored the boundaries of his kingdom. But the awesome range of talents which encouraged the Cowboys to make Smith the 17th player selected were soon evident. With power, determination, a magnetic sense of north-south orientation and a gyroscopic balance as he sheered away from collisions, Smith settled into the position, his destiny, which had awaited him. His first 100-yards-rushing outing, on Week Five, brought Dallas back into the picture after three straight losses. His second century, on Week Twelve against Washington, gave momentum to the Cowboys' playoff bid, while his third of the campaign, on Week Fifteen, left the team poised on the brink of postseason involvement. Smith ended the campaign as the leading NFL rookie running back with 937 yards but the Cowboys' march faltered and, eventually, failed. However, the postscript to the season shows Dallas winning all five of its games when Smith carried the ball 20 or more times. It is a message that will not have fallen on deaf ears.

Steve Christie had been picked Division I-AA All-America by AP after ending his career as William & Mary's all-time leading scorer, yet he wasn't considered worthy even of a 12th-round pick and signed for Tampa Bay as a free agent. But that lowly status served only to amplify the value of a bargain acquisition, who would go on to set Buccaneers records with 23 field goals and a field goal accuracy percentage of 85.2. In addition, he became the Bucs' best ever on kickoffs, depositing the ball inside the end zone on 35 of his 66 attempts, putting opponents' kick return teams under pressure. Many felt that he was unlucky not to be selected to the Pro Bowl, a status for which he will renew his challenge in 1991.

The Miami Dolphins wanted a good offensive lineman. In **Richmond Webb**, who was the first at his position selected in the draft, and **Keith Sims**, who was the third behind center Bern Brostek, they found two great ones.

The position of left tackle is widely regarded as the

LEFT: Emmitt Smith showed the hallmark of class and authority expected of a Dallas running back.

ABOVE: Operating at left tackle, Richmond Webb could secure the Dolphins' offensive line for a decade.

most demanding on the offensive line but assistant coach John Sandusky, who is one of the all-time great specialists in this area, had no hesitation in handing Webb the job on opening day. By the end of the season, Webb had become the first rookie in NFL history to be selected to the Pro Bowl in that position, as backup to the peerless Anthony Munoz of Cincinnati and Patriots star Bruce Armstrong. Not even Munoz and the likes of Dan Dierdorf, Joe Jacoby and Jim Covert made the Pro Bowl trip as a rookie. Blessed with enormous strength, quick feet for adjustment, outstanding coordination and an unbreakable spirit, Webb was one of the few tackles who even came close to handling Buffalo defensive end Bruce Smith. In the AFC playoffs, Smith, a perennial All-Pro, was restricted to just three tackles and no sacks.

Making a full contribution on an offensive line which gave up an NFL-low 16 sacks, Sims slotted in at left guard, the perfect partner for Webb. His only absences came early in the season when he missed two games following successful arthroscopic surgery on his left knee. At 6-2, 305 pounds, Sims is unexpectedly light on his feet and presents a very wide barrier. He adjusts rapidly with the timing and positioning of a matador and only rarely is caught off balance when dropping back into pass protection. When it is time to go to war, on run blocking, he unleashes a tremendous surge of power. Modestly, the Dolphins describe him as versatile, able to play all three of tackle, guard and center positions. Perhaps the best assessment of him comes from Bobby Beathard, part-builder of the famed Washington 'Hogs' offensive line and now general manager of the San Diego Chargers, who said, "Boy, do I wish we could have traded for an extra number 1 (pick) or a high number 2 to get Sims."

James Francis brought penetration to the Cincinnati pass rush and can take on the best of running backs.

1990 was considered to be a vintage year for linebackers, seven being picked in the first round and five in the second. Inevitably, some took time to settle while others, such as Tampa Bay's Keith McCants, simply could not fight their way past veteran starters. But a few leapt to instant stardom.

Some observers feel that it was only for a lack of intensity at linebacker that the ultimate goal of a Super Bowl title has eluded Cincinnati. **James Francis** went a long way towards solving that perceived weakness with a combination of composure, authority and aggression which quickly elevated him to the leadership of the defense. Starting all 16 games at right outside linebacker, the 6-5, 252-pounder topped the club in total tackles (78) and sacks with eight of the team-total 25. A raw-boned young man of great range and explosiveness, after registering seven of his sacks in the first seven games, he attracted the level of double-team blocking that is the greatest compliment that opposing coaches can bestow.

Selected ahead of Francis, in fifth position, **Junior Seau** was considered by some scouts to offer the closest comparison in value with the quintessential NFL linebacker, Lawrence Taylor. A contractual dispute meant that Seau missed all but two practice sessions in training camp but, by Week Two, he was installed as the Chargers' right inside linebacker and came second on the team with 85 tackles. Seau's selection as the second non-travelling reserve to the Pro Bowl was an indication of things to come.

Percy Snow joined Chris Martin, Dino Hackett and Derrick Thomas, completing a Kansas City unit which is poised to make its claim to be the AFC's most formidable quartet. **Chris Singleton** was another who missed much of the training camp, but his superior talents were evident as, gradually, he worked his way into the Patriots' first-string lineup, starting on Week Seven and then, in three late-season games, tasting success with three sacks.

Having traded away their first-round option, the Redskins had to wait until way down in the second round before selecting **Andre Collins** in 46th place. The latest high-class linebacker to come off the Penn

Outside linebacker Aaron Wallace was a major success as a specialist pass rusher.

State assembly line, Collins moved in to start on the left outside on opening day and powered from strength to strength. Entering the season, opponents knew that they had to pay special attention to right outside linebacker Wilber Marshall, a former Pro Bowler, but they quickly learned the folly of underestimating Collins, whose unexpected speed and awareness saw him play much of his game in the enemy backfield. With 93 total tackles to rank fifth on the team, he carried his share of the burden, and with six sacks he ranked second behind specialist pass rusher Fred Stokes.

Aaron Wallace had set a Texas A&M record with 42 career sacks. As a senior, even though bothered with injuries, he'd been a dominant force and had been nominated for the Butkus Award given annually to collegiate football's premier linebacker. Yet some scouts questioned his intensity, attaching the label of 'underachiever'. But the Raiders have a way of motivating men, young and old. And Wallace would quickly silence his detractors. Following the Raiders' Week Three victory over Pittsburgh, Steelers head coach Chuck Noll reflected, "The Raiders played good, old-fashioned, knock-your-head-off football." He might have had in mind Wallace, who that day registered two of the team's six sacks. Wallace did not start a game all season. His special rôle was that of designated destroyer and he played it to perfection, logging nine sacks to come third on the team behind Greg Townsend and Scott Davis.

Shortly after the 1990 draft, New England Director of Player Operations Joe Mendes summed up **Ray Agnew's** attitude to the game, saying, "...if it were up to him, the season would start yesterday." Agnew joined a defense which would feel the pressure all year, ending the campaign ranked 27th in the league. But Agnew didn't buckle. Though hampered by calf and knee injuries which caused him grudgingly to miss four games, Agnew kept up the pressure at defensive right end, hammering away at an opponent who usually represents the strength of the offensive line. Stronger than most and with the kind of disposition which comes in handy when the going gets tough – he's mean – Agnew also showed an intuitive reaction to the cunningly devised pro blocking schemes. Equally tough against the run and on rushing the passer, he was selected to most all-rookie teams.

Chapter Five

American Football Conference

Team Rankings

	Offense						Defense					
	Total Yds.	Rushing	Passing	Points For	No. Intercepted	No. Sacked	Total Yds.	Rushing	Passing	Points Against	Interceptions	Sacks
Buffalo	2	4	5	1	=3	4	5	7	4	4	=6	5
Cincinnati	5	3	7	4	=13	=6	12	11	14	10	8	14
Cleveland	12	14	6	13	=13	11	9	12	9	14	=10	12
Denver	4	8	3	7	8	12	10	9	11	12	13	=8
Houston	1	11	1	2	=6	8	7	2	8	8	2	=6
Indianapolis	14	13	8	12	12	13	13	13	12	11	14	13
Kansas City	3	6	4	3	1	3	8	5	10	3	3	1
L.A. Raiders	9	5	12	5	2	5	2	6	2	5	=10	2
Miami	6	10	2	6	5	1	4	8	3	2	=4	=3
New England	13	12	10	14	=10	14	14	14	7	13	9	=10
N.Y. Jets	8	2	11	10	=3	=9	11	10	13	9	=6	=6
Pittsburgh	11	7	14	11	=6	=6	1	4	1	1	1	=8
San Diego	7	1	13	8	9	2	3	1	5	6	=4	=3
Seattle	10	9	9	9	=10	=9	6	3	6	7	12	=10

Afc Passers

	Att	Comp	% Comp	Yards	Ave Gain	TD	% TD	Long	Int	% Int	Rating Points
Kelly, Jim, *Buff.*	346	219	63.3	2829	8.18	24	6.9	71	9	2.6	101.2
Moon, Warren, *Hou.*	584	362	62.0	4689	8.03	33	5.7	t87	13	2.2	96.8
DeBerg, Steve, *K.C.*	444	258	58.1	3444	7.76	23	5.2	t90	4	0.9	96.3
Schroeder, Jay, *Raiders*	334	182	54.5	2849	8.53	19	5.7	t68	9	2.7	90.8
Marino, Dan, *Mia.*	531	306	57.6	3563	6.71	21	4.0	t69	11	2.1	82.6
Brister, Bubby, *Pitt.*	387	223	57.6	2725	7.04	20	5.2	90	14	3.6	81.6
Elway, John, *Den.*	502	294	58.6	3526	7.02	15	3.0	66	14	2.8	78.5
O'Brien, Ken, *Jets*	411	226	55.0	2855	6.95	13	3.2	t69	10	2.4	77.3
Esiason, Boomer, *Cin.*	402	224	55.7	3031	7.54	24	6.0	53	22	5.5	77.0
George, Jeff, *Ind.*	334	181	54.2	2152	6.44	16	4.8	75	13	3.9	73.8
Krieg, Dave, *Sea.*	448	265	59.2	3194	7.13	15	3.3	t63	20	4.5	73.6
Tolliver, Billy Joe, *S.D.*	410	216	52.7	2574	6.28	16	3.9	t45	16	3.9	68.9
Kosar, Bernie, *Clev.*	423	230	54.4	2562	6.06	10	2.4	50	15	3.5	65.7
Wilson, Marc, *N.E.*	265	139	52.5	1625	6.13	6	2.3	t36	11	4.2	61.6
Non-qualifiers											
Carlson, Cody, *Hou.*	55	37	67.3	383	6.96	4	7.3	t53	2	3.6	96.3
Reich, Frank, *Buff.*	63	36	57.1	469	7.44	2	3.2	43	0	0.0	91.3
Trudeau, Jack, *Ind.*	144	84	58.3	1078	7.49	6	4.2	73	6	4.2	78.4
Grogan, Steve, *N.E.*	92	50	54.3	615	6.68	4	4.3	48	3	3.3	76.1
Hodson, Tommy, *N.E.*	156	85	54.5	968	6.21	4	2.6	56	5	3.2	68.5
Friesz, John, *S.D.*	22	11	50.0	98	4.45	1	4.5	17	1	4.5	58.5
Eason, Tony, *Jets*	28	13	46.4	155	5.54	0	0.0	31	1	3.6	49.0
Pagel, Mike, *Clev.*	148	69	46.6	819	5.53	3	2.0	32	8	5.4	48.2
Vlasic, Mark, *S.D.*	40	19	47.5	168	4.20	1	2.5	27	2	5.0	46.7
Kubiak, Gary, *Den.*	22	11	50.0	145	6.59	0	0.0	36	4	18.2	31.6

t = touchdown
Leader based on rating points, minimum 220 attempts

AFC Receivers – Most Receptions

	No	Yards	Ave	Long	TD
Jeffires, Haywood, *Hou.*	74	1048	14.2	t87	8
Hill, Drew, *Hou.*	74	1019	13.8	57	5
Williams, John L., *Sea.*	73	699	9.6	60	0
Givins, Ernest, *Hou.*	72	979	13.6	t80	9
Reed, Andre, *Buff.*	71	945	13.3	t56	8
Bentley, Albert, *Ind.*	71	664	9.4	73	2
Duncan, Curtis, *Hou.*	66	785	11.9	t37	1
Paige, Stephone, *K.C.*	65	1021	15.7	t86	5
Miller, Anthony, *S.D.*	63	933	14.8	t31	7
Brooks, Bill, *Ind.*	62	823	13.3	75	5
Slaughter, Webster, *Clev.*	59	847	14.4	50	4
Jackson, Mark, *Den.*	57	926	16.2	66	4
Toon, Al, *Jets*	57	757	13.3	t46	6
Metcalf, Eric, *Clev.*	57	452	7.9	35	1
Hester, Jessie, *Ind.*	54	924	17.1	t64	6
Fryar, Irving, *N.E.*	54	856	15.9	56	4
Johnson, Vance, *Den.*	54	747	13.8	49	3
Fernandez, Mervyn, *Raiders*	52	839	16.1	t66	5
Duper, Mark, *Mia.*	52	810	15.6	t69	5
Kane, Tommy, *Sea.*	52	776	14.9	t63	4
Cook, Marv, *N.E.*	51	455	8.9	t35	5
Gault, Willie, *Raiders*	50	985	19.7	t68	3
Lipps, Louis, *Pitt.*	50	682	13.6	37	3
Thomas, Thurman, *Buff.*	49	532	10.9	63	2
Blades, Brian, *Sea.*	49	525	10.7	24	3
Harmon, Ronnie, *S.D.*	46	511	11.1	t36	2
Langhorne, Reggie, *Clev.*	45	585	13.0	39	2
Brennan, Brian, *Clev.*	45	568	12.6	28	2
Brown, Eddie, *Cin.*	44	706	16.0	t50	9
Moore, Rob, *Jets*	44	692	15.7	t69	6
Jensen, Jim, *Mia.*	44	365	8.3	18	1
McGee, Tim, *Cin.*	43	737	17.1	52	1
Mack, Kevin, *Clev.*	42	360	8.6	30	2
Thomas, Robb, *K.C.*	41	545	13.3	t47	4
Harry, Emile, *K.C.*	41	519	12.7	60	2

t = touchdown

AFC Receivers – Most Yards

	Yards	No	Ave	Long	TD
Jeffires, Haywood, *Hou.*	1048	74	14.2	t87	8
Paige, Stephone, *K.C.*	1021	65	15.7	t86	5
Hill, Drew, *Hou.*	1019	74	13.8	57	5
Gault, Willie, *Raiders*	985	50	19.7	t68	3
Givins, Ernest, *Hou.*	979	72	13.6	t80	9
Reed, Andre, *Buff.*	945	71	13.3	t56	8
Miller, Anthony, *S.D.*	933	63	14.8	t31	7
Jackson, Mark, *Den.*	926	57	16.2	66	4
Hester, Jessie, *Ind.*	924	54	17.1	t64	6
Fryar, Irving, *N.E.*	856	54	15.9	56	4
Slaughter, Webster, *Clev.*	847	59	14.4	50	4
Fernandez, Mervyn, *Raiders*	839	52	16.1	t66	5
Brooks, Bill, *Ind.*	823	62	13.3	75	5
Duper, Mark, *Mia.*	810	52	15.6	t69	5
Duncan, Curtis, *Hou.*	785	66	11.9	t37	1
Kane, Tommy, *Sea.*	776	52	14.9	t63	4
Toon, Al, *Jets*	757	57	13.3	t46	6
Johnson, Vance, *Den.*	747	54	13.8	49	3
McGee, Tim, *Cin.*	737	43	17.1	52	1
Lofton, James, *Buff.*	712	35	20.3	71	4
Brown, Eddie, *Cin.*	706	44	16.0	t50	9
Williams, John L., *Sea.*	699	73	9.6	60	0
Moore, Rob, *Jets*	692	44	15.7	t69	6
Lipps, Louis, *Pitt.*	682	50	13.6	37	3
Bentley, Albert, *Ind.*	664	71	9.4	73	2
Holman, Rodney, *Cin.*	596	40	14.9	53	5
Langhorne, Reggie, *Clev.*	585	45	13.0	39	2
Brennan, Brian, *Clev.*	568	45	12.6	28	2
Dykes, Hart Lee, *N.E.*	549	34	16.1	t35	2
Thomas, Robb, *K.C.*	545	41	13.3	t47	4
Thomas, Thurman, *Buff.*	532	49	10.9	63	2
Blades, Brian, *Sea.*	525	49	10.7	24	3
Harry, Emile, *K.C.*	519	41	12.7	60	2
Harmon, Ronnie, *S.D.*	511	46	11.1	t36	2
McNair, Todd, *K.C.*	507	40	12.7	65	2

t = touchdown

Haywood Jeffires led the AFC both in receptions and yards receiving.

AFC RUSHERS

	Att	Yards	Ave	Long	TD
Thomas, Thurman, *Buff.*	271	1297	4.8	t80	11
Butts, Marion, *S.D.*	265	1225	4.6	52	8
Humphrey, Bobby, *Den.*	288	1202	4.2	t37	7
Word, Barry, *K.C.*	204	1015	5.0	t53	4
Brooks, James, *Cin.*	195	1004	5.1	t56	5
Fenner, Derrick, *Sea.*	215	859	4.0	36	14
Smith, Sammie, *Mia.*	226	831	3.7	33	8
Stephens, John, *N.E.*	212	808	3.8	26	2
Okoye, Christian, *K.C.*	245	805	3.3	32	7
Hoge, Merril, *Pitt.*	203	772	3.8	t41	7
Williams, John L., *Sea.*	187	714	3.8	25	3
Mack, Kevin, *Clev.*	158	702	4.4	26	5
White, Lorenzo, *Hou.*	168	702	4.2	22	8
Jackson, Bo, *Raiders*	125	698	5.6	88	5
Allen, Marcus, *Raiders*	179	682	3.8	28	12
Dickerson, Eric, *Ind.*	166	677	4.1	43	4
Thomas, Blair, *Jets*	123	620	5.0	41	1
Bernstine, Rod, *S.D.*	124	589	4.8	t40	4
Bentley, Albert, *Ind.*	137	556	4.1	t26	4
Baxter, Brad, *Jets*	124	539	4.3	t28	6
McNeil, Freeman, *Jets*	99	458	4.6	29	6
Worley, Tim, *Pitt.*	109	418	3.8	38	0
Williams, Warren, *Pitt.*	68	389	5.7	t70	3
Hector, Johnny, *Jets*	91	377	4.1	22	2
Harmon, Ronnie, *S.D.*	66	363	5.5	41	0
Green, Harold, *Cin.*	83	353	4.3	39	1
Smith, Steve, *Raiders*	81	327	4.0	17	2
Logan, Marc, *Mia.*	79	317	4.0	17	2
Davis, Kenneth, *Buff.*	64	302	4.7	47	4
Pinkett, Allen, *Hou.*	66	268	4.1	19	0
Woods, Ickey, *Cin.*	64	268	4.2	32	6
Elway, John, *Den.*	50	258	5.2	21	3
Metcalf, Eric, *Clev.*	80	248	3.1	17	1
Allen, Marvin, *N.E.*	63	237	3.8	29	1
Taylor, Craig, *Cin.*	51	216	4.2	24	2
Moon, Warren, *Hou.*	55	215	3.9	17	2
Mueller, Jamie, *Buff.*	59	207	3.5	20	2
Foster, Barry, *Pitt.*	36	203	5.6	38	1
Bell, Greg, *Raiders*	47	164	3.5	21	1
Esiason, Boomer, *Cin.*	50	157	3.1	21	0
Hoard, Leroy, *Clev.*	58	149	2.6	42	3
Stradford, Troy, *Mia.*	37	138	3.7	15	1
Fullwood, Brent, *G.B.-Clev.*	44	124	2.8	16	1
Winder, Sammy, *Den.*	42	120	2.9	19	2
Krieg, Dave, *Sea.*	32	115	3.6	25	0
Adams, George, *N.E.*	28	111	4.0	13	0

t = touchdown

RIGHT: Thurman Thomas, unquestioned superstar, was the AFC leading rusher.

OPPOSITE: The immensely powerful Derrick Fenner led the AFC with 15 touchdowns.

AFC SCORING – Kickers

	XP	XPA	FG	FGA	PTS
Lowery, Nick, *K.C.*	37	38	34	37	139
Norwood, Scott, *Buff.*	50	52	20	29	110
Treadwell, David, *Den.*	34	36	25	34	109
Johnson, Norm, *Sea.*	33	34	23	32	102
Leahy, Pat, *Jets*	32	32	23	26	101
Stoyanovich, Pete, *Mia.*	37	37	21	25	100
Anderson, Gary, *Pitt.*	32	32	20	25	92
Breech, Jim, *Cin.*	41	44	17	21	92
Jaeger, Jeff, *Raiders*	40	42	15	20	85
Carney, John, *S.D.*	27	28	19	21	84
Biasucci, Dean, *Ind.*	32	33	17	24	83
Garcia, Teddy, *Hou.*	26	28	14	20	68
Staurovsky, Jason, *N.E.*	19	19	16	22	67
Kauric, Jerry, *Clev.*	24	27	14	20	66

AFC SCORING – Touchdowns

	TD	TDR	TDP	TDM	PTS
Fenner, Derrick, *Sea.*	15	14	1	0	90
Allen, Marcus, *Raiders*	13	12	1	0	78
Thomas, Thurman, *Buff.*	13	11	2	0	78
White, Lorenzo, *Hou.*	12	8	4	0	72
Hoge, Merril, *Pitt.*	10	7	3	0	60
Brooks, James, *Cin.*	9	5	4	0	54
Brown, Eddie, *Cin.*	9	0	9	0	54
Givins, Ernest, *Hou.*	9	0	9	0	54
Smith, Sammie, *Mia.*	9	8	1	0	54
Butts, Marion, *S.D.*	8	8	0	0	48
Jeffires, Haywood, *Hou.*	8	0	8	0	48
Reed, Andre, *Buff.*	8	0	8	0	48
Green, Eric, *Pitt.*	7	0	7	0	42
Humphrey, Bobby, *Den.*	7	7	0	0	42
Mack, Kevin, *Clev.*	7	5	2	0	42
Miller, Anthony, *S.D.*	7	0	7	0	42
Okoye, Christian, *K.C.*	7	7	0	0	42
Baxter, Brad, *Jets*	6	6	0	0	36
Bentley, Albert, *Ind.*	6	4	2	0	36
Hester, Jessie, *Ind.*	6	0	6	0	36
Jones, Tony, *Hou.*	6	0	6	0	36
McNeil, Freeman, *Jets*	6	6	0	0	36
Moore, Rob, *Jets*	6	0	6	0	36
Paige, Tony, *Mia.*	6	2	4	0	36
Toon, Al, *Jets*	6	0	6	0	36
Woods, Ickey, Cin.	6	6	0	0	36

AFC KICKOFF RETURNERS

	No	Yards	Ave	Long	TD
Clark, Kevin, *Den.*	20	505	25.3	75	0
Elder, Donnie, *S.D.*	24	571	23.8	90	0
Ball, Eric, *Cin.*	16	366	22.9	38	0
Lewis, Nate, *S.D.*	17	383	22.5	39	0
Woodson, Rod, *Pitt.*	35	764	21.8	49	0
Warren, Chris, *Sea.*	23	478	20.8	71	0
Martin, Sammy, *N.E.*	25	515	20.6	38	0
Holland, Jamie, *Raiders*	32	655	20.5	87	0
McNeil, Gerald, *Hou.*	27	551	20.4	64	0
Metcalf, Eric, *Clev.*	52	1052	20.2	t101	2
Jennings, Stanford, *Cin.*	29	584	20.1	33	0
Smith, Don, *Buff.*	32	643	20.1	38	0
Loville, Derek, *Sea.*	18	359	19.9	29	0
Verdin, Clarence, *Ind.*	18	350	19.4	44	0
Brown, Ron, *Raiders*	30	575	19.2	34	0
Logan, Marc, *Mia.*	20	367	18.4	35	0
Mathis, Terance, *Jets*	43	787	18.3	35	0
Simmons, Stacey, *Ind.*	19	348	18.3	34	0

AFC Punters

	No	Yards	Long	Ave	TB	Blk	Opp Ret	Ret Yds	In 20	Net Ave
Montgomery, Greg, *Hou.*	34	1530	60	45.0	5	0	23	186	7	36.6
Horan, Mike, *Den.*	58	2575	67	44.4	6	1	22	159	14	38.9
Stark, Rohn, *Ind.*	71	3084	61	43.4	3	1	42	334	24	37.4
Johnson, Lee, *Cin.*	64	2705	70	42.3	8	0	36	352	12	34.3
Roby, Reggie, *Mia.*	72	3022	62	42.0	3	0	40	397	20	35.6
Hansen, Brian, *N.E.*	90	3752	69	41.7	8	2	50	503	18	33.6
Donnelly, Rick, *Sea.*	67	2722	54	40.6	8	0	29	254	18	34.4
Prokop, Joe, *Jets*	59	2363	58	40.1	3	0	33	257	18	34.7
Kidd, John, *S.D.*	61	2442	59	40.0	2	1	28	131	14	36.6
Tuten, Rick, *Buff.*	53	2107	55	39.8	4	0	26	214	12	34.2
Wagner, Bryan, *Clev.*	74	2879	65	38.9	2	4	41	425	13	30.9
Barker, Bryan, *K.C.*	64	2479	56	38.7	1	0	38	324	16	33.4
Gossett, Jeff, *Raiders*	60	2315	57	38.6	4	2	24	153	18	33.6
Stryzinski, Dan, *Pitt.*	65	2454	51	37.8	5	1	16	105	18	34.1

Leader based on gross average, minimum 34 punts

AFC Sackers

	No
Thomas, Derrick, *K.C.*	20.0
Smith, Bruce, *Buff.*	19.0
O'Neal, Leslie, *S.D.*	13.5
Byrd, Dennis, *Jets*	13.0
Green, Jacob, *Sea.*	12.5
Jones, Sean, *Hou.*	12.5
Townsend, Greg, *Raiders*	12.5
Cross, Jeff, *Mia.*	11.5
Perry, Michael Dean, *Clev.*	11.5
Fletcher, Simon, *Den.*	11.0
Davis, Scott, *Raiders*	10.0
Grossman, Burt, *S.D.*	10.0
Smith, Neil, *K.C.*	9.5
Wallace, Aaron, *Raiders*	9.0
Childress, Ray, *Hou.*	8.0
Francis, James, *Cin.*	8.0
Fuller, William, *Hou.*	8.0
Clancy, Sam, *Ind.*	7.5
Williams, Lee, *S.D.*	7.5
Saleaumua, Dan, *K.C.*	7.0
Junior, E.J., *Mia.*	6.0
Long, Howie, *Raiders*	6.0
Williams, Brent, *N.E.*	6.0
Williams, Gerald, *Pitt.*	6.0
Bryant, Jeff, *Sea.*	5.5
Griggs, David, *Mia.*	5.5
Maas, Bill, *K.C.*	5.5
Martin, Chris, *K.C.*	5.5
Davis, Darrell, *Jets*	5.0
Mecklenburg, Karl, *Den.*	5.0
Porter, Rufus, *Sea.*	5.0
Willis, Keith, *Pitt.*	5.0
Wright, Jeff, *Buff.*	5.0
Banks, Chip, *Ind.*	4.5
Bickett, Duane, *Ind.*	4.5
Lloyd, Greg, *Pitt.*	4.5
Mersereau, Scott, *Jets*	4.5
Tuatagaloa, Natu, *Cin.*	4.5
Washington, Marvin, *Jets*	4.5
Bennett, Cornelius, *Buff.*	4.0
Golic, Bob, *Raiders*	4.0
Herrod, Jeff, *Ind.*	4.0
Lageman, Jeff, *Jets*	4.0
Powers, Warren, *Den.*	4.0
Seals, Leon, *Buff.*	4.0
Talley, Darryl, *Buff.*	4.0
Wilson, Karl, *Mia.*	4.0

AFC INTERCEPTORS

	No	Yards	Ave	Long	TD
Johnson, Richard, *Hou.*	8	100	12.5	35	1
Byrd, Gill, *S.D.*	7	63	9.0	24	0
Ross, Kevin, *K.C.*	5	97	19.4	40	0
McMillan, Erik, *Jets*	5	92	18.4	25	0
Oliver, Louis, *Mia.*	5	87	17.4	35	0
Williams, Jarvis, *Mia.*	5	82	16.4	t42	1
Woodson, Rod, *Pitt.*	5	67	13.4	34	0
Lippett, Ronnie, *N.E.*	4	94	23.5	73	0
Griffin, Larry, *Pitt.*	4	75	18.8	36	0
Kinard, Terry, *Hou.*	4	75	18.8	47	0
Hurst, Maurice, *N.E.*	4	61	15.3	36	0
Dishman, Cris, *Hou.*	4	50	12.5	42	0
McKyer, Tim, *Mia.*	4	40	10.0	21	0
Bussey, Barney, *Cin.*	4	37	9.3	18	0
Fulcher, David, *Cin.*	4	20	5.0	18	C
Marion, Fred, *N.E.*	4	17	4.3	16	0
Woodruff, Dwayne, *Pitt.*	3	110	36.7	59	0
Robinson, Eugene, *Sea.*	3	89	29.7	39	0
Harper, Dwayne, *Sea.*	3	69	23.0	47	0
Prior, Mike, *Ind.*	3	66	22.0	36	0
Wright, Felix, *Clev.*	3	56	18.7	36	0
Anderson, Eddie, *Raiders*	3	49	16.3	31	0
Clifton, Kyle, *Jets*	3	49	16.3	39	0
Cherry, Deron, *K.C.*	3	40	13.3	21	0
Billups, Lewis, *Cin.*	3	39	13.0	29	0
Petry, Stan, *K.C.*	3	33	11.0	t33	1
Donaldson, Jeff, *K.C.*	3	28	9.3	14	0
Washington, Brian, *Jets*	3	22	7.3	13	0
McDaniel, Terry, *Raiders*	3	20	6.7	15	0
Harden, Mike, *Raiders*	3	19	6.3	15	0
Jackson, Kirby, *Buff.*	3	16	5.3	14	0
Everett, Thomas, *Pitt.*	3	2	0.7	2	0

t = touchdown

AFC PUNT RETURNERS

	No	FC	Yards	Ave	Long	TD
Verdin, Clarence, *Ind.*	31	3	396	12.8	36	0
Woodson, Rod, *Pitt.*	38	8	398	10.5	t52	1
Warren, Chris, *Sea.*	28	16	269	9.6	39	0
Townsell, JoJo, *Jets*	17	4	154	9.1	20	0
Brown, Tim, *Raiders*	34	8	295	8.7	39	0
Price, Mitchell, *Cin.*	29	14	251	8.7	t66	1
Clark, Kevin, *Den.*	21	1	159	7.6	32	0
Worthen, Naz, *K.C.*	25	3	180	7.2	37	0
McNeil, Gerald, *Hou.*	30	20	172	5.7	26	0
Martin, Tony, *Mia.*	26	9	140	5.4	35	0
Fryar, Irving, *N.E.*	28	10	133	4.8	17	0

t = touchdown
Leader based on average return, minimum 17 returns

LEFT: Mike Horan led the NFL both in gross and net punting average.

RIGHT: Richard Johnson enjoyed his best year as a pro, leading the AFC in interceptions.

BUFFALO BILLS

Address One Bills Drive, Orchard Park, New York 14127.
Stadium Rich Stadium, Orchard Park. *Capacity* 80,290 *Playing Surface* AstroTurf.
Team Colours Royal Blue, Scarlet Red, and White.
Head Coach Marv Levy – 6th year; 11th NFL.
Championships Division 1980,'88,'89,'90; AFL 1964,'65; Conference 1990.
History AFL 1960-69, AFC 1970-

The 1990 Bills may well be the best team not to have won the Super Bowl. They have excellent management and are extremely well coached. At a stroke, in the collegiate draft they may have found immediate help for their one area of possible need, the defensive secondary, and they must enter the 1991 season favoured to return to the hottest cauldron of all.

The Bills' successes and quarterback Jim Kelly's first NFL passing title were not mere coincidence. They were inextricably linked and marked the completion of a process which has its origins in 1986, when Kelly joined the club. A careful start to the rebuilding process gained momentum with the arrival of head coach Marv Levy halfway through the 1986 campaign. Levy's willingness to experiment, to innovate with the adoption of a no-huddle offense when appropriate, and to enthuse, brought his offense to the point of perfection. If Levy is the navigator and Kelly is the driver, then running back Thurman Thomas represents the multi-option gearbox transforming motive power into application. Comparisons with Hall-of-Famer and former Bills player O.J. Simpson are silly – their styles are quite different. And while Simpson was almost the entire offense, Thomas is just a major part. But the final analysis just might place Thomas, who is more versatile than Simpson was, alongside the great man. Fullback Jamie Mueller does the heavy work. As a target for Kelly, Thomas fits in nicely with starting wide receivers Andre Reed and James Lofton, the latter who has rekindled the fire of his All-Pro years. There are convenient options of blocking and receiving at the tight end position, where Keith McKeller sees more action than Pete Metzelaars.

The firepower is unleashed from a point of calm offered by an offensive line which, only recently, has been given the credit it deserves. The starting unit has Will Wolford and Howard Ballard at tackle, Jim Ritcher and John Davis in the guard positions and Pro Bowler Kent Hull at center.

No offense can function undamaged and here the Bills are comfortable, with quarterback Frank Reich,

Darryl Talley, for so long overshadowed by expressive teammates, achieved league-wide acclaim for the first time in his career.

1991 SCHEDULE OF GAMES		
September		
1	MIAMI	4:00
8	PITTSBURGH	1:00
15	at New York Jets	4:00
22	at Tampa Bay	4:00
29	CHICAGO	1:00
October		
7	at Kansas City (Mon.)	8:00
13	INDIANAPOLIS	1:00
21	CINCINNATI (Mon.)	9:00
27	Open Date	
November		
3	NEW ENGLAND	1:00
10	vs Green Bay at Milwaukee	12:00
18	at Miami (Mon.)	9:00
24	at New England	1:00
December		
1	NEW YORK JETS	1:00
8	at Los Angeles Raiders	1:00
15	at Indianapolis (Sun. night)	8:00
22	DETROIT	1:00

wide receivers Don Beebe and the effervescent Steve Tasker, running back Kenneth Davis and the pair of linemen, Glenn Parker and Mitch Frerotte.

Steady placekicking by Scott Norwood ensures that drives inside the opponents' 25-yard line usually produce points, though he does not have long-range strength. Rick Tuten, too, punts more for precision than distance.

If there is a weakness in defense, it is in the safety positions where Mark Kelso has had injuries and Leonard Smith might be exposed by the speed and variety of the modern passing offenses. John Hagy did well enough as Kelso's deputy but he has been lost to Plan-B free agency. The starters will need to keep an eye on top draftee Henry Jones. Of the other draftees, Darryl Wren has the great speed of a cornerback and Shawn Wilbourn, who was barely considered by most clubs, may surprise one or two opponents with the power of his hitting.

As for the front seven, what more can be said of a group which sent defensive end Bruce Smith and linebackers Cornelius Bennett, Shane Conlan and Darryl Talley (the special selection by coach Art Shell) to the Pro Bowl? Smith is the best at his position in the NFL, Bennett may be the fastest at his, Conlan is as determined and tough as they come and Talley may just sum up all the qualities of an NFL linebacker. The remaining three, defensive end Leon Seals, nose tackle Jeff Wright and inside linebacker Ray Bentley, hardly could be dismissed as making up the numbers. It is unlikely that draftee Phil Hansen will break into the three-man front but, when the Bills adjust to the 4-3, he'll be ready to go.

1991 Draft

Round	Name	Pos.	Ht.	Wt.	College
1.	Jones, Henry	CB	5-11	197	Illinois
2.	Hansen, Phil	DE	6-5	258	North Dakota State
3.	Wren, Darryl	CB	5-11	186	Pittsburg, Kansas
5.	Wilbourn, Shawn	DB	5-11	197	Cal State-Long Beach
6.	Hamilton, Millard	WR	5-9	172	Clark, Georgia
7.	Rasul, Amir	RB	5-11	190	Florida A&M
8.	Lamb, Brad	WR	5-9	171	Anderson, Ind.
9.	Maddox, Mark	LB	6-2	230	Northern Michigan
10.	DeLorenzo, Tony	G	6-3	282	New Mexico State
11.	Kirkland, Dean	G	6-2	297	Washington
12.	Clark, Stephen	TE	6-5	242	Texas

VETERAN ROSTER

No.	Name	Pos.	Ht.	Wt.	NFL Year	College
54	Bailey, Carlton	LB	6-3	235	4	North Carolina
92	Baldinger, Gary	NT	6-3	270	5	Wake Forest
75	Ballard, Howard	T	6-6	325	4	Alabama A&M
	Bavaro, David	LB	6-0	236	2	Syracuse
82	Beebe, Don	WR	5-11	183	3	Chadron State, Neb.
97	Bennett, Cornelius	LB	6-2	238	5	Alabama
50	Bentley, Ray	LB	6-2	235	6	Central Michigan
61	Burton, Leonard	T	6-3	277	5	South Carolina
58	Conlan, Shane	LB	6-3	230	5	Penn State
65	Davis, John	G-T	6-4	310	5	Georgia Tech
23	Davis, Kenneth	RB	5-10	209	6	Texas Christian
45	Drane, Dwight	S	6-2	205	6	Oklahoma
85	Edwards, Al	WR	5-8	168	2	Northwestern State, La.
59	Frerotte, Mitch	G-C	6-3	285	3	Penn State
33	Fuller, Eddie	RB	5-9	199	1	Louisiana State
35	Gardner, Carwell	RB	6-2	235	2	Louisville
99	Garner, Hal	LB	6-4	238	5	Utah State
7	Gilbert, Gale	QB	6-3	210	4	California
	Glover, Deval	WR	5-11	184	1	Syracuse
26	Hale, Chris	CB	5-8	165	3	Southern California
27	Hicks, Clifford	CB	5-10	188	5	Oregon
67	Hull, Kent	C	6-5	275	6	Mississippi State
47	Jackson, Kirby	CB	5-10	180	5	Mississippi State
12	Kelly, Jim	QB	6-3	218	6	Miami
38	Kelso, Mark	S	5-11	185	6	William & Mary
63	Lingner, Adam	C	6-4	263	9	Illinois
73	Lodish, Mike	NT	6-3	270	2	UCLA
80	Lofton, James	WR	6-3	190	14	Stanford
84	McKeller, Keith	TE	6-4	245	4	Jacksonville State
88	Metzelaars, Pete	TE	6-7	250	10	Wabash
57	Monger, Matt	LB	6-1	235	6	Oklahoma State
41	Mueller, Jamie	RB	6-1	224	5	Benedictine
11	Norwood, Scott	K	6-0	207	7	James Madison
37	Odomes, Nate	CB	5-10	188	5	Wisconsin
74	Parker, Glenn	T	6-5	304	2	Arizona
53	Patton, Marvcus	LB	6-2	223	2	UCLA
94	Pike, Mark	DE	6-4	272	5	Georgia Tech
29	Pool, David	CB	5-9	188	2	Carson-Newman
83	Reed, Andre	WR	6-2	190	7	Kutztown State
14	Reich, Frank	QB	6-4	210	7	Maryland
51	Ritcher, Jim	G	6-3	275	12	North Carolina State
87	Rolle, Butch	TE	6-3	245	6	Michigan State
96	Seals, Leon	DE	6-5	270	5	Jackson State
	Smiley, Tim	S	6-0	190	1	Arkansas State
78	Smith, Bruce	DE	6-4	275	7	Virginia Tech
46	Smith, Leonard	S	5-11	202	9	McNeese State
56	Talley, Darryl	LB	6-4	235	9	West Virginia
89	Tasker, Steve	WR-KR	5-9	185	7	Northwestern
34	Thomas, Thurman	RB	5-10	198	4	Oklahoma State
	Tucker, Brett	CB	5-11	194	1	Northern Illinois
10	Tuten, Rick	P	6-2	218	2	Florida State
31	Williams, James	CB	5-10	175	2	Fresno State
69	Wolford, Will	T	6-5	295	6	Vanderbilt
91	Wright, Jeff	NT	6-3	270	4	Central Missouri State

INDIANAPOLIS COLTS

Address P.O. Box 535000, Indianapolis, Indiana 46253.
Stadium Hoosier Dome, Indianapolis. *Capacity* 60,127 *Playing Surface* AstroTurf.
Team Colours Royal Blue and White.
Head Coach Ron Meyer – 6th year; 9th NFL.
Championships Division 1970,'75,'76,'77,'87; Conference 1970; NFL 1958,'59,'68; Super Bowl 1970.
History NFL 1953-69, AFC 1970-
(Until 1984, they were known as the Baltimore Colts. A team of the same name played in the AAFC, from 1947 to 1949, and in the NFL in 1950, at the end of which they went out of business.)

The Colts took a chance, releasing Chris Hinton and Andre Rison in the trade which enabled them to draft junior quarterback Jeff George. And they came out well, for not only did George settle in without too many problems but, also, the emergence of other players cushioned the loss of the veterans. Rather quicker than anticipated, then, the Colts may be ready to make a serious bid for honours.

Without question, the success of the offense rests on two players, George and running back Eric Dickerson, each with his supporting cast. George did enough over the final half of the season to show that he can be far more than just a high-class quarterback. Also, he emerged as a leader. Help came from an unexpected source when wide receiver Jessie Hester, who had been discarded by the Raiders and, subsequently, Atlanta, discovered the confidence to match his undoubted talent. The club leader in receiving yardage, Hester also came top with six touchdowns. Even so, Bill Brooks, who attracts double-teaming, remains as the senior partner. Behind these two there is the speedy Stacey Simmons, the potential of Pro Bowl kick returner Clarence Verdin and the superstar of yester-year, Stanley Morgan. Tight end Pat Beach is mostly a blocker and it will be interesting to see if the Colts can find a way of invigorating Orson Mobley, who had his moments with the Broncos.

Dickerson can be seen either as a standard-bearer or plain infuriating, depending upon your position, but there's no ignoring the thrill of anticipation when he gears up to carry the ball. He should end the season second in the NFL all-time rushing list. His partner, Albert Bentley, is not likely to break any records but, in addition to his useful rushing and reliability, he has found a key responsibility in the passing offense and led the club with 71 catches in 1990. The offensive line slowly became accustomed to playing without Hinton and, helping in this process, the timely emergence of left tackle Zefross Moss was a factor. Brian Baldinger switched from right guard to right tackle following an injury to Kevin Call, giving Pat Tomberlin the chance to show his stuff. Left guard Randy Dixon is an accomplished performer but the anchor of the unit is center Ray Donaldson, who missed going to the Pro Bowl for the first time in five years. With Chris Conlin, William Schultz, Pat Cunningham and draftee Mark Vander Poel in reserve, the group should progress.

With their top two draft options, the club sought help for the defensive line and the secondary. However, defensive end Shane Curry will not displace either of starters Donnell Thompson and Jon Hand, the feeling being that initially he could be groomed for the rôle of third-down pass rusher, which is a job performed with credit by Sam Clancy. At nose tackle, Harvey Armstrong is not given much acclaim outside the club but he is a tough warrior with an instinct for finding the point of attack. Together with Thompson and Hand, he forms a solid veteran trio. Linebacking has been a Colts strength for some years now, but the retirement of Fredd Young and Plan-B losses have left a gap at right inside linebacker. For the lucky player chosen, it will be a privilege to join Jeff Herrod, Duane Bickett and the re-enthused Chip Banks. The early signs are that Plan-B signing Cedric Figaro will battle with Scott Radecic for the job.

Even though Indianapolis used a third-round option to select Dave McCloughan, this may be nothing more than in recognition of the fact that, these days, a team can not have too many defensive backs. Last year's starting foursome of cornerbacks Chris Goode and Eugene Daniel, and safeties Keith Taylor and Mike Prior, should still be intact on opening day.

Of his kickers, head coach Ron Meyer said, "We are extremely fortunate to have Rohn Stark and Dean Biasucci." Stark is the current Pro Bowl punter and Biasucci is always a danger, even from long range. Inside the 40, he's almost automatic.

1991 SCHEDULE OF GAMES

September	
1 NEW ENGLAND	3:00
8 at Miami	1:00
15 at Los Angeles Raiders	1:00
22 DETROIT	12:00
29 at Seattle	1:00
October	
6 PITTSBURGH (Sun. night)	7:00
13 at Buffalo	1:00
20 NEW YORK JETS	12:00
27 Open Date	
November	
3 MIAMI	4:00
10 at New York Jets	1:00
17 CHICAGO	1:00
24 vs Green Bay at Milwaukee	12:00
December	
1 CLEVELAND	1:00
8 at New England	1:00
15 BUFFALO (Sun. night)	8:00
22 at Tampa Bay	1:00

1991 Draft

Round	Name	Pos.	Ht.	Wt.	College
2.	Curry, Shane	DE	6-3	259	Miami
3.	McCloughan, Dave	DB	6-0	180	Colorado
4.	Vander Poel, Mark	T	6-6	303	Colorado
5.	Cash, Kerry	TE	6-4	247	Texas
6.	Agee, Mel	DT	6-5	282	Illinois
7.	Bradley, James	WR	5-11	193	Michigan State
8.	Bruton, Tim	TE	6-3	252	Missouri
9.	Griffith, Howard	RB	5-11	219	Illinois
10.	Giannetti, Frank	DE	6-2	265	Penn State
11.	Crafts, Jerry	T	6-4	284	Louisville
12.	Luedeke, Rob	C	6-5	269	Penn State

VETERAN ROSTER

No.	Name	Pos.	Ht.	Wt.	NFL Year	College
79	Armstrong, Harvey	NT	6-3	282	9	Southern Methodist
62	Baldinger, Brian	G	6-4	278	9	Duke
31	Ball, Michael	S	6-0	220	4	Southern
51	Banks, Chip	LB	6-4	254	9	Southern California
36	Baylor, John	CB	6-0	203	3	Southern Mississippi
81	Beach, Pat	TE	6-4	249	9	Washington State
20	Bentley, Albert	RB	5-11	217	7	Miami
4	Biasucci, Dean	K	6-0	190	7	Western Carolina
50	Bickett, Duane	LB	6-5	251	7	Southern California
80	Brooks, Bill	WR	6-0	189	6	Boston University
71	Call, Kevin	T	6-7	308	8	Colorado State
76	Clancy, Sam	DE	6-7	290	8	Pittsburgh
66	Conlin, Chris	G-C	6-4	287	3	Penn State
72	Cunningham, Pat	T	6-6	295	1	Texas A&M
38	Daniel, Eugene	CB	5-11	188	8	Louisiana State
95	Davis, Travis	NT	6-2	274	2	Michigan State
29	Dickerson, Eric	RB	6-3	224	9	Southern Methodist
69	Dixon, Randy	G	6-3	302	5	Pittsburgh
53	Donaldson, Ray	C	6-3	300	12	Georgia
58	Figaro, Cedric	LB	6-2	250	4	Notre Dame
11	George, Jeff	QB	6-4	221	2	Illinois
37	Goode, Chris	CB	6-0	196	5	Alabama
26	Grant, Alan	CB	5-10	187	2	Stanford
78	Hand, Jon	DE	6-7	301	6	Alabama
9	Herrmann, Mark	QB	6-4	220	11	Purdue
54	Herrod, Jeff	LB	6-0	246	4	Mississippi
84	Hester, Jessie	WR	5-11	172	6	Florida State
7	Hilger, Rusty	QB	6-4	209	6	Oklahoma State
25	Holloway, Cornell	DB	5-11	182	2	Pittsburgh
23	Johnson, Anthony	RB	6-0	222	2	Notre Dame
96	McDonald, Quintus	LB	6-3	263	3	Penn State
87	Mobley, Orson	TE	6-5	259	6	Salem College
86	Morgan, Stanley	WR	5-11	185	15	Tennessee
73	Moss, Zefross	T	6-6	338	3	Alabama State
39	Prior, Mike	S	6-0	210	6	Illinois State
52	Radecic, Scott	LB	6-3	236	8	Penn State
74	Schultz, William	T	6-5	293	2	Southern California
85	Simmons, Stacey	WR	5-9	183	2	Florida
98	Siragusa, Tony	NT	6-3	291	2	Pittsburgh
3	Stark, Rohn	P	6-3	203	10	Florida State
27	Taylor, Keith	S	5-11	206	4	Illinois
99	Thompson, Donnell	DE	6-4	280	11	North Carolina
68	Tomberlin, Pat	G	6-2	330	2	Florida State
10	Trudeau, Jack	QB	6-3	219	6	Illinois
83	Verdin, Clarence	WR-PR	5-8	162	6	Southwestern Louisiana
92	Walker, Tony	LB	6-3	235	2	Southeast Missouri St.

Left inside linebacker Jeff Herrod led the Colts with 155 tackles and had four sacks, despite missing three games.

MIAMI DOLPHINS

Address Joe Robbie Stadium, 2269 N.W. 199th Street, Miami, Florida 33056.
Stadium Joe Robbie Stadium, Miami. *Capacity* 73,000 *Playing Surface* Grass (PAT).
Team Colours Aqua, Coral, and White.
Head Coach Don Shula – 22nd year; 29th NFL.
Championships Division 1971,'72,'73,'74, '79,'81,'83,'84,'85; Conference 1971,'72, '73,'82,'84; Super Bowl 1972,'73.
History AFL 1966-69, AFC 1970-

Since Don Shula arrived in Miami in 1970, the Dolphins have been to the playoffs 13 times, their most recent visit after a four-year absence producing a fuse-blowing spectacular with Buffalo, when the teams combined for 78 points, the second-highest total in NFL playoff history. This was more like the real Miami Dolphins.

It seems only yesterday that second-year quarterback Dan Marino rewrote the NFL record book as he passed for 5,084 yards and 48 touchdowns, the latter eclipsing the previous single-season mark of 36. Subsequently, he has shown himself to be mortal but, as the quality of the supporting cast has fallen away, the daring of youth has developed into strength of character and poise, a rallying point which is now the launching pad for the great assault. Along the way, the passing axis of Marino and wide receiver Mark Clayton has become the most prolific in NFL annals, accounting for 65 touchdowns. This still is the lightning bolt which can transfix opponents, and when they shift their defenses to counter the threat, the other starter, Mark Duper, can run amok. And there's another potential destroyer surging into open field from the tight end position, Ferrell Edmunds, who has been voted to two Pro Bowls though barely beginning to call upon the full range of his potential.

For a time, as the offensive line struggled to develop cohesion, some felt that only Marino's quick release kept both him and the Dolphins alive. But the rapid re-establishment of the five-man front as a force can only mean trouble for the opposition. At a stroke, the arrival of draftees Richmond Webb and Keith Sims secured the left side. The other starters, center Jeff Uhlenhake and the right-side combination of Harry Galbreath and Mark Dennis, responded accordingly. If there is one question to be answered, it is at running back where Sammie Smith has smouldered but has not yet reached flash-point. Again, fullback Tony Paige has been a revelation since his days with the Jets but he's not likely to win a game on his own. The Dolphins don't need a game-winning combination at running back; rather, they need a genuine threat, a decoy on which to build a

Sammie Smith's contributions from the running back position could help to set up the Dan Marino air show.

1991 SCHEDULE OF GAMES

September		
1	at Buffalo	4:00
8	INDIANAPOLIS	1:00
15	at Detroit	1:00
22	GREEN BAY	1:00
29	at New York Jets	4:00
October		
6	at New England	1:00
13	at Kansas City	3:00
20	HOUSTON	1:00
27	Open Date	
November		
3	at Indianapolis	4:00
10	NEW ENGLAND (Sun. night)	8:00
18	BUFFALO (Mon.)	9:00
24	at Chicago	12:00
December		
1	TAMPA BAY	1:00
9	CINCINNATI (Mon.)	9:00
15	at San Diego	1:00
22	NEW YORK JETS	1:00

play-action passing game. Given this, they can reserve a spot in the playoffs.

On defense, the Dolphins may need to borrow a little more time at linebacker, where both Hugh Green and Cliff Odom will be entering their 11th NFL seasons. Perhaps this was the reason why Miami traded for Houston starter John Grimsley, who will compete for a job to line up in company with David Griggs and Pro Bowler John Offerdahl. Up front, defensive right end Jeff Cross fought his way into the Pro Bowl squad with 11.5 sacks, but a corresponding development by nose tackle Shawn Lee and defensive left end T.J. Turner is overdue. It may be that former Pro Bowl nose tackle Brian Sochia can regain his full powers following an injury. It would be a fair assessment that, despite the presence of two current Pro Bowlers, the front seven is not overpowering, yet surprisingly the highest priority for this area in the draft was as low as round five, when linebacker Bryan Cox was selected.

The secondary, too, has not quite reached the levels expected of a group which was boosted by the use of high draft options to select the University of Florida pairing of safeties Louis Oliver and Jarvis Williams. The unit competes well but doesn't dominate as most potential champion teams do. Also, there will be a period of readjustment as a replacement for departed left cornerback Tim McKyer is found. Here, the loss of Plan-B free agent Rodney Thomas leaves veterans Paul Lankford, Vestee Jackson and Kerry Glenn in competition with draftees Chris Green and Roland Smith.

Punter Reggie Roby still finds a way of placing the ball into orbit while placekicker Pete Stoyanovich has established a hold which could last for many years.

1991 Draft

Round	Name	Pos.	Ht.	Wt.	College
1.	Hill, Randal	WR	5-10	177	Miami
3.	Craver, Aaron	RB	5-11	214	Fresno State
5.	Cox, Bryan	LB	6-3	235	Western Illinois
5.	Williams, Gene	G	6-1	308	Iowa State
7.	Green, Chris	CB	5-10	188	Illinois
8.	Smith, Roland	CB	5-8	180	Miami
9.	Miller, Scott	WR	5-10	179	UCLA
10.	Titley, Michael	TE	6-1	240	Iowa
11.	Rogers, Ernie	G	6-4	299	California
12.	Brunson, Joe	DT	6-4	291	Tennessee-Chattanooga

VETERAN ROSTER

No.	Name	Pos.	Ht.	Wt.	NFL Year	College
86	Banks, Fred	WR	5-10	185	6	Liberty
84	Baty, Greg	TE	6-5	240	5	Stanford
53	Bolcar, Ned	LB	6-1	235	2	Notre Dame
82	Brown, Andre	WR	6-3	210	3	Miami
37	Brown, J.B.	CB	6-0	192	3	Maryland
83	Clayton, Mark	WR	5-9	185	9	Louisville
50	Cooper, Louis	LB	6-2	238	7	Western Carolina
91	Cross, Jeff	DE	6-4	272	4	Missouri
65	Dellenbach, Jeff	T-C	6-6	285	7	Wisconsin
74	Dennis, Mark	T	6-6	295	5	Illinois
85	Duper, Mark	WR	5-9	192	10	Northwestern State, La.
80	Edmunds, Ferrell	TE	6-6	254	4	Maryland
22	Fullwood, Brent	RB	5-10	210	5	Auburn
62	Galbreath, Harry	G	6-1	275	4	Tennessee
35	Glenn, Kerry	CB	5-9	178	5	Minnesota
55	Green, Hugh	LB	6-2	230	11	Pittsburgh
92	Griggs, David	LB	6-3	248	3	Virginia
59	Grimsley, John	LB	6-2	238	8	Kentucky
45	Harden, Bobby	S	6-0	192	1	Miami
21	Higgs, Mark	RB-KR	5-7	195	4	Kentucky
29	Hobley, Liffort	S	6-0	202	6	Louisiana State
38	Holt, Leroy	RB	5-10	224	1	Southern California
24	Jackson, Vestee	CB	6-0	186	6	Washington
11	Jensen, Jim	WR-RB	6-4	224	11	Boston University
54	Junior, E.J.	LB	6-3	242	11	Alabama
44	Lankford, Paul	CB	6-1	191	10	Penn State
98	Lee, Shawn	NT	6-2	285	4	North Alabama
32	Limbrick, Garrett	RB	6-2	240	2	Oklahoma State
20	Logan, Marc	RB	5-11	222	5	Kentucky
13	Marino, Dan	QB	6-4	224	9	Pittsburgh
89	Martin, Tony	WR	6-0	180	2	Mesa, Colorado
28	McGruder, Michael	CB	5-11	190	1	Kent State
19	Mitchell, Scott	QB	6-6	236	1	Utah
27	Moore, Stevon	S	5-11	204	2	Mississippi
93	Odom, Cliff	LB	6-2	243	11	Texas-Arlington
56	Offerdahl, John	LB	6-3	238	6	Western Michigan
96	Oglesby, Alfred	NT	6-3	278	2	Houston
25	Oliver, Louis	S	6-2	226	3	Florida
49	Paige, Tony	RB	5-10	235	8	Virginia Tech
90	Price, Terry	DE	6-4	272	2	Texas A&M
52	Reichenbach, Mike	LB	6-2	240	8	East Stroudsburg State
4	Roby, Reggie	P	6-2	246	9	Iowa
81	Schwedes, Scott	WR-PR	6-0	185	5	Syracuse
9	Secules, Scott	QB	6-3	220	4	Virginia
88	Sievers, Eric	TE	6-4	238	11	Maryland
69	Sims, Keith	G	6-2	305	2	Iowa State
30	Smith, Don	RB	5-11	200	5	Mississippi State
33	Smith, Sammie	RB	6-2	230	3	Florida State
70	Sochia, Brian	DE-NT	6-3	278	9	N.W. Oklahoma State
10	Stoyanovich, Pete	K	5-10	185	3	Indiana
95	Turner, T.J.	DE	6-4	280	6	Houston
63	Uhlenhake, Jeff	C	6-3	284	3	Ohio State
78	Webb, Richmond	T	6-6	298	2	Texas A&M
60	Weidner, Bert	C	6-3	284	2	Kent State
26	Williams, Jarvis	S	5-11	200	4	Florida

NEW ENGLAND PATRIOTS

Address Foxboro Stadium, Route 1, Foxboro, Mass. 02035.
Stadium Foxboro Stadium, Foxboro.
Capacity 60,794 *Playing Surface* Grass.
Team Colours Red, White, and Blue.
Head Coach Dick MacPherson – 1st year.
Championships Division 1978,'86; Conference 1985.
History AFL 1960-69, AFC 1970-
(Until 1971, they were known as the Boston Patriots.)

In the 1985 season, the Patriots contested Super Bowl XX, but the 1990 campaign saw them slip to the NFL's poorest record. Along the way, Victor K. Kiam II, the president and chief executive officer of Remington Products, decided that he liked the product so much he'd buy the team. Entering his third full season as owner and chairman, Mr. Kiam's investment may be ready to pay off.

Trading down from prime position in the draft brought the advantage of expanding the Patriots' range of choice and, without question, produced a package of draftees and veterans which could invigorate the squad in more than a few areas. First-round pick Pat Harlow should step in to start at right tackle, ahead of veteran David Viaene, and it is possible that third-rounder Calvin Stephens could fill a left guard spot which the club accepts as being open for bids. Viaene may replace the retired Damian Johnson at right guard. Danny Villa has become a key feature at center and the great All-Pro Bruce Armstrong anchors the unit at left tackle.

After 16 seasons, most of them at the top, Steve Grogan has been put out to pasture. This, coupled with the retirement of Marc Wilson, means that Tom Hodson will be the unchallenged starter at quarterback. As a 1990 rookie, Hodson did well enough under difficult circumstances. He shapes up as a solid NFL quarterback and the club will have decent backup strength in Hugh Millen. At wide receiver there is explosive speed in depth, with Irving Fryar and Hart Lee Dykes the starters. Behind these two, Greg McMurtry hovers as a player of polish and stature, while Michael Timpson awaits his chance as the fastest member of the group. In 1990 tight end Marv Cook was the most prolific at his position in the AFC. A solid blocker, he may develop as the cement which holds the passing game together, with the experienced Zeke Mowatt ready to move in when the offense uses a double-tight end formation.

RIGHT: Left tackle Bruce Armstrong is widely accepted as being the Patriots' best lineman.

The draft produced yet another potential starter in Leonard Russell, who, in partnership with John Stephens, could give the Patriots the priceless asset of two speedy, heavyweight running backs. The AP Rookie of the Year in 1988, Stephens may just have found the ideal foil.

Defensively, the Patriots are in transition yet, throughout the unit, there are assured starters providing a framework for the development of a cohesive force. Starting with the three-man line, Brent Williams, who has led the team in sacks for the past three seasons, is highly respected while second-year powerhouse Ray Agnew should develop into a star performer. Nose tackle Tim Goad is a solid player. With a little luck, the Patriots could once again offer a feared prospect at linebacker. With complete rehabilitation from injury, Ed Reynolds and Johnny Rembert would provide a ferocious partnership on the inside. On the left outside, former All-Pro Andre Tippett may never regain his full powers following an early-1989 injury, but he remains an outstanding exponent of the art. Completing the foursome, right outside linebacker Chris Singleton, a 1990 first-round pick, has a point to make, never really coming to grips with the pace after missing most of the training camp. The intense Eugene Lockhart and David Howard, who were obtained as part of a trade with Dallas, join the depth.

Turning to the defensive secondary, it is with refreshing frankness that the Patriots assign right cornerback Maurice Hurst as the only pencilled-in starter. This is not to say that the remainder of a decent group, safeties Fred Marion and Roland James, and left cornerback Ronnie Lippett, will not retain their starting positions. But it is recognised that they will be pressed by the youthful talent of Junior Robinson, Tim Gordon and three draftees led by second-round pick Jerome Henderson. As the placekicker, Jason Staurovsky is not under threat but, following the loss of Plan-B free agent Brian Hansen, the punting job is wide open.

1991 SCHEDULE OF GAMES

September		
1	at Indianapolis	3:00
8	CLEVELAND	1:00
15	at Pittsburgh	1:00
22	HOUSTON	1:00
29	at Phoenix	1:00
October		
6	MIAMI	1:00
13	Open Date	
20	MINNESOTA	1:00
27	DENVER	1:00
November		
3	at Buffalo	1:00
10	at Miami (Sun. night)	8:00
17	NEW YORK JETS	1:00
24	BUFFALO	1:00
December		
1	at Denver	2:00
8	INDIANAPOLIS	1:00
15	at New York Jets	1:00
22	at Cincinnati	1:00

1991 Draft

Round	Name	Pos.	Ht.	Wt.	College
1.	Harlow, Pat	T	6-6	288	Southern California
1.	Russell, Leonard	RB	6-1	237	Arizona State
2.	Henderson, Jerome	CB	5-10	189	Clemson
3.	Stephens, Calvin	G	6-1	285	South Carolina
4.	Zolak, Scott	QB	6-5	222	Maryland
5.	Vaughn, Jon	RB	5-9	203	Michigan
5.	Coates, Ben	TE	6-4	243	Livingstone
6.	Key, David	CB	5-9	199	Michigan
7.	Miller, Blake	C	6-1	281	Louisiana State
8.	Colon, Harry	S	5-11	203	Missouri
9.	Glenn, O'Neil	G	6-2	292	Maryland
10.	Bethel, Randy	TE	6-0	243	Miami
11.	Moore, Vince	WR	5-10	200	Tennessee
11.	Alsbury, Paul	P	6-1	203	Southwest Texas State
12.	Edwards, Tim	DT	6-2	274	Delta State

VETERAN ROSTER

No.	Name	Pos.	Ht.	Wt.	NFL Year	College
33	Adams, George	RB	6-1	225	7	Kentucky
92	Agnew, Ray	DE	6-3	272	2	North Carolina State
39	Allen, Marvin	RB	5-10	208	4	Tulane
78	Armstrong, Bruce	T	6-4	284	5	Louisville
59	Brown, Vincent	LB	6-2	245	4	Mississippi Valley State
63	Chilton, Gene	C	6-3	286	5	Texas
76	Clayton, Stan	G	6-3	265	4	Penn State
22	Coleman, Eric	CB	6-0	190	3	Wyoming
46	Cook, Marv	TE	6-4	234	3	Iowa
65	Crawford, Elbert	C-G	6-3	280	2	Arkansas
71	DeRiggi, Fred	NT	6-2	268	1	Syracuse
88	Dykes, Hart Lee	WR	6-4	218	3	Oklahoma State
	Francis, Ron	CB	5-9	188	5	Baylor
80	Fryar, Irving	WR-PR	6-0	200	8	Nebraska
74	Gambol, Chris	T	6-6	303	4	Iowa
91	Gannon, Chris	DE	6-6	260	3	Southwest Louisiana
43	Gibson, Ernest	CB	5-10	185	7	Furman
72	Goad, Tim	NT	6-3	280	4	North Carolina
28	Gordon, Tim	S	6-0	188	5	Tulsa
58	Harvey, Richard	LB	6-1	227	2	Tulane
60	Hobby, Marion	DE	6-4	277	2	Tennessee
13	Hodson, Tom	QB	6-3	195	2	Louisiana State
	Howard, David	LB	6-2	233	7	Cal State-Long Beach
	Hunter, Ivy Joe	RB	6-0	247	3	Kentucky
37	Hurst, Maurice	CB	5-10	185	3	Southern
38	James, Roland	S	6-2	191	12	Tennessee
50	Jarostchuk, Ilia	LB	6-3	245	5	New Hampshire
	Jones, Victor	RB	5-8	212	2	Louisiana State
35	Landry, Anthony	RB	5-9	200	1	Stephen F. Austin
42	Lippett, Ronnie	CB	5-11	180	8	Miami
	Lockhart, Eugene	LB	6-2	229	8	Houston
31	Marion, Fred	S	6-2	191	10	Miami
82	Martin, Sammy	WR-KR	5-11	175	4	Louisiana State
86	McMurtry, Greg	WR	6-2	207	2	Michigan
64	Melander, Jon	G	6-7	280	1	Minnesota
7	Millen, Hugh	QB	6-5	216	5	Washington
81	Mowatt, Zeke	TE	6-3	240	8	Florida State
52	Rembert, Johnny	LB	6-3	234	9	Clemson
95	Reynolds, Ed	LB	6-5	242	9	Virginia
27	Robinson, Junior	CB	5-9	181	2	East Carolina
55	Singleton, Chris	LB	6-2	247	2	Arizona
97	Smith, Sean	DE	6-7	280	2	Georgia Tech
4	Staurovsky, Jason	K	5-9	170	5	Tulsa
44	Stephens, John	RB	6-1	215	4	Northwestern State, La.
53	Tardits, Richard	LB	6-2	218	2	Georgia
45	Timpson, Michael	WR	5-10	175	2	Penn State
56	Tippett, Andre	LB	6-3	241	9	Iowa
90	Veris, Garin	DE	6-4	255	6	Stanford
70	Viaene, Dave	T	6-5	300	3	Minnesota-Duluth
75	Villa, Danny	T	6-5	305	5	Arizona State
	Wagner, Bryan	P	6-1	200	5	Cal State-Northridge
21	Washington, Mickey	CB	5-9	187	2	Texas A&M
96	Williams, Brent	DE	6-4	275	6	Toledo
25	Zackery, Tony	S	6-2	200	1	Washington

NEW YORK JETS

Address 1000 Fulton Avenue, Hempstead, New York 11550.
Stadium Giants Stadium, East Rutherford, N.J. *Capacity* 76,891 *Playing Surface* AstroTurf.
Team Colours Kelly Green and White.
Head Coach Bruce Coslet – 2nd year.
Championships AFL 1968; Super Bowl 1968.
History AFL 1960-69, AFC 1970-
(Until 1963, they were known as the New York Titans.)

"In a nut shell, we accomplished a lot this year, but we haven't even scratched the surface," reflected Jets head coach Bruce Coslet about a squad, much of which bears the hallmark of that master designer, general manager Dick Steinberg.

The Jets led at half time in 11 games but couldn't hold opponents off, and the need for improving the defense was confirmed in a draft which saw only two offensive players taken before round ten. There is a framework of high-class players upon which to build, starting with 'Eagle' defensive tackle Dennis Byrd, through middle linebacker Kyle Clifton and ending with a secondary featuring cornerback James Hasty and free safety Erik McMillan. Byrd had a fine season with 13 sacks and was the leading tackler on the defensive line with 79. The offseason trade of starting defensive left end Ron Stallworth acknowledges the progress made by backups Darrell Davis and Marvin Washington, who combined for 9.5 sacks. The other starter at defensive end, Jeff Lageman, a former first-round draftee outside linebacker, has yet to come through as a major force. Former Raider Bill Pickel and ex-Dolphin John Bosa could add bite.

Clifton's importance to the defense is underlined by his total of 199 tackles, more than double those of the next best, McMillan, who had 95. The rawhide-tough Clifton could use a little extra sparkle from the outsides and it may have arrived in the shape of third-round draftee Morris Lewis, who comes over as an unpredictable, opportunistic player who might just be what the pass rush needs. The secondary can be breathtakingly exciting and needs only to tidy up its collective application. Combining well with Hasty and McMillan, rookie left cornerback Tony Stargell overcame his early-season difficulties while strong safety Brian Washington's emergence reflected his new-found enthusiasm for the game.

On offense, almost all the pieces have been assembled for a scoring machine and, while Tony Eason, Troy Taylor and top draftee Browning Nagle will press for playing time, it still should be established veteran Ken O'Brien who lights the fuse. Few AFC clubs can boast a better pair of starting wide receivers than the majestic Al Toon and last-year's supplemental first-round pick Rob Moore. And there's no shortage of genuine class in backups Chris Burkett and JoJo Townsell. "He's not a deep receiving threat but he knocks your butt off," was Coslet's description of the starting tight end, Mark Boyer, whom he regards as ideal for his system. The backups are Chris Dressel and Doug Wellsandt, each of whom fits the same description, primarily a blocker who can catch.

At running back, the Jets have a reassuring blend of youth and experience, with the latter represented by the pairing of Freeman McNeil and Johnny Hector. For much of his career, McNeil has been close to superstardom and only a susceptibility to injury has robbed him of his place with the gods. However, it is the partnership of Blair Thomas and Brad Baxter which probably will continue to start. Thomas has immense potential as an athlete and the priceless quality of professional dedication. After a slow start to his career following contractual negotiations and niggling injuries, Thomas should be ready to produce. Baxter is not as gifted but he makes very few errors and everyone respects his toughness.

Though possessing impact players in abundance, the whole show depends upon the continued development of the offensive line. Jim Sweeney is the rock at center and, ordinarily, he would be flanked by guards Dave Cadigan and Mike Haight. However, a superior showing by rookie Dwayne White when Cadigan was injured may mean that the healthy Cadigan shifts to play tackle, displacing one of Jeff Criswell and Brett Miller. Trevor Matich is a decent reserve guard while new signings Irv Eatman and Ron Mattes will fit somewhere into the picture at tackle.

Placekicker Pat Leahy, voted club MVP by his teammates, goes on and on, while punter Joe Prokop seems to have found a home after stays with Green Bay and San Diego.

1991 SCHEDULE OF GAMES

September		
1	TAMPA BAY	1:00
8	at Seattle	1:00
15	BUFFALO	4:00
23	at Chicago (Mon.)	8:00
29	MIAMI	4:00
October		
6	at Cleveland	1:00
13	HOUSTON	4:00
20	at Indianapolis	12:00
27	Open Date	
November		
3	GREEN BAY	1:00
10	INDIANAPOLIS	1:00
17	at New England	1:00
24	SAN DIEGO	4:00
December		
1	at Buffalo	1:00
8	at Detroit	4:00
15	NEW ENGLAND	1:00
22	at Miami	1:00

Middle linebacker Kyle Clifton was the Jets' leading tackler with 195, a total which was 103 more than the next best.

1991 Draft

Round	Name	Pos.	Ht.	Wt.	College
2.	Nagle, Browning	QB	6-2	220	Louisville
3.	Lewis, Morris	LB	6-3	240	Georgia
4.	Gunn, Mark	DE	6-4	295	Pittsburgh
6.	Bryant, Blaise	RB	5-11	198	Iowa State
6.	Riley, Mike	CB	5-10	178	Tulane
7.	Parrish, Doug	CB	5-10	190	San Francisco State
8.	James, Tim	S	6-1	207	Colorado
9.	Glonek, Paul	DT	6-4	275	Arizona
10.	Baker, Al	RB	5-11	223	Kentucky
11.	Keeton, Rocen	LB	6-2	241	UCLA
12.	Hayes, Mark	T	6-6	283	Arizona State

VETERAN ROSTER

No.	Name	Pos.	Ht.	Wt.	NFL Year	College
30	Baxter, Brad	RB	6-1	235	2	Alabama State
	Bosa, John	DE	6-4	275	4	Boston College
80	Boyer, Mark	TE	6-4	242	7	Southern California
	Brim, Michael	CB	6-0	190	4	Virginia Union
29	Brown, A.B.	RB	5-9	215	2	West Virginia
87	Burkett, Chris	WR	6-4	200	7	Jackson State
90	Byrd, Dennis	DE	6-5	270	3	Tulsa
66	Cadigan, Dave	G-T	6-4	285	4	Southern California
59	Clifton, Kyle	LB	6-4	236	8	Texas Christian
61	Criswell, Jeff	T	6-7	291	5	Graceland
49	Curtis, Travis	S	5-10	180	5	West Virginia
98	Davis, Darrell	DE	6-2	258	2	Texas Christian
89	Dawkins, Dale	WR	6-1	190	2	Miami
84	Dressel, Chris	TE	6-4	239	7	Stanford
62	Duffy, Roger	C	6-3	285	2	Penn State
	Eatman, Irv	T	6-7	298	6	UCLA
44	Egu, Patrick	RB	5-11	206	2	Nevada-Reno
91	Frase, Paul	DE-DT	6-5	260	3	Syracuse
52	Galvin, John	LB	6-3	230	4	Boston College
79	Haight, Mike	G-T	6-4	279	6	Iowa
40	Hasty, James	CB	6-0	201	4	Washington State
34	Hector, Johnny	RB	5-11	207	9	Texas A&M
	Houston, Bobby	LB	6-2	234	1	North Carolina State
26	Johnson, Ken	S	6-2	208	2	Florida A&M
95	Johnson, Troy	LB	6-2	236	4	Oklahoma
58	Kelly, Joe	LB	6-2	235	6	Washington
19	Kelly, Pat	TE	6-6	252	3	Syracuse
	Kors, R.J.	S	6-0	195	1	Cal State-Long Beach
56	Lageman, Jeff	DE-LB	6-5	255	3	Virginia
5	Leahy, Pat	K	6-0	200	18	St Louis
81	Mathis, Terance	WR-KR	5-10	170	2	New Mexico
64	Matich, Trevor	C-T-G	6-4	282	7	Brigham Young
	Mattes, Ron	T	6-6	302	6	Virginia
23	Mayes, Michael	CB	5-10	173	2	Louisiana State
22	McMillan, Erik	S	6-2	200	4	Missouri
92	McNeil, Emanuel	DT	6-3	277	1	Tennessee-Martin
24	McNeil, Freeman	RB	5-11	208	11	UCLA
94	Mersereau, Scott	DT-DE	6-3	273	5	Southern Connecticut
72	Miller, Brett	T	6-7	293	9	Iowa
85	Moore, Rob	WR	6-3	205	2	Syracuse
51	Mott, Joe	LB	6-4	243	3	Iowa
77	Nichols, Gerald	DT-DE	6-2	260	5	Florida State
7	O'Brien, Ken	QB	6-4	212	9	California-Davis
21	Odegard, Don	CB	6-0	180	2	Nevada-Las Vegas
	Pickel, Bill	DT	6-5	260	9	Rutgers
20	Price, Dennis	CB	6-1	175	3	UCLA
6	Prokop, Joe	P	6-2	225	6	Cal Poly-Pomona
45	Stargell, Tony	CB	5-11	190	2	Tennessee State
57	Stephens, Mac	LB	6-3	220	2	Minnesota
53	Sweeney, Jim	C-G	6-4	275	8	Pittsburgh
14	Taylor, Troy	QB	6-4	200	2	California
32	Thomas, Blair	RB	5-10	195	2	Penn State
88	Toon, Al	WR	6-4	205	7	Wisconsin
83	Townsell, JoJo	WR-KR	5-9	182	7	UCLA
48	Washington, Brian	S	6-1	220	3	Nebraska
97	Washington, Marvin	DE-DT	6-6	276	3	Idaho
86	Wellsandt, Doug	TE	6-3	248	2	Washington State
67	White, Dwayne	G	6-2	312	2	Alcorn State
63	Zawatson, Dave	G-T	6-5	287	3	California

CINCINNATI BENGALS

Address 200 Riverfront Stadium, Cincinnati, Ohio 45202.
Stadium Riverfront Stadium, Cincinnati. *Capacity* 59,755 *Playing Surface* AstroTurf-8.
Team Colours Black, Orange, and White.
Head Coach Sam Wyche – 8th year.
Championships Division 1970,'73,'81,'88,'90; Conference 1981,'88.
History AFL 1968-69, AFC 1970-

One of the few teams which might match the excitement and scoring power of the Buffalo Bills, though with not quite the same overall authority on defense, is Cincinnati. And it was with defense in mind that the club used its top three options in the draft.

Of the starting trio, nose tackle Tim Krumrie and defensive ends Skip McClendon and David Grant, only Krumrie is unchallenged. While McClendon and Grant pressure opponents, the Bengals need players who go out and devour people. From the second and third rounds of the draft came a pair of immensely powerful defensive ends in Lamar Rogers and Bob Dahl. If only one came through as a force, the club would be satisfied. Such is the strategy of pro football that the best help may have arrived with top draftee Alfred Williams, who won the Butkus Award given annually to the best linebacker in college football. He really is explosive and shapes up as the best news possible for the Bengals' right outside linebacker, James Francis, who quickly gained the ultimate respect from opponents who were obliged to assign double-teaming in the attempt to contain him. As the horns of a crazed buffalo, Francis and Williams could transform the defense in a flash. On the insides at linebacker Carl Zander and Kevin Walker have faced up to the task of stopping the run with tenacity and must surely be helped by the overall strengthening of the unit.

A step behind them, in the secondary, it is freedom from injuries as much as new talent that is needed. Thus, while the departure of Plan-B free agent Solomon Wilcots leaves the Bengals thin at free safety, the return of a healthy Rickey Dixon to compete with Barney Bussey would take care of things. Eric Thomas and Lewis Billups form a classy pairing at cornerback and few ball carriers relish any form of contact with Pro Bowl strong safety David Fulcher. Reserve cornerback Rod Jones, a former first-round pick of Tampa Bay, has extensive experience as a starter.

Paradoxically, the Bengals' offense begins when punter Lee Johnson sends his kickoffs deep into the opposing end zone. In his major rôle, he delivers the ball with good accuracy, hang-time and length. Placekicker Jim Breech is the reliable sort, almost deadly inside the 40 and not bad from further out. Placing him

1991 SCHEDULE OF GAMES

September		
1	at Denver	2:00
8	HOUSTON (Sun. night)	8:00
15	at Cleveland	1:00
22	WASHINGTON	1:00
29	Open Date	
October		
6	SEATTLE	1:00
13	at Dallas	12:00
21	at Buffalo (Mon.)	9:00
27	at Houston	12:00
November		
3	CLEVELAND	1:00
10	PITTSBURGH	1:00
17	at Philadelphia	1:00
24	LOS ANGELES RAIDERS	1:00
December		
1	NEW YORK GIANTS	4:00
9	at Miami (Mon.)	9:00
15	at Pittsburgh	1:00
22	NEW ENGLAND	1:00

in position for his PATs and field goals, Boomer Esiason has all the weapons any quarterback would need. There's little which now separates wide receivers Eddie Brown and Tim McGee, a pair of high-class operatives, except possibly when it comes to the knockout punch. Last year, Brown outscored McGee by nine touchdowns to one. There is the great potential of untapped quality in Reggie Rembert, who spent last year on injured reserve and has yet to enter the fray. At tight end, Pro Bowler Rodney Holman is an integral part of the passing offense, and while backup Eric Kattus is the man for the heavy work of blocking, he too can hang on to a touchdown pass.

Esiason's options continue into the backfield, where both James Brooks and Ickey Woods offer a distinct receiving threat. However, it is their rushing, the mix of speed, elusiveness and power, for which they are truly feared. Behind them, there is the reassuring presence of Harold Green and Eric Ball.

When it comes to opening the holes and keeping opponents at bay, Cincinnati have one of the better offensive lines in the AFC. For the greater part of the last ten years, left tackle Anthony Munoz has been considered the finest in the game. Joe Walter handles the right tackle spot with dominance and reliability. In the middle, nobody shoves around the trio of Bruce Reimers, Ken Moyer and center Bruce Kozerski. As backups, Brian Blados, Paul Jetton and Mike Brennan represent a blend of proven experience and youthful promise.

LEFT: Wide receiver Tim McGee confirmed his status as the perfect foil for starting partner Eddie Brown.

1991 Draft

Round	Name	Pos.	Ht.	Wt.	College
1.	Williams, Alfred	LB	6-6	237	Colorado
2.	Rogers, Lamar	DT	6-3	275	Auburn
3.	Dahl, Bob	DT	6-4	267	Notre Dame
4.	Hollas, Donald	QB	6-3	215	Rice
4.	Carpenter, Rob	WR	6-1	183	Syracuse
5.	Arthur, Mike	C	6-3	271	Texas A&M
6.	Fain, Richard	CB	5-10	183	Florida
7.	Vinson, Fernandus	S	5-10	197	North Carolina State
8.	Dingle, Mike	RB	6-2	240	South Carolina
9.	Garrett, Shane	WR	5-9	187	Texas A&M
10.	Lavin, Jim	G	6-3	282	Georgia Tech
11.	Smith, Chris	TE	6-4	239	Brigham Young
12.	Bennett, Antoine	DB	5-11	185	Florida A&M

VETERAN ROSTER

No.	Name	Pos.	Ht.	Wt.	NFL Year	College
42	Ball, Eric	RB	6-2	214	3	UCLA
86	Barber, Mike	WR	5-11	172	3	Marshall
53	Barker, Leo	LB	6-2	230	8	New Mexico State
24	Billups, Lewis	CB	5-11	182	6	North Alabama
74	Blados, Brian	G	6-5	296	8	North Carolina
55	Brady, Ed	LB	6-2	236	8	Illinois
3	Breech, Jim	K	5-6	161	13	California
60	Brennan, Mike	T	6-5	274	2	Notre Dame
21	Brooks, James	RB	5-10	182	11	Auburn
81	Brown, Eddie	WR	6-0	185	7	Miami
99	Buck, Jason	DE	6-5	264	5	Brigham Young
27	Bussey, Barney	S	6-0	210	6	South Carolina State
45	Carter, Carl	CB	5-11	180	6	Texas Tech
57	Clark, Bernard	LB	6-2	248	2	Miami
29	Dixon, Rickey	S-CB	5-11	188	4	Oklahoma
7	Esiason, Boomer	QB	6-5	220	8	Maryland
50	Francis, James	LB	6-5	252	2	Baylor
33	Fulcher, David	S	6-3	238	6	Arizona State
	Gordon, Alex	LB	6-5	245	5	Cincinnati
98	Grant, David	NT	6-5	278	4	West Virginia
28	Green, Harold	RB	6-2	222	2	South Carolina
82	Holman, Rodney	TE	6-3	238	10	Tulane
80	James, Lynn	WR	6-0	191	2	Arizona State
36	Jennings, Stanford	RB-KR	6-1	212	8	Furman
68	Jetton, Paul	G	6-4	288	3	Texas
11	Johnson, Lee	P	6-2	200	7	Brigham Young
25	Jones, Rod	CB	6-0	185	6	Southern Methodist
84	Kattus, Eric	TE	6-5	251	6	Michigan
64	Kozerski, Bruce	C	6-4	287	8	Holy Cross
69	Krumrie, Tim	NT	6-2	274	9	Wisconsin
72	McClendon, Skip	DE	6-7	287	5	Arizona State
85	McGee, Tim	WR	5-10	183	6	Tennessee
73	Moyer, Ken	G	6-7	297	3	Toledo
78	Munoz, Anthony	T	6-6	284	12	Southern California
52	Ogletree, Craig	LB	6-2	236	2	Auburn
32	Price, Mitchell	CB-PR	5-9	181	2	Tulane
75	Reimers, Bruce	G	6-7	298	8	Iowa State
88	Rembert, Reggie	WR	6-4	200	1	West Virginia
87	Riggs, Jim	TE	6-5	245	5	Clemson
76	Scrafford, Kirk	T	6-6	255	2	Montana
83	Smith, Kendal	WR	5-10	189	3	Utah State
20	Taylor, Craig	RB	6-0	228	3	West Virginia
22	Thomas, Eric	CB	5-11	181	5	Tulane
96	Tuatagaloa, Natu	DE	6-4	274	3	California
59	Walker, Kevin	LB	6-3	244	4	Maryland
63	Walter, Joe	T	6-7	292	7	Texas Tech
51	White, Leon	LB	6-3	242	6	Brigham Young
4	Wilhelm, Erik	QB	6-3	217	3	Oregon State
30	Woods, Ickey	RB	6-2	232	3	Nevada-Las Vegas
91	Zander, Carl	LB	6-2	235	7	Tennessee

CLEVELAND BROWNS

Address Tower B, Cleveland Stadium, Cleveland, Ohio 44114.
Stadium Cleveland Stadium, Cleveland. *Capacity* 80,098 *Playing Surface* Grass.
Team Colours Seal Brown, Orange, and White.
Head Coach Bill Belichick – 1st year.
Championships Division 1971,'80,'85,'86,'87,'89; AAFC 1946,'47,'48,'49; NFL 1950,'54,'55,'64.
History AAFC 1946-49, NFL 1950-69, AFC 1970-

So dramatically can fortunes change in the NFL. After an outstanding five-year period in which they contested the AFC Championship Game in 1986, 1987 and 1989, won the division title in 1985 and went to the playoffs as a wild card in 1988, the Browns slumped to a 3-13-0 record, the lowest win percentage in franchise history. It has to rank as a conspiracy of fates that the effects of retirements, contractual holdouts, young players not coming through and veterans playing below par were focused in a five-month period. And the worry is that the rehabilitation process may take some years.

But even the worst damage can be limited to form a basis for improvement. It would help if the offensive line veterans could turn up healthy and stay that way. Left tackle Paul Farren, center Mike Baab and right guard Gregg Rakoczy form a steady nucleus, with left guard Ralph Tamm and right tackle Tony Jones promising to be better for having gained valuable experience in 1990. The rehabilitation of Dan Fike, who started 70 games at right guard before suffering a knee injury late in the 1989 season, would be an enormous boost, while Plan-B free agent John Rienstra, who was a 1986 first-round pick of Pittsburgh, might be a factor. Second-round draftee guard Ed King may need the season to adjust after joining the pros as a junior.

Much depends upon the form of quarterback Bernie Kosar, who suffered through a disappointing 1990 campaign. On his day he can pick opponents apart ruthlessly. It is the combination of his blend of thoughtful interpretation, skill and occasional daring which has nursed big performances out of an otherwise steady set of wide receivers. Of the senior trio, club leader Webster Slaughter has the speed, a touch ahead of Reggie Langhorne, while Brian Brennan has the sure hands. The time is overdue for Lawyer Tillman, a 1989 second-round draftee with immense potential, to come through. It may be that the Browns see Tillman as ripe for conversion to tight end, where the retirement of the fabled Ozzie Newsome has created a conspicuous void. On the surface, Plan-B free agent signing Charles Arbuckle is a prime candidate for the job but he remains an unknown quantity after missing what would have been his rookie year with an injury.

New head coach Bill Belichick will expect the running backs to carry a load with Kevin Mack the likely beast of burden. On hand will be the solid Leroy Hoard and Eric Metcalf, the latter a mercurial runner who latched onto the pace over the final seven games of last season when he averaged 4.6 yards per carry. Lee Rouson, the former Giants player who is well known to Belichick, provides cover at both backfield positions.

Despite having only one player of outstanding ability for the defensive line, the Browns seem likely to continue with their 4-3 system. That one player, All-Pro Michael Dean Perry, led the club in 1990 with 11.5 quarterback sacks. He is a rallying point for young defensive ends Rob Burnett and Anthony Pleasant, and defensive left tackle Tom Gibson. At linebacker there is no shortage of heart. Clay Matthews has ranked among the league's best for most of his 13 pro years. He operates on the left side of the competitive Mike Johnson, who led the club with 161 total tackles last season. David Grayson and Van Waiters share the right side. The defensive secondary has lost stalwart strong safety Felix Wright but top draftee Eric Turner should be the instant replacement. Elsewhere, fine veterans continue, with Thane Gash operating at free safety, and the pairing of Raymond Clayborn and Frank Minnifield at cornerback.

Following the release of punter Bryan Wagner, Plan-B signing Brian Hansen appears to have an edge over his rivals. For the job of placekicker, former Giants first-year player Matt Stover appears to be a solid candidate.

RIGHT: Cleveland may feel the loss of strong safety Felix Wright, who was quickly spotted and signed up by Minnesota as a Plan-B free agent.

1991 SCHEDULE OF GAMES

September		
1	DALLAS	1:00
8	at New England	1:00
15	CINCINNATI	1:00
22	at New York Giants	1:00
29	Open Date	
October		
6	NEW YORK JETS	1:00
13	at Washington	1:00
20	at San Diego	1:00
27	PITTSBURGH	1:00
November		
3	at Cincinnati	1:00
10	PHILADELPHIA	1:00
17	at Houston (Sun. night)	7:00
24	KANSAS CITY	1:00
December		
1	at Indianapolis	1:00
8	DENVER	1:00
15	HOUSTON	1:00
22	at Pittsburgh	1:00

1991 Draft

Round	Name	Pos.	Ht.	Wt.	College
1.	Turner, Eric	S	6-0	206	UCLA
2.	King, Ed	G	6-4	297	Auburn
3.	Jones, James	NT	6-1	299	Northern Iowa
4.	Sagapolutele, Pio	NT	6-5	285	San Diego State
6.	Jackson, Michael	WR	6-3	190	Southern Mississippi
8.	Conover, Frank	DT	6-4	310	Syracuse
9.	Irvin, Raymond	DB	5-10	172	Central Florida
9.	Wiggins, Shawn	WR	5-9	164	Wyoming
10.	Greenfield, Brian	P	5-11	222	Pittsburgh
11.	Jones, Todd	G	6-2	325	Henderson, Ark.
12.	Austin, Elijah	NT	6-2	278	North Carolina State

VETERAN ROSTER

No.	Name	Pos.	Ht.	Wt.	NFL Year	College
48	Arbuckle, Charles	TE	6-2	238	1	UCLA
61	Baab, Mike	C	6-4	275	10	Texas
37	Barnett, Harlon	S	5-11	200	2	Michigan State
24	Blaylock, Tony	CB	5-11	190	4	Winston-Salem State
36	Braggs, Stephen	S	5-9	180	5	Texas
58	Brandon, David	LB	6-4	230	4	Memphis State
86	Brennan, Brian	WR	5-10	185	8	Boston College
52	Brown, Richard	LB	6-3	240	4	San Diego State
90	Burnett, Rob	DE	6-4	270	2	Syracuse
26	Clayborn, Raymond	CB	6-1	190	15	Texas
74	Farren, Paul	T-G	6-6	270	9	Boston University
69	Fike, Dan	G	6-7	285	7	Florida
13	Francis, Jeff	QB	6-4	225	2	Tennessee
27	Gainer, Derrick	RB	5-11	235	2	Florida A&M
81	Galbraith, Scott	TE	6-3	260	2	Southern California
30	Gash, Thane	S	6-0	195	4	East Tennessee State
71	Gibson, Tom	DL	6-8	275	3	Northern Arizona
56	Grayson, David	LB	6-2	230	5	Fresno State
11	Hansen, Brian	P	6-4	220	7	Sioux Falls
23	Harper, Mark	CB	5-9	185	6	Alcorn State
39	Hilliard, Randy	CB	5-11	160	2	Northwestern State, La.
33	Hoard, Leroy	RB	5-11	230	2	Michigan
62	Jefferson, Ben	T	6-9	330	2	Maryland
51	Johnson, Eddie	LB	6-1	235	11	Louisville
59	Johnson, Mike	LB	6-1	230	6	Virginia Tech
80	Joines, Vernon	WR	6-2	210	2	Maryland
55	Jones, Jock	LB	6-2	230	2	Virginia Tech
66	Jones, Tony	T	6-5	290	4	Western Carolina
19	Kosar, Bernie	QB	6-5	215	7	Miami
40	Kramer, Kyle	S	6-3	190	2	Bowling Green
88	Langhorne, Reggie	WR	6-2	205	7	Elizabeth City State
34	Mack, Kevin	RB	6-0	230	7	Clemson
57	Matthews, Clay	LB	6-2	245	14	Southern California
21	Metcalf, Eric	RB	5-10	190	3	Texas
31	Minnifield, Frank	CB	5-9	180	8	Louisville
67	Morris, Mike	C	6-5	285	4	Northeast Missouri St.
22	Newsome, Vince	S	6-1	186	9	Washington
89	Oliphant, Mike	WR	5-9	171	2	Puget Sound
92	Perry, Michael Dean	DT	6-1	285	4	Clemson
17	Philcox, Todd	QB	6-4	209	2	Syracuse
98	Pleasant, Anthony	DE	6-5	258	2	Tennessee State
73	Rakoczy, Gregg	G-C	6-5	295	5	Miami
77	Reeves, Ken	T	6-5	277	7	Texas A&M
70	Rienstra, John	G	6-5	272	6	Temple
72	Robbins, Kevin	G	6-6	295	2	Michigan State
44	Rouson, Lee	RB	6-1	222	7	Colorado
83	Rowell, Eugene	WR	6-1	180	2	Southern Mississippi
84	Slaughter, Webster	WR	6-1	170	6	San Diego State
3	Stover, Matt	K	5-11	178	1	Louisiana State
87	Talley, John	TE	6-5	245	2	West Virginia
65	Tamm, Ralph	G	6-4	280	2	West Chester State
85	Tillman, Lawyer	WR	6-5	230	2	Auburn
50	Waiters, Van	LB	6-4	250	4	Indiana
91	Weston, Rhondy	DE	6-5	280	2	Florida
78	Woods, Rob	T	6-5	275	1	Arizona

HOUSTON OILERS

Address 6910 Fannin Street, Houston, Texas 77030.
Stadium Astrodome, Houston.
Capacity 60,502 *Playing Surface* AstroTurf-8.
Team Colours Columbia Blue, Scarlet, and White.
Head Coach Jack Pardee – 2nd year; 8th NFL.
Championships AFL 1960,'61.
History AFL 1960-69, AFC 1970-

On its day, the Oilers' multiple passing offense can leave opponents in disarray, yet it was the crucial requirement for perfection at quarterback which, in the playoffs, was their undoing. With Warren Moon injured, the complexities of the system, coupled with the temperature of the occasion, were just too much for backup Cody Carlson and the Oilers slid to a heavy defeat. Yet the system does work and it will remain unchanged as they attempt to become the only AFC club to reach the playoffs for a fifth successive year.

It might be likened to the charge of the Light Brigade as four wide receivers flood into the open spaces but, unlike those ill-fated heroics of more than a century ago, each Oilers foray is a carefully intentioned attempt to dismantle the opposing defense and, when it works, it is a remarkable sight. Last year Houston wide receivers finished first, second, fourth and seventh in the AFC list. In order, Haywood Jeffires, Drew Hill, Ernest Givins and Curtis Duncan will once again rattle a few cages. The system doesn't use a tight end, and means that the lone running back faces a greater range of responsibilities and, with them, opportunities. Lorenzo White took every available option to play his part, rushing for 702 yards and catching 39 passes. In a conventional pro set, he'd probably be a 1,000-yard rusher bu- that's simply not the way of things. Such is the class of backup Allen Pinkett that he slips into the system with ease.

There are few more beautiful sights in the game than Moon, sliding, fading and watching, adjusting to the shifting colours of the mosaic in motion before triggering the pass. It is a one-dimensional approach but, despite its vulnerabilities, the system remains and it means that, somehow, Carlson will have to be given more practice time to master the problems. The offensive line emerges from a secure unit, though there will be some adjustment of personnel to accommodate a vacancy at center. Pro Bowl guard Bruce Matthews may take on the job, with another Pro Bowler, Mike Munchak, at left guard. Don Maggs and David Williams are the tackles, leaving Dean Steinkuhler, Doug Dawson, and draftees John Flannery and Kevin Donnalley as the pieces available for completing the puzzle.

On defense, the Oilers are sound, but the quest for perfection saw them take three defensive backs with their top four options. AFC-leading interceptor Richard Johnson and Cris Dishman are good, speedy cornerbacks while, at strong safety, the outstanding Bubba

Wide receiver Drew Hill caught passes for over 1,000 yards for the fourth time in his career.

McDowell rules his territory without compassion. Free safety Terry Kinard is still close to his best but the challengers, among them former Bills starter John Hagy and top draftee Mike Dumas, are gathering.

The defensive linemen adjusted well to the 4-3 system, left tackle Ray Childress going to the Pro Bowl and defensive right end Sean Jones having his best sack total, a club-leading 12.5, since 1986. Defensive left end William Fuller prospered, even defensing seven passes, while right tackle Doug Smith threw his weight around with his usual force. There is no reason to disturb the formation. Behind them, at linebacker, Lamar Lathon moves in on the left side with Al Smith resuming in the middle. But there could be changes, depending upon the progress of Lathon and the desire for playing time which will come from Johnny Meads, Scott Kozak and Eugene Seale.

The departure of Plan-B free agent placekicker Tony Zendejas, who missed the final ten games through injury, takes the pressure off his replacement, Teddy Garcia. It may well be that Garcia had done enough the retain his spot. Only restricted opportunities – with 34 punts he was short of the qualifying number by six – prevented Greg Montgomery from taking top place in the official NFL list with a gross average of 45 yards.

1991 SCHEDULE OF GAMES

September		
1	LOS ANGELES RAIDERS	3:00
8	at Cincinnati (Sun. night)	8:00
16	KANSAS CITY (Mon.)	8:00
22	at New England	1:00
29	Open Date	
October		
6	DENVER	12:00
13	at New York Jets	4:00
20	at Miami	1:00
27	CINCINNATI	12:00
November		
3	at Washington	1:00
10	DALLAS	12:00
17	CLEVELAND (Sun. night)	7:00
24	at Pittsburgh	1:00
December		
2	PHILADELPHIA (Mon.)	8:00
8	PITTSBURGH	12:00
15	at Cleveland	1:00
21	at New York Giants (Sat.)	12:30

1991 Draft

Round	Name	Pos.	Ht.	Wt.	College
2.	Dumas, Mike	S	5-10	178	Indiana
2.	Lewis, Darryl	CB	5-8	193	Arizona
2.	Flannery, John	C	6-3	304	Syracuse
3.	Jackson, Steve	CB	5-8	182	Purdue
3.	Donnalley, Kevin	T	6-5	290	North Carolina
4.	Rocker, David	DT	6-3	265	Auburn
4.	Robertson, Marcus	CB	5-11	197	Iowa State
5.	Wellman, Gary	WR	5-8	173	Southern California
7.	Freeman, Kyle	LB	6-0	235	Angelo State
8.	Brown, Gary	RB	5-10	220	Penn State
9.	Jefferson, Shawn	WR	5-11	172	Central Florida
10.	Moore, Curtis	LB	6-1	236	Kansas
11.	Smith, James	S	6-2	202	Richmond
12.	Johnson, Alex	WR	5-8	168	Miami

VETERAN ROSTER

No.	Name	Pos.	Ht.	Wt.	NFL Year	College
76	Alm, Jeff	DT	6-6	269	2	Notre Dame
97	Banks, Robert	DE	6-5	255	5	Notre Dame
37	Bergeson, Eric	S	5-11	192	2	Brigham Young
14	Carlson, Cody	QB	6-3	202	5	Baylor
79	Childress, Ray	DT	6-6	272	7	Texas A&M
66	Dawson, Doug	G-C	6-3	288	4	Texas
28	Dishman, Cris	CB	6-0	178	4	Purdue
80	Duncan, Curtis	WR	5-11	184	5	Northwestern
51	Fairs, Eric	LB	6-3	244	6	Memphis State
88	Ford, Bernard	WR	5-10	171	3	Central Florida
95	Fuller, William	DE	6-3	265	6	North Carolina
8	Garcia, Teddy	K	5-9	172	4	Northeast Louisiana
81	Givins, Ernest	WR	5-9	172	6	Louisville
93	Graf, Rick	LB	6-5	245	5	Wisconsin
22	Hagy, John	S	6-0	185	4	Texas
83	Harris, Leonard	WR-KR	5-8	162	6	Texas Tech
85	Hill, Drew	WR	5-9	172	12	Georgia Tech
90	Johnson, Ezra	DE	6-4	257	15	Morris Brown
84	Jeffires, Haywood	WR	6-2	201	5	North Carolina State
23	Johnson, Richard	CB	6-1	195	7	Wisconsin
86	Jones, Cedric	WR	6-1	184	10	Duke
96	Jones, Sean	DE	6-7	264	8	Northeastern
82	Jones, Tony	WR	5-7	139	2	Texas
27	Kinard, Terry	S	6-1	198	9	Clemson
21	Knight, Leander	S	6-1	192	3	Montclair State
56	Kozak, Scott	LB	6-3	222	3	Oregon
57	Lathon, Lamar	LB	6-3	244	2	Houston
78	Maggs, Don	T	6-5	290	5	Tulane
74	Matthews, Bruce	G-C	6-5	291	9	Southern California
25	McDowell, Bubba	S	6-1	198	3	Miami
89	McNeil, Gerald	WR-PR	5-8	142	6	Baylor
91	Meads, Johnny	LB	6-2	226	8	Nicholls State
94	Montgomery, Glenn	DT	6-0	268	3	Houston
9	Montgomery, Greg	P	6-4	215	4	Michigan State
1	Moon, Warren	QB	6-3	212	8	Washington
63	Munchak, Mike	G	6-3	284	10	Penn State
64	Norgard, Erik	C-G	6-1	278	2	Colorado
26	Orlando, Bo	S	5-10	180	2	West Virginia
72	Peguese, Willis	DE	6-4	267	2	Miami
20	Pinkett, Allen	RB	5-9	196	6	Notre Dame
31	Porter, Kerry	RB	6-1	220	4	Washington State
53	Seale, Eugene	LB	5-10	253	5	Lamar
10	Slack, Reggie	QB	6-1	221	2	Auburn
54	Smith, Al	LB	6-1	244	5	Utah State
99	Smith, Doug	DT	6-6	314	7	Auburn
70	Steinkuhler, Dean	T	6-3	287	8	Nebraska
68	Stewart, Alex	DE	6-4	260	1	Cal State-Fullerton
36	Thomas, Dee	DB	5-10	176	2	Nicholls State
44	White, Lorenzo	RB	5-11	222	4	Michigan State
73	Williams, David	T	6-5	292	3	Florida

PITTSBURGH STEELERS

Address Three Rivers Stadium, 300 Stadium Circle, Pittsburgh, Pennsylvania 15212.
Stadium Three Rivers Stadium, Pittsburgh. *Capacity* 59,000 *Playing Surface* AstroTurf.
Team Colours Black and Gold.
Head Coach Chuck Noll – 23rd year.
Championships Division 1972,'74,'75,'76,'77,'78, '79,'83,'84; Conference 1974,'75,'78,'79; Super Bowl 1974,'75,'78,'79.
History NFL 1933-69, AFC 1970-
(Until 1940, they were known as the Pittsburgh Pirates.)

For several years now, analyzing the Steelers has not been easy as, with shifts and turns, no clear picture of development has emerged. Only now is a shape materializing. But one thing has remained certain, and that is a guarantee of the very best in coaching by the formidable Chuck Noll.

Noll has a fine body of offensive linemen and goes to war with four certain starters, Pro Bowler Tunch Ilkin and John Jackson at tackle, Terry Long at right guard and Dermontti Dawson at center. Brian Blankenship started 13 games at left guard but the Steelers do not disguise their optimism over the prospects for Carlton Haselrig, who preferred wrestling to football in college and moved from nose tackle to guard in the 1990 offseason. He is still learning the business but it is significant that he was the only guard protected under Plan B. Although Haselrig probably will start, Blankenship is of great value, both as a backup and a long-snapper.

With a regular set protecting him, it is not surprising that quarterback Bubby Brister is coming off a season when he established personal highs in every category, notably a passer rating of 81.6 and the most touchdown passes (20) by a Steeler since 1981. On his day able to reach into the depths and pull out an exciting hybrid of dash and nerve, Brister occasionally has shown the style of former Steeler Terry Bradshaw. He needs only to develop greater consistency. The club has confidence in backup Rick Strom.

There's little doubt that improvement in the tight end position, with good contributions from veteran Mike Mularkey and the emergence of the gargantuan Eric Green, was an unexpected bounty. At running back, however, there has been stagnation. The group is steady enough but, last year, rarely looked like taking an opponent apart. The slow progress of Tim Worley has been a disappointment but, entering camp, he is seen as a starter in tandem with the honest Merril Hoge. It is at wide receiver that hopes for real progress abound. Top-class assistance for the primary target, veteran Louis Lipps, was sought in the draft. And the signs are that one of Jeff Graham and Ernie Mills may offer the solution to a problem that has lingered.

Defensively, the Steelers don't usually give much away and, last year, they gave less than any other team in the league. Surprisingly, for the top-rated defense, the pass rush wasn't that terrifying, logging only 34 sacks compared with Kansas City's NFL-leading 60. Perhaps because of this, Florida's Huey Richardson was the club's premier selection in the draft. Richardson, an outside linebacker in college, probably will be used as a stand-up pass-rushing specialist. Otherwise, the defensive lineup will be much as last year. The three-man front will have hard man Gerald Williams at nose tackle and Keith Willis to his left. Aaron Jones, who until now has shown only flashes, is being asked to come through at the expense of Donald Evans at defensive right end. At linebacker, maintaining the Steelers' historic tradition for quality, intensity and intelligence, the quartet of Bryan Hinkle, Hardy Nickerson, David Little and Greg Lloyd will continue to start. Jerry Olsavsky and Jerrol Williams remain as backups only because of the quality ahead of them.

Young, effervescent and bent on destruction, the defensive secondary is a fighting force of some renown. Pro Bowl right cornerback Rod Woodson is a multiple weapon, always likely to return an interception for a score, while left cornerback David Johnson has made remarkable progress. Carnell Lake and Thomas Everett form an uncompromising pairing at safety. Larry Griffin has emerged from an impressive list of backups to carve out a key rôle in the dime package.

When it comes to punting, the Steelers are more concerned with field position than pure distance and do not see Dan Stryzinski's modest average as a weakness. And there are no worries over placekicker Gary Anderson, whose field goal accuracy bounces around the top three marks in NFL history.

LEFT: Merril Hoge, who is coming off his best year as a pro, will carry the load until Tim Worley begins to show his full potential.

1991 Draft

Round	Name	Pos.	Ht.	Wt.	College
1.	Richardson, Huey	DE-LB	6-4	238	Florida
2.	Graham, Jeff	WR	6-1	198	Ohio State
3.	Mills, Ernie	WR	5-10	176	Florida
4.	Walker, Sammy	CB	5-10	192	Texas Tech
4.	Cooper, Adrian	TE	6-4	253	Oklahoma
6.	Thompson, Leroy	RB	5-9	210	Penn State
7.	Jones, Andre	LB	6-2	213	Notre Dame
8.	Dingman, Dean	G	6-1	286	Michigan
9.	McGonnigal, Bruce	TE	6-4	229	Virginia
10.	Solomon, Ariel	T	6-4	273	Colorado
11.	Thomas, Efrum	DB	5-11	187	Alabama
12.	Brady, Jeff	LB	6-0	230	Kentucky

VETERAN ROSTER

No.	Name	Pos.	Ht.	Wt.	NFL Year	College
1	Anderson, Gary	K	5-11	184	10	Syracuse
60	Blankenship, Brian	G-C	6-1	280	5	Nebraska
6	Brister, Bubby	QB	6-3	208	6	Northeast Louisiana
88	Calloway, Chris	WR	5-10	185	2	Michigan
64	Davidson, Kenny	DE	6-5	272	2	Louisiana State
89	Davis, Lorenzo	WR	5-11	185	2	Youngstown State
63	Dawson, Dermontti	C	6-2	279	4	Kentucky
96	Dunbar, Karl	DE	6-4	275	1	Louisiana State
66	Evans, Donald	DE	6-2	265	3	Winston-Salem State
27	Everett, Thomas	S	5-9	182	5	Baylor
80	Fair, Ron	WR	5-11	190	1	Arizona State
29	Foster, Barry	RB	5-10	223	2	Arkansas
68	Freeman, Lorenzo	NT-DE	6-5	319	5	Pittsburgh
86	Green, Eric	TE	6-5	274	2	Liberty
22	Griffin, Larry	S	6-0	202	6	North Carolina
35	Hall, Delton	CB	6-1	208	5	Clemson
77	Haselrig, Carlton	G	6-1	291	2	Pitt-Johnstown
53	Hinkle, Bryan	LB	6-2	220	10	Oregon
33	Hoge, Merril	RB	6-2	229	5	Idaho State
62	Ilkin, Tunch	T	6-3	274	12	Indiana State
65	Jackson, John	T	6-6	290	4	Eastern Kentucky
99	Jenkins, A.J.	LB-DE	6-2	237	3	Cal State-Fullerton
44	Johnson, David	CB	6-0	185	3	Kentucky
97	Jones, Aaron	DE	6-5	269	4	Eastern Kentucky
25	Jones, Gary	S	6-1	203	2	Texas A&M
37	Lake, Carnell	S	6-1	207	3	UCLA
51	Lanza, Chuck	C	6-2	265	3	Notre Dame
83	Lipps, Louis	WR	5-10	186	8	Southern Mississippi
50	Little, David	LB	6-1	236	11	Florida
95	Lloyd, Greg	LB	6-2	225	4	Fort Valley State
74	Long, Terry	G	5-11	278	8	East Carolina
	McGovern, Rob	LB	6-2	234	3	Holy Cross
84	Mularkey, Mike	TE	6-4	238	9	Florida
54	Nickerson, Hardy	LB	6-2	225	5	California
14	O'Donnell, Neil	QB	6-3	221	1	Maryland
55	Olsavsky, Jerry	LB	6-1	218	3	Pittsburgh
85	O'Shea, Terry	TE	6-4	238	3	California, Pa.
71	Ricketts, Tom	T	6-5	293	3	Pittsburgh
20	Stone, Dwight	WR-RB	6-0	190	5	Middle Tennessee State
11	Strom, Rick	QB	6-2	201	3	Georgia Tech
4	Stryzinski, Dan	P	6-1	193	2	Indiana
73	Strzelczyk, Justin	T	6-5	291	2	Maine
91	Veasey, Craig	DE	6-2	280	2	Houston
98	Williams, Gerald	NT	6-3	291	6	Auburn
57	Williams, Jerrol	LB	6-5	244	3	Purdue
42	Williams, Warren	RB	6-0	201	4	Miami
93	Willis, Keith	DE	6-1	263	9	Northeastern
49	Woodruff, Dwayne	CB	6-0	196	12	Louisville
26	Woodson, Rod	CB-KR	6-0	197	5	Purdue
38	Worley, Tim	RB	6-2	223	3	Georgia
	Wyatt, Willie	NT	6-0	275	2	Alabama

1991 SCHEDULE OF GAMES

Date	Game	Time
September		
1	SAN DIEGO	4:00
8	at Buffalo	1:00
15	NEW ENGLAND	1:00
22	at Philadelphia	1:00
29	Open Date	
October		
6	at Indianapolis (Sun. night)	7:00
14	NEW YORK GIANTS (Mon.)	9:00
20	SEATTLE	1:00
27	at Cleveland	1:00
November		
3	at Denver (Sun. night)	6:00
10	at Cincinnati	1:00
17	WASHINGTON	1:00
24	HOUSTON	1:00
28	at Dallas (Thanksgiving)	3:00
December		
8	at Houston	12:00
15	CINCINNATI	1:00
22	CLEVELAND	1:00

DENVER BRONCOS

Address 13655 East Dove Valley Parkway, Englewood, Colorado 80112.
Stadium Denver Mile High Stadium. *Capacity* 76,273 *Playing Surface* Grass (PAT).
Team Colours Orange, Royal Blue, and White.
Head Coach Dan Reeves – 11th year.
Championships Division 1977,'78,'84,'86,'87,'89; Conference 1977,'86,'87,'89.
History AFL 1960-69, AFC 1970-

It defies all reason that a team which had been to three of the previous four Super Bowls and may even have improved its squad over that period, suddenly collapsed to finish last in its division. The answer may lie in turnovers, those turnovers "that'll kill ya", as is often said. The Broncos' 32 handouts led to 121 points, a fraction lower than one third of their opponents' total, and were critical in eight losses. In contrast, opponents' turnovers helped towards only two wins for Denver. Few observers feel that this was the real Denver Broncos and a great many more think that this club, with its positive ownership and outstanding head coach, to say nothing of players blessed with true greatness, will quickly turn around.

If there is a weakness, certainly a hole to be filled, it is at left tackle, the position dominated by the club's best lineman, Gerald Perry, who was traded in an arrangement which may benefit both parties. The other spots are held down firmly by Jim Juriga, Keith Kartz, Doug Widell and Ken Lanier. There may be shifts of personnel, with Juriga moving to tackle and former Cowboy Crawford Ker coming in at left guard. Darrell Hamilton, Sean Farrell and Dave Widell will also be involved in the equation.

Turning to the areas of strength, the running back position is boosted by the arrival of Gaston Green. Never really given an extended run with the talent-laden Rams, Green needs to shake off the tag of being injury-prone but could add sparkle to the unquestioned power of Bobby Humphrey. In his second year, Humphrey built on his promise as he crashed and finessed for 1,202 yards. He is the ideal foil for a passing game directed by the man, John Elway, whom many scouts still insist is among the very best in the business. Adjusting to the harshness of experience, Elway softened his line, completing a career-high 58.6% of his passes. A lot of them were to wide receiver Mark Jackson, whose haul was three better than that of Vance Johnson. This pairing hopes to be reunited with the 'Third Amigo', Ricky Nattiel. With ample talent in reserve and mindful of tight end Clarence Kay's inconsistency, the Broncos invested a second-round option in Reggie Johnson.

Defensively, improvement is needed and steps were taken with the selection of linebackers Mike Croel and Keith Traylor. Croel is expected to step in at left outside linebacker, at the expense of Tim Lucas, and could pay immediate dividends with his ferocious pass rushing complementing the club's best blitzer, right outside linebacker Simon Fletcher. Traylor can play outside or inside and may be groomed to take over from Karl Mecklenburg, who is feeling the effects of persistent injury. The tough Michael Brooks completes the quartet. The loss of Alphonso Carreker in September 1990, was a blow. Without him, the production from the defensive line was muted. Correspondingly, his return from injury to join nose tackle Greg Kragen and defensive right end Ron Holmes could bring about immediate improvement.

If there is uncertainty surrounding the front seven, given the rehabilitation of cornerback Tyrone Braxton the lineup in the defensive secondary is established. The combination of Braxton's ball-hawking, free safety Steve Atwater's fearsome tackling, the experience of strong safety Dennis Smith and the calm reliability of right cornerback Wymon Henderson adds up to a solid unit. The reserves are led by Randy Robbins and the aggressive Alton Montgomery.

Kicking in Mile High Stadium is not often easy and, under those circumstances, David Treadwell satisfies the requirements. For punter Mike Horan, the cold hinders but the rarefied air may compensate. He dealt with the difficulties well, ending up with the NFL's best gross average of 44.4 yards.

RIGHT: In only his second NFL year, free safety Steve Atwater was named All-Pro and emerged as a focal point in the Denver secondary.

1991 SCHEDULE OF GAMES		
September		
1	CINCINNATI	2:00
8	at Los Angeles Raiders	1:00
15	SEATTLE	2:00
22	SAN DIEGO	2:00
29	at Minnesota (Sun. night)	7:00
October		
6	at Houston	12:00
13	Open Date	
20	KANSAS CITY	2:00
27	at New England	1:00
November		
3	PITTSBURGH (Sun. night)	6:00
10	LOS ANGELES RAIDERS	2:00
17	at Kansas City	12:00
24	at Seattle	1:00
December		
1	NEW ENGLAND	2:00
8	at Cleveland	1:00
15	PHOENIX	2:00
22	at San Diego	1:00

1991 Draft

Round	Name	Pos.	Ht.	Wt.	College
1.	Croel, Mike	LB	6-2	231	Nebraska
2.	Johnson, Reggie	TE	6-1	256	Florida State
3.	Traylor, Keith	LB	6-2	260	Central State, Okla.
4.	Russell, Derek	WR	6-0	179	Arkansas
5.	Lewis, Greg	RB	5-10	214	Washington
6.	Subis, Nick	T	6-4	280	San Diego State
8.	Walker, Kenny	DE	6-2	246	Nebraska
9.	Gibson, Don	NT	6-2	268	Southern California
10.	Mayfield, Curtis	WR	5-11	174	Oklahoma State
11.	Moore, Shawn	QB	6-1	215	Virginia

VETERAN ROSTER

No.	Name	Pos.	Ht.	Wt.	NFL Year	College
27	Atwater, Steve	S	6-3	213	3	Arkansas
64	Beavers, Scott	G	6-4	277	2	Georgia Tech
32	Bratton, Melvin	RB	6-1	225	3	Miami
34	Braxton, Tyrone	CB	5-11	185	5	North Dakota State
56	Brooks, Michael	LB	6-1	235	5	Louisiana State
92	Carreker, Alphonso	DE	6-6	272	7	Florida State
20	Clark, Kevin	DB-KR	5-10	185	3	San Jose State
25	Corrington, Kip	S	6-0	175	3	Texas A&M
58	Curtis, Scott	LB	6-1	230	4	New Hampshire
62	Davidson, Jeff	G	6-5	309	2	Ohio State
55	Dennison, Rick	LB	6-3	220	10	Colorado State
	Dimry, Charles	CB	6-0	175	4	Nevada-Las Vegas
7	Elway, John	QB	6-3	215	9	Stanford
35	Ezor, Blake	RB	5-9	183	2	Michigan State
63	Farrell, Sean	G	6-3	260	10	Penn State
73	Fletcher, Simon	LB	6-5	240	7	Houston
99	Galloway, David	DE	6-3	265	10	Florida
	Green, Gaston	RB	5-11	192	4	UCLA
87	Green, Paul	TE	6-3	230	2	Southern California
93	Haliburton, Ronnie	LB	6-4	230	2	Louisiana State
69	Hamilton, Darrell	T	6-5	298	3	North Carolina
24	Henderson, Wymon	CB	5-9	186	5	Nevada-Las Vegas
90	Holmes, Ron	DE	6-4	265	7	Washington
2	Horan, Mike	P	5-11	190	8	Cal State-Long Beach
26	Humphrey, Bobby	RB	6-1	201	3	Alabama
80	Jackson, Mark	WR	5-9	180	6	Purdue
82	Johnson, Vance	WR	5-11	185	7	Arizona
66	Juriga, Jim	G	6-6	275	4	Illinois
72	Kartz, Keith	C	6-4	270	5	California
88	Kay, Clarence	TE	6-2	237	8	Georgia
	Ker, Crawford	G	6-3	283	7	Florida
71	Kragen, Greg	NT	6-3	265	7	Utah State
8	Kubiak, Gary	QB	6-0	192	9	Texas A&M
21	Lang, Le-Lo	CB	5-11	185	2	Washington
76	Lanier, Ken	T	6-3	290	11	Florida State
59	Lucas, Tim	LB	6-3	230	5	California
77	Mecklenburg, Karl	LB	6-3	240	9	Minnesota
52	Mills, Jeff	LB	6-3	238	2	Nebraska
22	Montgomery, Alton	CB	6-0	195	2	Houston
84	Nattiel, Ricky	WR	5-9	180	5	Florida
75	Parkinson, Brent	T	6-5	267	1	Southern California
	Perryman, Robert	RB	6-1	233	5	Michigan
91	Powers, Warren	DE	6-6	287	3	Maryland
48	Robbins, Randy	S	6-2	189	8	Arizona
30	Sewell, Steve	RB-WR	6-3	210	7	Oklahoma
81	Sharpe, Shannon	WR	6-2	225	2	Savannah State
49	Smith, Dennis	S	6-3	200	11	Southern California
28	Smith, Elliott	CB	6-2	192	3	Alcorn State
65	Smith, Monte	G	6-4	270	2	North Dakota
85	Stallworth, Tim	WR	5-10	185	1	Washington State
94	Szymanski, Jim	DE	6-5	268	2	Michigan State
53	Thompson, Anthony	LB	6-1	227	2	East Carolina
61	Townsend, Andre	DE-NT	6-3	265	8	Mississippi
9	Treadwell, David	K	6-1	175	3	Clemson
86	Verhulst, Chris	TE	6-2	249	4	Chico State
79	Widell, Dave	T	6-6	292	4	Boston College
67	Widell, Doug	G	6-4	287	3	Boston College
83	Young, Michael	WR	6-1	183	7	UCLA

KANSAS CITY CHIEFS

Address One Arrowhead Drive, Kansas City, Missouri 64129.
Stadium Arrowhead Stadium, Kansas City. *Capacity* 78,067 *Playing Surface* AstroTurf-8.
Team Colours Red, Gold, and White.
Head Coach Marty Schottenheimer – 3rd year; 8th NFL.
Championships Division 1971; AFL 1962,'66,'69; Super Bowl 1969.
History AFL 1960-69, AFC 1970-
(Until 1963, they were known as the Dallas Texans.)

It was just like the 'old times' of the late 1960s in the AFL as Kansas City and the Raiders went at it, nose-to-nose, with the division crown at stake. By a combined total of five points the Chiefs won both games but, in the end, they had to settle for a wild-card spot in the playoffs. Their exit came in heartbreaking manner, an infringement taking them just beyond the limit of place-kicker Nick Lowery's range in the final minute of the first-round playoff game against Miami. Significantly, though, Kansas City's 11-5 record was its best since that era of greatness more than 20 years ago. Few would question their right to preseason favouritism for a playoff spot.

It is no coincidence that the revival has come under head coach Marty Schottenheimer, whose Cleveland teams went to the playoffs in every one of his four full seasons with the AFC Central club. Schottenheimer, who had six years playing linebacker with Buffalo and the Patriots, has developed this experience to a level of specialist excellence and, in double-quick time, has assembled a quartet which has emerged as one of the most feared in the NFL.

Dino Hackett and Percy Snow occupy the inside spots, with former New Orleans and Minnesota veteran Chris Martin on the left and the NFL 1990 sack leader, Derrick Thomas, on the right. And that's just the core. Up front, the three-man line of defensive ends Neil Smith and Bill Maas, and nose tackle Dan Saleaumua has firmed up into an impressive group while, hovering as the rear-guard, the defensive secondary has Pro Bowlers Albert Lewis and Kevin Ross at cornerback, Kevin Porter at strong safety and the great veteran, Deron Cherry, at free safety. One or two of the defensive backs are in their early 30s and it made sense for Kansas City to use the middle rounds of the draft, not a high priority area, in the search for youth.

Running the offense, Kansas City has the venerable Steve DeBerg, a veteran quarterback of 14 NFL years with stops in San Francisco, Denver and Tampa Bay along the way. DeBerg is coming off his finest season as a pro and there is no reason to feel that he could not continue at that level. It was clear, however, that there was a need to bolster the receiving corps and classy help has arrived in the form of Plan-B free agent tight end Pete Holohan. Of the starters at wide receiver, Stephone Paige, who at one time held the NFL single-game record with 309 yards receiving, is the senior player ahead of Robb Thomas.

The only problem at running back centres around the most efficient use of Barry Word and Christian Okoye, two heavyweights each of whom has rushed for 1,000 yards in a season. Ordinarily, they might play in tandem but the Chiefs frequently employ a one-back system. It was all the more curious that the Chiefs used their first-round draft option to acquire Harvey Williams. Word, who came along with a rattle last year after a troubled career, would appear to have the advantage but it is a slight worry that he was not effective in the playoffs. Charged with the responsibility for taking care of the heavy work, a young offensive line has been reinforced by second-round draftee tackle Joe Valerio, who will put pressure on John Alt and Rich Baldinger to start with guards David Szott and David Lutz, and center Tim Grunhard.

The special team is always likely to block half-a-dozen kicks and you couldn't ask for much better than the boot of Nick Lowery to finish off a drive.

RIGHT: Cornerback Kevin Ross led the Chiefs with five interceptions and went to his second Pro Bowl.

1991 SCHEDULE OF GAMES

September		
1	ATLANTA	12:00
8	NEW ORLEANS	12:00
16	at Houston (Mon.)	8:00
22	SEATTLE	3:00
29	at San Diego	1:00
October		
7	BUFFALO (Mon.)	8:00
13	MIAMI	3:00
20	at Denver	2:00
28	LOS ANGELES RAIDERS (Mon.)	8:00
November		
3	Open Date	
10	at Los Angeles Rams	1:00
17	DENVER	12:00
24	at Cleveland	1:00
December		
1	at Seattle	1:00
8	SAN DIEGO	12:00
14	at San Francisco (Sat.)	1:00
22	at Los Angeles Raiders	1:00

1991 Draft

Round	Name	Pos.	Ht.	Wt.	College
1.	Williams, Harvey	RB	6-1	215	Louisiana State
2.	Valerio, Joe	T	6-4	293	Pennsylvania
3.	Barnett, Tim	WR	6-1	201	Jackson State
5.	Mincy, Charles	DB	5-11	185	Washington
6.	Malone, Darrell	CB	5-10	180	Jacksonville State
7.	Ellison, Bernard	CB	6-0	192	Nevada-Reno
8.	Dohring, Tom	T	6-6	289	Michigan
9.	Keen, Robbie	K	6-3	213	California
10.	Ramsey, Eric	CB	5-11	189	Auburn
11.	Olive, Bobby	WR	5-11	161	Ohio State
12.	Shipley, Ron	G	6-3	299	New Mexico

VETERAN ROSTER

No.	Name	Pos.	Ht.	Wt.	NFL Year	College
76	Alt, John	T	6-7	300	8	Iowa
77	Baldinger, Rich	G-T	6-4	292	10	Wake Forest
4	Barker, Bryan	P	6-1	187	2	Santa Clara
99	Bell, Mike	DE	6-4	266	11	Colorado State
	Bell, Richard	RB	6-0	200	2	Nebraska
88	Birden, J.J.	WR	5-9	160	2	Oregon
34	Burruss, Lloyd	S	6-0	211	11	Maryland
20	Cherry, Deron	S	5-11	205	11	Rutgers
17	DeBerg, Steve	QB	6-3	214	15	San Jose State
10	Elkins, Mike	QB	6-3	225	3	Wake Forest
22	Gamble, Kenny	RB	5-10	204	2	Colgate
74	Graham, Derrick	T	6-4	305	2	Appalachian State
98	Griffin, Leonard	DE	6-4	272	6	Grambling
61	Grunhard, Tim	C	6-2	302	2	Notre Dame
56	Hackett, Dino	LB	6-3	230	6	Appalachian State
86	Harry, Emile	WR	5-11	178	5	Stanford
85	Hayes, Jonathan	TE	6-5	254	7	Iowa
44	Heard, Herman	RB	5-10	194	7	Southern Colorado
	Holohan, Pete	H-B	6-4	232	11	Notre Dame
43	Jones, Bill	RB	5-11	222	2	Southwest Texas State
80	Jones, Fred	WR	5-9	175	2	Grambling
29	Lewis, Albert	CB	6-2	198	9	Grambling
8	Lowery, Nick	K	6-4	205	12	Dartmouth
72	Lutz, David	G-T	6-6	303	9	Georgia Tech
63	Maas, Bill	DE-NT	6-5	277	8	Pittsburgh
57	Martin, Chris	LB	6-2	245	9	Auburn
48	McNair, Todd	RB	6-1	185	3	Temple
	Munford, Marc	LB	6-2	231	5	Nebraska
35	Okoye, Christian	RB	6-1	260	5	Azusa Pacific
83	Paige, Stephone	WR	6-2	185	9	Fresno State
24	Pearson, Jayice	CB	5-11	185	6	Washington
11	Pelluer, Steve	QB	6-4	212	8	Washington
45	Petry, Stan	CB	5-11	175	3	Texas Christian
27	Porter, Kevin	S	5-10	219	4	Auburn
52	Rogers, Tracy	LB	6-2	235	2	Fresno State
31	Ross, Kevin	CB	5-9	182	8	Temple
	Sadowski, Troy	TE	6-5	265	2	Georgia
97	Saleaumua, Dan	NT	6-0	289	5	Arizona State
21	Saxon, James	RB	5-11	225	3	San Jose State
	Shaw, Ricky	LB	6-4	240	4	Oklahoma State
95	Sims, Tom	NT	6-2	273	1	Pittsburgh
90	Smith, Neil	DE	6-4	271	4	Nebraska
59	Snow, Percy	LB	6-2	244	2	Michigan State
	Stallworth, Ron	DE-DT	6-5	260	3	Auburn
	Stradford, Troy	RB	5-9	195	5	Boston College
79	Szott, David	G	6-4	273	2	Penn State
58	Thomas, Derrick	LB	6-3	244	3	Alabama
81	Thomas, Robb	WR	5-11	171	3	Oregon State
	Vlasic, Mark	QB	6-3	206	4	Iowa
46	Washington, Charles	CB	6-1	208	3	Cameron, Oklahoma
82	Whitaker, Danta	TE	6-4	243	2	Mississippi Valley State
65	Winters, Frank	C-G	6-3	280	5	Western Illinois
23	Word, Barry	RB	6-2	240	3	Virginia

LOS ANGELES RAIDERS

Address 332 Center Street, El Segundo, California 90245.
Stadium Los Angeles Memorial Coliseum. *Capacity* 92,488 *Playing Surface* Grass.
Team Colours Silver and Black.
Head Coach Art Shell – 3rd year.
Championships Division 1970,'72,'73,'74,'75,'76, '83,'85,'90; Conference 1976,'80,'83; AFL 1967; Super Bowl 1976,'80,'83.
History AFL 1960-69, AFC 1970-
(Until 1982, they were known as the Oakland Raiders.)

After entering the campaign not widely fancied, wouldn't you know that the Raiders would confound everyone with their best regular-season record since 1985 to take the division title? They were even able to absorb two losses to the 'old enemy', Kansas City. It is a stronger squad which resumes the battle.

Browsing through the list reveals one area which may need attention, the defensive tackle position, which lost an outstanding backup with the Plan-B departure of Bill Pickel. The solution may rest on the impact of last year's first-round pick, Anthony Smith, who missed the entire campaign with an injury. If Smith can come in at defensive left end, Howie Long could move inside where he is comfortable, partnering Scott Davis with Greg Townsend at defensive right end. Potentially a better sacking crew than those hooligans who brought ancient Rome to its knees, this could be the Raiders' finest line in recent memory. They might even raise the art of terror to new heights with the kind of contribution projected for outside linebacker Aaron Wallace, who had nine sacks in his rookie season. It remains to be seen if Wallace can become an every-down player but, given this, the linebacking trio he would form with some combination of Jerry Robinson, Riki Ellison, Tom Benson and the recently acquired former Tampa Bay starter, Winston Moss, could present real problems for the opposition.

There certainly is no shortage of experience in the defensive secondary and it now welcomes the most experienced of all, the best at his position for almost a decade and a legend in his own time, the great Ronnie Lott. Unprotected by the 49ers, with whom he won four Super Bowl Championship rings, Lott has been troubled by injuries but still ranks as an outstanding competitor and incomparable leader. These days he's seen as a free safety but he is able to move around. The final pairing at safety will emerge from experiments in the preseason with Lott, Eddie Anderson and Mike Harden the principal contenders. The corners are looking increasingly safe under the custodianship of Terry McDaniel and Lionel Washington, but it would be unwise to discount the prospects for backup Garry Lewis, who had beaten out McDaniel to start, entering the 1990 campaign, before suffering an injury.

With the criticism waning and draftee Todd Marinovich some way from challenging, Jay Schroeder can settle in more comfortably at quarterback. He might even enjoy life a little more and why not with the likes of Mervyn Fernandez, Willie Gault and Tim Brown as wide receivers? Backups Sam Graddy and Jamie Holland have blazing speed. There will be a competition at tight end, with Ethan Horton and Mike Dyal probably coming out even. The Raiders will find ways of using each player to his best advantage.

Using the talent at running back may be a bigger problem. With Marcus Allen, Greg Bell, Vance Mueller and former 49er Roger Craig available to start in the speedster spot, the Raiders may use a rotation with the idea of keeping everyone fresh. But some players simply need the carries to work up a head of steam and this may present difficulties, especially if Bo Jackson recovers full fitness. Steve Smith has seniority at fullback for his blocking, steady rushing and occasional shock receiving.

Perhaps the greatest improvement has been shown by the offensive line, which now has Max Montoya and Steve Wisniewski at guard and Don Mosebar at center, Pro Bowlers all. It says a great deal for the development of tackles Rory Graves and Steve Wright that Bruce Wilkerson could not regain a starting spot. Behind Wilkerson, James FitzPatrick, Todd Peat and Plan-B signing Joel Patten await their chances.

Jeff Jaeger and Jeff Gossett take care of the kicking game. Jaeger might sensibly attempt field goals from 50 yards, his longest success last year. Gossett is coming off the poorest gross average of his career, but he was required to kick for position as distinct from length and nobody is complaining.

1991 SCHEDULE OF GAMES

September		
1	at Houston	3:00
8	DENVER	1:00
15	INDIANAPOLIS	1:00
22	at Atlanta	1:00
29	SAN FRANCISCO	1:00
October		
6	SAN DIEGO	1:00
13	at Seattle (Sun. night)	4:30
20	LOS ANGELES RAMS	1:00
28	at Kansas City (Mon.)	8:00
November		
3	Open Date	
10	at Denver	2:00
17	SEATTLE	1:00
24	at Cincinnati	1:00
December		
1	at San Diego (Sun. night)	5:00
8	BUFFALO	1:00
16	at New Orleans (Mon.)	8:00
22	KANSAS CITY	1:00

Pro Bowl guard Steve Wisniewski has started 31 of a possible 32 games since joining the Raiders.

1991 Draft

Round	Name	Pos.	Ht.	Wt.	College
1.	Marinovich, Todd	QB	6-4	210	Southern California
2.	Bell, Nick	RB	6-2	252	Iowa
4.	Ismail, Raghib	WR	5-10	175	Notre Dame
6.	Harrison, Nolan	DT	6-5	289	Indiana
8.	Jones, Brian	LB	6-1	242	Texas
8.	Woulard, Todd	LB	6-2	225	Alabama A&M
9.	Lewis, Tahaun	CB	5-10	175	Nebraska
10.	Glover, Andrew	TE	6-6	220	Grambling
12.	Johnson, Dennis	WR	5-10	174	Winston-Salem State

VETERAN ROSTER

No.	Name	Pos.	Ht.	Wt.	NFL Year	College
	Adams, Stefon	DB-KR	5-10	190	6	East Carolina
80	Alexander, Mike	WR	6-3	195	2	Penn State
32	Allen, Marcus	RB	6-2	210	10	Southern California
	Alston, O'Brien	LB	6-6	248	3	Maryland
33	Anderson, Eddie	S	6-1	205	6	Fort Valley State
28	Bell, Greg	RB	5-10	210	8	Notre Dame
54	Benson, Tom	LB	6-2	240	8	Oklahoma
7	Beuerlein, Steve	QB	6-2	210	4	Notre Dame
24	Brown, Ron	CB-KR	5-11	190	8	Arizona State
81	Brown, Tim	WR-KR	6-0	195	3	Notre Dame
97	Burton, Ron	LB	6-1	245	5	North Carolina
	Craig, Roger	RB	6-0	224	9	Nebraska
70	Davis, Scott	DE	6-7	270	4	Illinois
46	Dorn, Torin	CB	6-0	190	2	North Carolina
84	Dyal, Mike	TE	6-2	240	3	Texas A&I
50	Ellison, Riki	LB	6-2	230	8	Southern California
11	Evans, Vince	QB	6-2	210	12	Southern California
86	Fernandez, Mervyn	WR	6-3	200	5	San Jose State
73	FitzPatrick, James	T	6-7	330	6	Southern California
83	Gault, Willie	WR	6-1	175	9	Tennessee
	Glenn, Vencie	S	6-0	192	6	Indiana State
79	Golic, Bob	DT	6-2	275	12	Notre Dame
6	Gossett, Jeff	P	6-2	195	10	Eastern Illinois
85	Graddy, Sam	WR	5-10	175	4	Tennessee
60	Graves, Rory	T	6-6	295	4	Ohio State
45	Harden, Mike	S	6-1	200	12	Michigan
62	Harrell, Newt	G	6-5	290	1	West Texas State
82	Holland, Jamie	WR	6-1	195	5	Ohio State
88	Horton, Ethan	TE	6-4	240	5	North Carolina
34	Jackson, Bo	RB	6-1	235	5	Auburn
18	Jaeger, Jeff	K	5-11	195	4	Washington
58	Jimerson, A.J.	LB	6-3	230	2	Norfolk State
	Klostermann, Bruce	LB	6-3	236	5	South Dakota State
25	Land, Dan	CB	6-0	195	3	Albany State
21	Lewis, Garry	CB	5-11	185	2	Alcorn State
75	Long, Howie	DE	6-5	270	11	Villanova
	Lott, Ronnie	S	6-0	200	11	Southern California
41	McCallum, Napoleon	RB	6-2	220	3	Navy
36	McDaniel, Terry	CB	5-10	180	3	Tennessee
65	Montoya, Max	G	6-5	290	13	UCLA
72	Mosebar, Don	C	6-6	280	9	Southern California
	Moss, Winston	LB	6-3	235	5	Miami
42	Mueller, Vance	RB	6-0	220	6	Occidental
	Patten, Joel	T	6-7	307	7	Duke
43	Patterson, Elvis	S	5-11	195	8	Kansas
64	Peat, Todd	G	6-2	315	4	Northern Illinois
57	Robinson, Jerry	LB	6-2	230	13	UCLA
78	Rother, Tim	T	6-7	280	3	Nebraska
13	Schroeder, Jay	QB	6-4	215	8	UCLA
94	Smith, Anthony	DE	6-3	265	1	Arizona
35	Smith, Steve	RB	6-1	240	5	Penn State
93	Townsend, Greg	DE	6-3	270	9	Texas Christian
67	Turk, Dan	C	6-4	275	6	Wisconsin
51	Wallace, Aaron	LB	6-3	230	2	Texas A&M
48	Washington, Lionel	CB	6-0	190	9	Tulane
68	Wilkerson, Bruce	T	6-5	295	5	Tennessee
90	Wise, Mike	DE	6-7	270	5	California-Davis
76	Wisniewski, Steve	G	6-4	280	3	Penn State
66	Wright, Steve	T	6-6	280	9	Northern Iowa

TM

SAN DIEGO CHARGERS

Address San Diego Jack Murphy Stadium, P.O. Box 20666, San Diego, California 92120.
Stadium San Diego Jack Murphy Stadium. *Capacity* 60,750 *Playing Surface* Grass.
Team Colours Navy Blue, White, and Gold.
Head Coach Dan Henning – 3rd year; 7th NFL.
Championships Division 1979,'80,'81; AFL 1963.
History AFL 1960-69, AFC 1970-
(For 1960 only, they were known as the Los Angeles Chargers.)

1990 saw the Chargers improve in almost every category but they couldn't quite find the punch to put opponents away. Thirteen of their games were decided by a touchdown or less, and it is that level of competitiveness which gives grounds for optimism.

Under the Plan-B arrangements which allow teams to protect only 37 players, the Chargers lost 11, more than any other organization, and it can be of little consolation that other clubs were anxious to sign what they felt was good talent. The defense suffered most with the departure of seven but only one, free safety Vencie Glenn, was a true starter. His loss, together with a commitment to enhancing what was a powerful group anyway, influenced San Diego to draft a superior safety, Stanley Richard, and defensive tackle George Thornton in the first two rounds. Richard could move in right away to partner strong safety Martin Bayless, teaming up with cornerbacks Sam Seale and Gill Byrd. Bayless has started since he joined the Chargers in 1987, while the ball-hawking Byrd has intercepted seven passes in each of the last three seasons, more than any other player in the NFL. Moving forward, the linebacking quartet is the ideal combination of hard-nosed tackling and predatory pass rushing. Left inside linebacker Gary Plummer takes the brunt of the run, operating in tandem with emerging star Junior Seau. Swooping from the right outside spot, Leslie O'Neal was the team leader with 13.5 sacks and went to his second consecutive Pro Bowl. The loss of the other starter, Billy Ray Smith, for five full games, was felt heavily.

San Diego uses a three-man defensive line with Pro Bowler Lee Williams on the left and Burt Grossman on the right. This pairing ranks among the league's best in rushing the passer. Sadly, senior nose tackle Joe Phillips was missed after sustaining a non-football-related injury in late September. With the departure of Les Miller, George Hinkle is the obvious backup for Phillips but draftee Thornton will want a say in things.

On offense, San Diego is particularly strong in some areas, notably at running back where Marion Butts is virtually unstoppable. He ranked third in the NFL last season and you wonder just what converted tight end Rod Bernstine, who is now an H-back, might achieve were he to be featured. The long-striding Bernstine averaged 4.8 yards per rush. With Ronnie Harmon on hand, there was little need for reinforcement but Eric Bieniemy was too good not to select in the second round. At wide receiver, Anthony Miller stands apart from the rest. A current Pro Bowl starter, Miller demands total respect but he could use a partner of stature. The hope is that Nate Lewis, who showed promise before a broken wrist on Week Thirteen ended his season, will come through. Otherwise, in an area not deep in experience, there's a clear opportunity for draftee Yancey Thigpen.

An asset of the offensive line is the versatility which allows players to shift positions. Thus, starting right tackle Broderick Thompson has played at guard while starting right guard Dave Richards has played at tackle. Also, starting left guard Courtney Hall switched from center, making room for rookie Frank Cornish. Even with three players swapping around at left tackle, the line conceded only 20 sacks, second in the NFL to Miami. Leo Goeas could make the left tackle spot his own but there may be further rearrangements as the Chargers attempt to involve second-round draftee guard Eric Moten and Plan-B signing Mark May. Not to be underestimated is the considerable blocking contribution made by tight end Arthur Cox, who has not failed to answer the bell in eight seasons.

It goes without saying that the maturing of quarterback Billy Joe Tolliver is crucial to the Chargers' fortunes. At the end of his second NFL campaign, he was under a little pressure from John Friesz, but he is expected to retain his seniority.

Plan-B signings John Carney and John Kidd confirmed the Chargers' judgement. Carney set a Chargers record, kicking 19 of 21 field goals, while Kidd averaged a steady 40 yards on his 61 punts.

1991 SCHEDULE OF GAMES

September		
1	at Pittsburgh	4:00
8	at San Francisco	1:00
15	ATLANTA	1:00
22	at Denver	2:00
29	KANSAS CITY	1:00
October		
6	at Los Angeles Raiders	1:00
13	at Los Angeles Rams	1:00
20	CLEVELAND	1:00
27	at Seattle	1:00
November		
3	Open Date	
10	SEATTLE	1:00
17	NEW ORLEANS	1:00
24	at New York Jets	4:00
December		
1	L.A. RAIDERS (Sun. night)	5:00
8	at Kansas City	12:00
15	MIAMI	1:00
22	DENVER	1:00

1991 Draft

Round	Name	Pos.	Ht.	Wt.	College
1.	Richard, Stanley	S	6-1	199	Texas
2.	Thornton, George	DT	6-3	301	Alabama
2.	Bieniemy, Eric	RB	5-7	208	Colorado
2.	Moten, Eric	G	6-3	307	Michigan State
4.	Thigpen, Yancey	WR	6-0	207	Winston-Salem State
5.	Young, Duane	TE	6-1	293	Michigan State
5.	Fields, Floyd	S	6-1	208	Arizona State
6.	Laister, Jimmy	T	6-4	300	Oregon Tech
7.	Jones, David	WR	6-2	213	Delaware State
7.	Beauford, Terry	G	6-1	285	Florida A&M
9.	Katoa, Andy	LB	6-2	230	Southern Oregon
10.	Poles, Roland	RB	6-0	251	Tennessee
10.	Heldt, Mike	C	6-0	285	Notre Dame
11.	Weinberg, Joaquim	WR	5-11	197	Johnson C. Smith
12.	Samuels, Chris	RB	5-10	209	Texas

VETERAN ROSTER

No.	Name	Pos.	Ht.	Wt.	NFL Year	College
44	Bayless, Martin	S	6-2	212	8	Bowling Green
82	Bernstine, Rod	RB	6-3	238	5	Texas A&M
71	Brown, Dean	G-T	6-3	311	1	Notre Dame
35	Butts, Marion	RB	6-1	248	3	Florida State
22	Byrd, Gill	CB	5-11	198	9	San Jose State
46	Caravello, Joe	H-B	6-3	262	5	Tulane
3	Carney, John	K	5-11	170	3	Notre Dame
29	Carrington, Darren	CB	6-1	189	3	Northern Arizona
63	Cornish, Frank	C	6-4	295	2	UCLA
88	Cox, Arthur	TE	6-2	277	9	Texas Southern
28	Elder, Donnie	CB-KR	5-9	178	6	Memphis State
61	Floyd, Eric	T	6-5	300	2	Auburn
27	Frank, Donald	CB	6-0	200	2	Winston-Salem State
17	Friesz, John	QB	6-4	209	1	Idaho
16	Gagliano, Bob	QB	6-3	196	7	Utah State
67	Goeas, Leo	T	6-4	285	2	Hawaii
92	Grossman, Burt	DE	6-4	255	3	Pittsburgh
53	Hall, Courtney	C	6-1	269	3	Rice
33	Harmon, Ronnie	RB	5-11	200	6	Iowa
34	Hendrickson, Steve	H-B	6-0	250	3	California
97	Hinkle, George	DE	6-5	269	4	Arizona
48	Humphery, Bobby	CB-KR	5-10	180	8	New Mexico State
10	Kidd, John	P	6-3	208	8	Northwestern
80	Kyles, Troy	WR	6-0	180	2	Howard
81	Lewis, Nate	WR	5-11	189	2	Oregon Tech
73	May, Mark	G-T	6-6	295	10	Pittsburgh
31	McEwen, Craig	H-B	6-1	220	5	Utah
83	Miller, Anthony	WR	5-11	185	4	Tennessee
91	O'Neal, Leslie	LB	6-4	259	5	Oklahoma State
37	Orr, Terry	TE	6-3	235	6	Texas
75	Phillips, Joe	NT	6-5	315	6	Southern Methodist
	Pike, Chris	DT	6-8	300	3	Tulsa
50	Plummer, Gary	LB	6-2	240	6	California
65	Richards, David	G-T	6-5	310	4	UCLA
64	Rodenhauser, Mark	C	6-5	263	4	Illinois State
57	Rolling, Henry	LB	6-2	225	4	Nevada-Reno
79	Savage, Tony	NT	6-3	300	1	Washington State
30	Seale, Sam	CB	5-9	185	8	Western St., Colorado
55	Seau, Junior	LB	6-3	250	2	Southern California
23	Shelton, Anthony	CB	6-1	195	2	Tennessee State
68	Simmonds, Mike	G	6-4	295	2	Indiana State
54	Smith, Billy Ray	LB	6-3	236	9	Arkansas
72	Swayne, Harry	T	6-5	270	5	Rutgers
85	Taylor, Kitrick	WR-KR	5-11	191	4	Washington State
56	Thaxton, Galand	LB	6-1	242	2	Wyoming
76	Thompson, Broderick	G-T	6-5	295	6	Kansas
11	Tolliver, Billy Joe	QB	6-1	218	3	Texas Tech
89	Walker, Derrick	TE	6-0	244	2	Michigan
99	Williams, Lee	DE	6-5	271	8	Bethune-Cookman
84	Wilson, Walter	WR	5-10	185	2	East Carolina
70	Zandofsky, Mike	G	6-2	285	3	Washington

Marion Butts set a Chargers record with 1,225 yards rushing.

RIGHT: Fullback John L. Williams is the Seahawks' great dual-purpose threat.

SEATTLE SEAHAWKS

Address 11220 N.E. 53rd Street, Kirkland, Washington 98033.
Stadium Kingdome, Seattle.
Capacity 64,984 *Playing Surface* AstroTurf.
Team Colours Blue, Green, and Silver.
Head Coach Chuck Knox – 9th year; 19th NFL.
Championships Division 1988.
History NFC 1976, AFC 1977-

While most attention focused on the running battle between the Raiders and Kansas City, Seattle, almost unnoticed, were just a whisker away from reaching the playoffs, ending up level with Houston and Pittsburgh but losing the tie-breaker to Houston, a team they'd beaten during the regular season. That they achieved this level with not the best squad in their history is a remarkable tribute to head coach Chuck Knox and general manager Tom Flores.

Strangely, the Seahawks were not very active in the Plan-B market for free agents, signing only two players, neither of whom is likely to be more than a third-stringer. However in the draft, they really disturbed the pool, selecting quarterback Dan McGwire, who, at almost 6'8" and 245 lbs, will be the biggest ever to play that position in the NFL. Dave Krieg is the starter and, despite his ups and downs, has held the job on merit ahead of Jeff Kemp and Kelly Stouffer, the latter who was seen as the heir apparent. Furthermore, Krieg has four years of a very lucrative contract still to run. But, with the arrival of McGwire, it must be that the Seahawks' long-term hopes no longer rest with Stouffer, for whom they traded a first- and two fifth-round draft options in 1988. There is fresh talent at wide receiver, too, where the arrival of draftees Doug Thomas and David Daniels will put pressure on current starters Tommy Kane and Brian Blades. If there is uncertainty in the passing game, the rushing component is quite clearly established, with the thrusting, clubbing, hammering Derrick Fenner as the running back, supported by the blocking and more selective running of John L. Williams, also who ranks as one of the best receivers coming out of the backfield. Seattle tight ends are not usually prolific and Travis McNeal maintains that tradition. Rather, McNeal is the sixth interior lineman, a steady blocker normally stationed at the shoulder of the right tackle. Last year, that player was Ronnie Lee, who settled in quickly after an illustrious career with Miami. Bryan Millard, Grant Feasel, Andy Heck and Edwin Bailey, the latter who is returning from an injury, complete a sound front line.

The selection of placekicker John Kasay as high as the fourth round means that incumbent Norm Johnson has a battle on his hands. Johnson has the better leg strength but has been considered inconsistent. Punter Rick Donnelly is not likely to be displaced.

The Seahawks experienced few problems in switching to a 4-3 defense and one bonus was the extra freedom available to their top lineman, defensive left end Jacob Green, who had 12.5 sacks, his best total since 1985. Again, defensive right end Tony Woods continued to make progress. Elsewhere for the line, the personnel is steady as distinct from explosive, and it is expected that last year's first-round draftee, defensive tackle Cortez Kennedy, will come through, meaning that one of Joe Nash and Jeff Bryant will adjust to a backup rôle. Using three linebackers eased the problems of a unit already lacking quality in depth and depleted further by injuries to Rufus Porter and promising rookie Terry Wooden. They will rejoin Dave Ahrens, David Wyman and Joe Cain in the scramble for playing time. The secondary usually is a Seattle strength and, last year, it received a welcome boost from strong safety Nesby Glasgow who, at 33 years old, was expected to be battling just to stay on the roster. Glasgow led the team both in tackles and inspirational speeches. Second-round draftee Robert Blackmon was expected to step in immediately but had to settle for working as the nickel back and on special teams. Gathering around Glasgow, cornerbacks Dwayne Harper and Patrick Hunter, and free safety Eugene Robinson, form a quartet which demands respect.

1991 SCHEDULE OF GAMES

September		
1	at New Orleans	12:00
8	NEW YORK JETS	1:00
15	at Denver	2:00
22	at Kansas City	3:00
29	INDIANAPOLIS	1:00
October		
6	at Cincinnati	1:00
13	L.A. RAIDERS (Sun. night)	4:30
20	at Pittsburgh	1:00
27	SAN DIEGO	1:00
November		
3	Open Date	
10	at San Diego	1:00
17	at Los Angeles Raiders	1:00
24	DENVER	1:00
December		
1	KANSAS CITY	1:00
8	SAN FRANCISCO	1:00
15	at Atlanta	1:00
22	LOS ANGELES RAMS (Sun. night)	5:00

1991 Draft

Round	Name	Pos.	Ht.	Wt.	College
1.	McGwire, Dan	QB	6-7	243	San Diego State
2.	Thomas, Doug	WR	5-9	176	Clemson
3.	Daniels, David	WR	6-0	192	Penn State
4.	Kasay, John	K	5-10	186	Georgia
5.	Davis, Harlan	CB	5-11	190	Tennessee
6.	Sinclair, Mike	DE	6-3	244	Eastern New Mexico
10.	Ringoen, Erik	LB	6-2	234	Hofstra
11.	Stewart, Tony	RB	6-0	199	Iowa
12.	Harris, Ike	G	6-3	276	South Carolina

VETERAN ROSTER

No.	Name	Pos.	Ht.	Wt.	NFL Year	College
50	Ahrens, Dave	LB	6-4	247	11	Wisconsin
51	Allert, Ty	LB	6-2	238	5	Texas
52	Andrews, Ricky	LB	6-2	236	2	Washington
65	Bailey, Edwin	G	6-4	279	11	South Carolina State
25	Blackmon, Robert	S	6-0	198	2	Baylor
89	Blades, Brian	WR	5-11	191	4	Miami
64	Brilz, Darrick	G	6-3	281	5	Oregon State
77	Bryant, Jeff	DT	6-5	281	10	Clemson
	Buczkowski, Bob	DE	6-5	260	3	Pittsburgh
59	Cain, Joe	LB	6-1	233	3	Oregon Tech
88	Chadwick, Jeff	WR	6-3	189	9	Grand Valley State
84	Clark, Louis	WR	6-0	198	5	Mississippi State
53	Comeaux, Darren	LB	6-1	239	10	Arizona State
	Cotton, Marcus	LB	6-3	235	4	Southern California
34	Davis, Brian	CB	6-2	190	4	Nebraska
3	Donnelly, Rick	P	6-0	209	7	Wyoming
75	Dyko, Chris	T	6-6	295	2	Washington State
54	Feasel, Grant	C	6-7	279	7	Abilene Christian
44	Fenner, Derrick	RB	6-3	228	3	North Carolina
22	Glasgow, Nesby	S	5-10	187	13	Washington
79	Green, Jacob	DE	6-3	256	12	Texas A&M
29	Harper, Dwayne	CB	5-11	174	4	South Carolina State
78	Hayes, Eric	DT	6-3	297	2	Florida State
66	Heck, Andy	T	6-6	286	3	Notre Dame
85	Heller, Ron	TE	6-3	242	5	Oregon State
27	Hunter, Patrick	CB	5-11	186	6	Nevada-Reno
26	Jefferson, James	CB	6-1	199	3	Texas A&I
9	Johnson, Norm	K	6-2	203	10	UCLA
30	Jones, James	RB	6-2	232	9	Florida
83	Junkin, Trey	TE	6-2	240	9	Louisiana Tech
81	Kane, Tommy	WR	5-11	181	4	Syracuse
15	Kemp, Jeff	QB	6-0	201	11	Dartmouth
96	Kennedy, Cortez	DT	6-3	293	2	Miami
17	Krieg, Dave	QB	6-1	192	12	Milton
63	Lee, Ronnie	T	6-3	295	13	Baylor
33	Loville, Derek	RB-KR	5-9	196	2	Oregon
31	McElroy, Vann	S	6-2	190	10	Baylor
86	McNeal, Travis	TE	6-3	244	3	Tennessee-Chattanooga
71	Millard, Bryan	G	6-5	277	8	Texas
99	Miller, Donald	LB	6-2	223	2	Idaho State
72	Nash, Joe	DT	6-3	278	10	Boston College
58	Newbill, Richard	LB	6-1	240	1	Miami
97	Porter, Rufus	LB	6-1	226	4	Southern
41	Robinson, Eugene	S	6-0	190	7	Colgate
82	Skansi, Paul	WR	5-11	187	9	Washington
94	Stephens, Rod	LB	6-1	237	3	Georgia Tech
11	Stouffer, Kelly	QB	6-3	207	3	Colorado State
	Thompson, Kevin	S	5-10	190	1	Oklahoma
87	Tice, Mike	TE	6-7	247	11	Maryland
56	Tofflemire, Joe	C	6-2	273	3	Arizona
42	Warren, Chris	RB	6-2	225	2	Ferrum
74	Wheat, Warren	G	6-6	274	2	Brigham Young
32	Williams, John L.	RB	5-11	231	6	Florida
90	Wooden, Terry	LB	6-3	232	2	Syracuse
57	Woods, Tony	DE	6-4	269	5	Pittsburgh
92	Wyman, David	LB	6-2	250	5	Stanford

Chapter Six

National Football Conference

Team Rankings

	OFFENSE						DEFENSE					
	Total Yds.	Rushing	Passing	Points For	No. Intercepted	No. Sacked	Total Yds.	Rushing	Passing	Points Against	Interceptions	Sacks
Atlanta	5	12	4	=6	=6	10	10	3	14	10	=7	11
Chicago	7	2	14	=6	2	=6	3	6	5	4	1	=6
Dallas	14	13	13	14	=12	=6	4	9	1	7	13	=8
Detroit	8	5	8	3	8	=8	14	14	10	14	=7	=6
Green Bay	11	14	5	11	9	14	12	10	11	9	=10	14
L.A. Rams	4	11	2	8	5	4	11	8	13	13	12	=12
Minnesota	6	7	6	5	=12	11	6	11	2	8	4	1
New Orleans	12	8	12	10	11	1	8	5	9	3	14	5
N.Y. Giants	9	4	11	9	1	3	1	4	3	1	3	=12
Philadelphia	2	1	7	1	3	12	5	1	12	5	6	2
Phoenix	10	6	10	12	=6	=8	9	13	4	12	=10	=8
San Francisco	1	9	1	4	4	5	2	2	6	2	=7	4
Tampa Bay	13	10	9	13	=12	13	13	12	8	11	2	10
Washington	3	3	3	2	10	2	7	7	7	6	5	3

NFC Passers

	Att	Comp	% Comp	Yards	Ave Gain	TD	% TD	Long	Int	% Int	Rating Points
Simms, Phil, *Giants*	311	184	59.2	2284	7.34	15	4.8	t80	4	1.3	92.7
Cunningham, Randall, *Phil.*	465	271	58.3	3466	7.45	30	6.5	t95	13	2.8	91.6
Montana, Joe, *S.F.*	520	321	61.7	3944	7.58	26	5.0	t78	16	3.1	89.0
Harbaugh, Jim, *Chi.*	312	180	57.7	2178	6.98	10	3.2	t80	6	1.9	81.9
Peete, Rodney, *Det.*	271	142	52.4	1974	7.28	13	4.8	t68	8	3.0	79.8
Everett, Jim, *Rams*	554	307	55.4	3989	7.20	23	4.2	t55	17	3.1	79.3
Miller, Chris, *Atl.*	388	222	57.2	2735	7.05	17	4.4	t75	14	3.6	78.7
Rypien, Mark, *Wash.*	304	166	54.6	2070	6.81	16	5.3	t53	11	3.6	78.4
Testaverde, Vinny, *T.B.*	365	203	55.6	2818	7.72	17	4.7	t89	18	4.9	75.6
Majkowski, Don, *G.B.*	264	150	56.8	1925	7.29	10	3.8	t76	12	4.5	73.5
Rosenbach, Timm, *Phoe.*	437	237	54.2	3098	7.09	16	3.7	t68	17	3.9	72.8
Gannon, Rich, *Minn.*	349	182	52.1	2278	6.53	16	4.6	t78	16	4.6	68.9
Walsh, Steve, *Dall.-N.O.*	336	179	53.3	2010	5.98	12	3.6	58	13	3.9	67.2
Aikman, Troy, *Dall.*	399	226	56.6	2579	6.46	11	2.8	t61	18	4.5	66.6
Non-qualifiers											
Young, Steve, *S.F.*	62	38	61.3	427	6.89	2	3.2	t34	0	0.0	92.6
Hostetler, Jeff, *Giants*	87	47	54.0	614	7.06	3	3.4	t44	1	1.1	83.2
Rutledge, Jeff, *Wash.*	68	40	58.8	455	6.69	2	2.9	40	1	1.5	82.7
Millen, Hugh, *Atl.*	63	34	54.0	427	6.78	1	1.6	53	0	0.0	80.6
Wilson, Wade, *Minn.*	146	82	56.2	1155	7.91	9	6.2	t75	8	5.5	79.6
Kiel, Blair, *G.B.*	85	51	60.0	504	5.93	2	2.4	22	2	2.4	74.8
Gagliano, Bob, *Det.*	159	87	54.7	1190	7.48	10	6.3	t47	10	6.3	73.6
Dilweg, Anthony, *G.B.*	192	101	52.6	1267	6.60	8	4.2	59	7	3.6	72.1
Campbell, Scott, *Atl.*	76	36	47.4	527	6.93	3	3.9	70	4	5.3	61.7
Humphries, Stan, *Wash.*	156	91	58.3	1015	6.51	3	1.9	44	10	6.4	57.5

t = touchdown Leader based on rating points, minimum 220 attempts

The incomparable Jerry Rice led the NFL in receptions, yards receiving and touchdown catches.

NFC RECEIVERS – Most Receptions

	No	Yards	Ave	Long	TD
Rice, Jerry, *S.F.*	100	1502	15.0	t64	13
Rison, Andre, *Atl.*	82	1208	14.7	t75	10
Byars, Keith, *Phil.*	81	819	10.1	54	3
Ellard, Henry, *Rams*	76	1294	17.0	t50	4
Clark, Gary, *Wash.*	75	1112	14.8	t53	8
Carter, Anthony, *Minn.*	70	1008	14.4	t56	8
Monk, Art, *Wash.*	68	770	11.3	44	5
Sharpe, Sterling, *G.B.*	67	1105	16.5	t76	6
Martin, Kelvin, *Dall.*	64	732	11.4	45	0
Johnson, Richard, *Det.*	64	727	11.4	t44	6
Martin, Eric, *N.O.*	63	912	14.5	58	5
Novacek, Jay, *Dall.*	59	657	11.1	41	4
Proehl, Ricky, *Phoe.*	56	802	14.3	t45	4
Jones, Brent, *S.F.*	56	747	13.3	t67	5
Sanders, Ricky, *Wash.*	56	727	13.0	38	3
Green, Roy, *Phoe.*	53	797	15.0	54	4
Clark, Robert, *Det.*	52	914	17.6	57	8
Anderson, Flipper, *Rams*	51	1097	21.5	t55	4
Jones, Hassan, *Minn.*	51	810	15.9	t75	7
Jackson, Keith, *Phil.*	50	670	13.4	t37	6
Carrier, Mark, *T.B.*	49	813	16.6	t68	4
Taylor, John, *S.F.*	49	748	15.3	t78	7
Holohan, Pete, *Rams*	49	475	9.7	28	2
Rathman, Tom, *S.F.*	48	327	6.8	28	0
Muster, Brad, *Chi.*	47	452	9.6	48	0
McGee, Buford, *Rams*	47	388	8.3	25	4
Jordan, Steve, *Minn.*	45	636	14.1	38	3
Kemp, Perry, *G.B.*	44	527	12.0	29	2
Jones, Ernie, *Phoe.*	43	724	16.8	t68	4
Hill, Bruce, *T.B.*	42	641	15.3	t48	5
Anderson, Neal, *Chi.*	42	484	11.5	t50	3
Davis, Wendell, *Chi.*	39	572	14.7	51	3
Meggett, Dave, *Giants*	39	410	10.5	38	1
Cobb, Reggie, *T.B.*	39	299	7.7	17	0

NFC RECEIVERS – Most Yards

	Yards	No	Ave	Long	TD
Rice, Jerry, *S.F.*	1502	100	15.0	t64	13
Ellard, Henry, *Rams*	1294	76	17.0	t50	4
Rison, Andre, *Atl.*	1208	82	14.7	t75	10
Clark, Gary, *Wash.*	1112	75	14.8	t53	8
Sharpe, Sterling, *G.B.*	1105	67	16.5	t76	6
Anderson, Flipper, *Rams*	1097	51	21.5	t55	4
Carter, Anthony, *Minn.*	1008	70	14.4	t56	8
Clark, Robert, *Det.*	914	52	17.6	57	8
Martin, Eric, *N.O.*	912	63	14.5	58	5
Byars, Keith, *Phil.*	819	81	10.1	54	3
Carrier, Mark, *T.B.*	813	49	16.6	t68	4
Jones, Hassan, *Minn.*	810	51	15.9	t75	7
Proehl, Ricky, *Phoe.*	802	56	14.3	t45	4
Green, Roy, *Phoe.*	797	53	15.0	54	4
Monk, Art, *Wash.*	770	68	11.3	44	5
Taylor, John, *S.F.*	748	49	15.3	t78	7
Jones, Brent, *S.F.*	747	56	13.3	t67	5
Martin, Kelvin, *Dall.*	732	64	11.4	45	0
Johnson, Richard, *Det.*	727	64	11.4	t44	6
Sanders, Ricky, *Wash.*	727	56	13.0	38	3
Jones, Ernie, *Phoe.*	724	43	16.8	t68	4
Barnett, Fred, *Phil.*	721	36	20.0	t95	8
Jackson, Keith, *Phil.*	670	50	13.4	t37	6
Novacek, Jay, *Dall.*	657	59	11.1	41	4
Hill, Bruce, *T.B.*	641	42	15.3	t48	5
Jordan, Steve, *Minn.*	636	45	14.1	38	3
Williams, Calvin, *Phil.*	602	37	16.3	t45	9
Davis, Wendell, *Chi.*	572	39	14.7	51	3
Baker, Stephen, *Giants*	541	26	20.8	t80	4
Kemp, Perry, *G.B.*	527	44	12.0	29	2
Collins, Shawn, *Atl.*	503	34	14.8	61	2

t = touchdown

NFC RUSHERS

	Att	Yards	Ave	Long	TD
Sanders, Barry, *Det.*	255	1304	5.1	t45	13
Byner, Earnest, *Wash.*	297	1219	4.1	22	6
Anderson, Neal, *Chi.*	260	1078	4.1	52	10
Cunningham, Randall, *Phil.*	118	942	8.0	t52	5
Smith, Emmitt, *Dall.*	241	937	3.9	t48	11
Johnson, Johnny, *Phoe.*	234	926	4.0	41	5
Gary, Cleveland, *Rams*	204	808	4.0	48	14
Anderson, Ottis, *Giants*	225	784	3.5	28	11
Walker, Herschel, *Minn.*	184	770	4.2	t58	5
Rozier, Mike, *Hou.-Atl.*	163	717	4.4	67	3
Sherman, Heath, *Phil.*	164	685	4.2	36	1
Muster, Brad, *Chi.*	141	664	4.7	28	6
Anderson, Gary, *T.B.*	166	646	3.9	22	3
Heyward, Craig, *N.O.*	129	599	4.6	t47	4
Mayes, Rueben, *N.O.*	138	510	3.7	18	7
Cobb, Reggie, *T.B.*	151	480	3.2	17	2
Riggs, Gerald, *Wash.*	123	475	3.9	20	6
Rosenbach, Timm, *Phoe.*	86	470	5.5	25	3
Carter, Dexter, *S.F.*	114	460	4.0	t74	1
Hampton, Rodney, *Giants*	109	455	4.2	41	2
Broussard, Steve, *Atl.*	126	454	3.6	t50	4
Toney, Anthony, *Phil.*	132	452	3.4	20	1
Craig, Roger, *S.F.*	141	439	3.1	26	1
Thompson, Anthony, *Phoe.*	106	390	3.7	40	4
Fenney, Rick, *Minn.*	87	376	4.3	27	2
Peete, Rodney, *Det.*	47	363	7.7	37	6
Fenerty, Gill, *N.O.*	73	355	4.9	t60	2
Harbaugh, Jim, *Chi.*	51	321	6.3	17	4
Rathman, Tom, *S.F.*	101	318	3.1	22	7
Haddix, Michael, *G.B.*	98	311	3.2	13	0
Hilliard, Dalton, *N.O.*	90	284	3.2	17	0
Testaverde, Vinny, *T.B.*	38	280	7.4	t48	1
Gannon, Rich, *Minn.*	52	268	5.2	27	1
Thompson, Darrell, *G.B.*	76	264	3.5	37	1
Green, Gaston, *Rams*	68	261	3.8	31	0
McGee, Buford, *Rams*	44	234	5.3	19	1
Tillman, Lewis, *Giants*	84	231	2.8	17	1
Agee, Tommie, *Dall.*	53	213	4.0	28	0
Sanders, Thomas, *Phil.*	56	208	3.7	39	1
Anderson, Alfred, *Minn.*	59	207	3.5	14	2
Hostetler, Jeff, *Giants*	39	190	4.9	30	2
Majkowski, Don, *G.B.*	29	186	6.4	24	1
Jones, Keith, *Atl.*	49	185	3.8	22	0
Woodside, Keith, *G.B.*	46	182	4.0	21	1
Aikman, Troy, *Dall.*	40	172	4.3	20	1
Sydney, Harry, *S.F.*	35	166	4.7	19	2
Meggett, Dave, *Giants*	22	164	7.5	51	0
Montana, Joe, *S.F.*	40	162	4.1	20	1
Young, Steve, *S.F.*	15	159	10.6	31	0
Gagliano, Bob, *Det.*	46	145	3.2	22	0
Carthon, Maurice, *Giants*	36	143	4.0	12	0
Byars, Keith, *Phil.*	37	141	3.8	23	0
Warner, Curt, *Rams*	49	139	2.8	9	1
Green, Mark, *Chi.*	27	126	4.7	14	0
Dilweg, Anthony, *G.B.*	21	114	5.4	22	0
Harvey, John, *T.B.*	27	113	4.2	14	0
Humphries, Stan, *Wash.*	23	106	4.6	17	2
Johnson, Tracy, *Atl.*	30	106	3.5	12	3

t = touchdown

RIGHT: Kickoff returner Dave Meggett.

OPPOSITE: Barry Sanders has been the NFC leading rusher in each of his two NFL years.

NFC SCORING – Touchdowns

	TD	TDR	TDP	TDM	PTS
Sanders, Barry, *Det.*	16	13	3	0	96
Gary, Cleveland, *Rams*	15	14	1	0	90
Anderson, Neal, *Chi.*	13	10	3	0	78
Rice, Jerry, *S.F.*	13	0	13	0	78
Anderson, Ottis, *Giants*	11	11	0	0	66
Smith, Emmitt, *Dall.*	11	11	0	0	66
Rison, Andre, *Atl.*	10	0	10	0	60
Walker, Herschel, *Minn.*	9	5	4	0	54
Williams, Calvin, *Phil.*	9	0	9	0	54
Barnett, Fred, *Phil.*	8	0	8	0	48
Carter, Anthony, *Minn.*	8	0	8	0	48
Clark, Gary, *Wash.*	8	0	8	0	48
Clark, Robert, *Det.*	8	0	8	0	48
Byner, Earnest, *Wash.*	7	6	1	0	42
Jones, Hassan, *Minn.*	7	0	7	0	42
Mayes, Rueben, *N.O.*	7	7	0	0	42
Rathman, Tom, *S.F.*	7	7	0	0	42
Taylor, John, *S.F.*	7	0	7	0	42
Jackson, Keith, *Phil.*	6	0	6	0	36
Johnson, Richard, *Det.*	6	0	6	0	36
Muster, Brad, *Chi.*	6	6	0	0	36
Peete, Rodney, *Det.*	6	6	0	0	36
Riggs, Gerald, *Wash.*	6	6	0	0	36
Sharpe, Sterling, *G.B.*	6	0	6	0	36

NFC SCORING – Kickers

	XP	XPA	FG	FGA	PTS
Lohmiller, Chip, *Wash.*	41	41	30	40	131
Butler, Kevin, *Chi.*	36	37	26	37	114
Cofer, Mike, *S.F.*	39	39	24	36	111
Ruzek, Roger, *Phil.*	45	48	21	29	108
Davis, Greg, *Atl.*	40	40	22	33	106
Jacke, Chris, G.B.	28	29	23	30	97
Christie, Steve, *T.B.*	27	27	23	27	96
Andersen, Morten, *N.O.*	29	29	21	27	92
Lansford, Mike, *Rams*	42	43	15	24	87
Del Greco, Al, *Phoe.*	31	31	17	27	82
Bahr, Matt, *Giants*	29	30	17	23	80
Willis, Ken, *Dall.*	26	26	18	25	80
Murray, Eddie, *Det.*	34	34	13	19	73
Reveiz, Fuad, S.D.-Minn.	26	27	13	19	65

NFC KICKOFF RETURNERS

	No	Yards	Ave	Long	TD
Atkins, Gene, *N.O.*	19	471	24.8	50	0
Meggett, Dave, *Giants*	21	492	23.4	58	0
Gray, Mel, *Det.*	41	939	22.9	65	0
Wilson, Charles, *G.B.*	35	798	22.8	36	0
Green, Gaston, *Rams*	25	560	22.4	t99	1
Walker, Herschel, *Minn.*	44	966	22.0	64	0
Sanders, Deion, *Atl.*	39	851	21.8	50	0
Gentry, Dennis, *Chi.*	18	388	21.6	59	0
Peebles, Danny, *T.B.*	18	369	20.5	55	0
Dixon, James, *Dall.*	36	736	20.4	47	0
Fenerty, Gill, *N.O.*	28	572	20.4	58	0

t = touchdown
Leader based on average return, minimum 18 returns

NFC PUNTERS

	No	Yards	Long	Ave	TB	Blk	Opp Ret	Ret Yds	In 20	Net Ave
Landeta, Sean, *Giants*	75	3306	67	44.1	11	0	41	291	24	37.3
Saxon, Mike, *Dall.*	79	3413	62	43.2	8	0	43	438	20	35.6
Camarillo, Rich, *Phoe.*	67	2865	63	42.8	5	0	41	258	16	37.4
Barnhardt, Tommy, *N.O.*	70	2990	65	42.7	6	1	43	302	20	36.2
Newsome, Harry, *Minn.*	78	3299	61	42.3	8	1	44	513	19	33.2
Feagles, Jeff, *Phil.*	72	3026	60	42.0	3	2	37	338	20	35.5
Fulhage, Scott, *Atl.*	70	2913	59	41.6	4	0	39	314	15	36.0
Arnold, Jim, *Det.*	63	2560	59	40.6	5	0	29	233	10	35.3
Buford, Maury, *Chi.*	76	3073	59	40.4	7	2	39	322	22	33.5
Royals, Mark, *T.B.*	72	2902	62	40.3	5	0	39	352	8	34.0
English, Keith, *Rams*	68	2663	58	39.2	2	1	46	420	8	31.9
Mojsiejenko, Ralf, *Wash.*	43	1687	53	39.2	0	1	25	182	17	34.2
Bracken, Don, *G.B.*	64	2431	59	38.0	2	1	34	266	17	32.7
Helton, Barry, *S.F.*	69	2537	56	36.8	8	1	30	215	15	30.9

Leader based on gross average, minimum 40 punts

NFC SACKERS

	No
Haley, Charles, *S.F.*	16.0
White, Reggie, *Phil.*	14.0
Greene, Kevin, *Rams*	13.0
Dent, Richard, *Chi.*	12.0
Doleman, Chris, *Minn.*	11.0
Swilling, Pat, *N.O.*	11.0
Taylor, Lawrence, *Giants*	10.5
Armstrong, Trace, *Chi.*	10.0
Cofer, Mike, *Det.*	10.0
Harvey, Ken, *Phoe.*	10.0
Fagan, Kevin, *S.F.*	9.5
Nunn, Freddie Joe, *Phoe.*	9.0
Turnbull, Renaldo, *N.O.*	9.0
Thomas, Henry, *Minn.*	8.5
Jones, Jimmie, *Dall.*	7.5
Joyner, Seth, *Phil.*	7.5
Simmons, Clyde, *Phil.*	7.5
Stokes, Fred, *Wash.*	7.5
Stubbs, Daniel, *Dall.*	7.5
Thomas, Broderick, *T.B.*	7.5
Clarke, Ken, *Minn.*	7.0
Harris, Tim, *G.B.*	7.0
Brown, Dennis, *S.F.*	6.0
Collins, Andre, *Wash.*	6.0
Green, Tim, *Atl.*	6.0
Jackson, Rickey, *N.O.*	6.0
Noga, Al, *Minn.*	6.0
Tolbert, Tony, *Dall.*	6.0
Holt, Pierce, *S.F.*	5.5
Mann, Charles, *Wash.*	5.5
Randle, Ervin, *T.B.*	5.5
Wilks, Jim, *N.O.*	5.5
Marshall, Wilber, *Wash.*	5.0
Piel, Mike, *Rams*	5.0
Tuggle, Jessie, *Atl.*	5.0
Marshall, Leonard, *Giants*	4.5
Noonan, Danny, *Dall.*	4.5
Brock, Matt, *G.B.*	4.0
Bruce, Aundray, *Atl.*	4.0
Hayworth, Tracy, *Det.*	4.0
Jackson, Greg, *Giants*	4.0
Martin, Wayne, *N.O.*	4.0
McMichael, Steve, *Chi.*	4.0
Murphy, Kevin, *T.B.*	4.0
Patterson, Shawn, *G.B.*	4.0
Perry, William, *Chi.*	4.0
Saddler, Rod, *Phoe.*	4.0
Strauthers, Thomas, *Minn.*	4.0

NFC PUNT RETURNERS

	No	FC	Yards	Ave	Long	TD
Bailey, Johnny, *Chi.*	36	13	399	11.1	t95	1
Meggett, Dave, *Giants*	43	12	467	10.9	t68	1
Gray, Mel, *Det.*	34	7	361	10.6	39	0
Henley, Darryl, *Rams*	19	4	195	10.3	26	0
Query, Jeff, *G.B.*	32	7	308	9.6	25	0
Sanders, Deion, *Atl.*	29	13	250	8.6	t79	1
Sikahema, Vai, *Phoe.*	36	6	306	8.5	20	0
Buck, Vince, *N.O.*	37	8	305	8.2	33	0
Taylor, John, *S.F.*	26	5	212	8.2	30	0
Drewrey, Willie, *T.B.*	23	15	184	8.0	16	0
Harris, Rod, *Dall.-Phil.*	28	8	214	7.6	30	0
Stanley, Walter, *Wash.*	24	8	176	7.3	32	0
Lewis, Leo, *Clev.-Minn.*	33	22	236	7.2	30	0
Shepard, Derrick, *Dall.*	20	1	121	6.1	13	0

t = touchdown
Leader based on average return, minimum 19 returns

NFC INTERCEPTORS

	No	Yards	Ave	Long	TD
Carrier, Mark, *Chi.*	10	39	3.9	14	0
Haddix, Wayne, *T.B.*	7	231	33.0	t65	3
Browner, Joey, *Minn.*	7	103	14.7	31	1
Waymer, Dave, *S.F.*	7	64	9.1	24	0
Mayhew, Martin, *Wash.*	7	20	2.9	15	0
Walls, Everson, *Giants*	6	80	13.3	40	1
Stinson, Lemuel, *Chi.*	6	66	11.0	30	0
White, William, *Det.*	5	120	24.0	48	1
Hopkins, Wes, *Phil.*	5	45	9.0	21	0
Hamilton, Harry, *T.B.*	5	39	7.8	27	0
Jackson, Greg, *Giants*	5	8	1.6	5	0
Robinson, Mark, *T.B.*	4	81	20.3	27	0
McDonald, Tim, *Phoe.*	4	63	15.8	38	0
Humphery, Bobby, *Rams*	4	52	13.0	t44	1
Newsome, Vince, *Rams*	4	47	11.8	22	0
Green, Darrell, *Wash.*	4	20	5.0	t18	1
Sanders, Deion, *Atl.*	3	153	51.0	t82	2
Merriweather, Mike, *Minn.*	3	108	36.0	73	0
Frizzell, William, *Phil.*	3	91	30.3	37	1
Bowles, Todd, *Wash.*	3	74	24.7	43	0
Holt, Issiac, *Dall.*	3	72	24.0	t64	1
Reynolds, Ricky, *T.B.*	3	70	23.3	46	0
Taylor, Jay, *Phoe.*	3	50	16.7	34	0
Butler, LeRoy, *G.B.*	3	42	14.0	28	0
Holmes, Jerry, *G.B.*	3	39	13.0	24	0
Case, Scott, *Atl.*	3	38	12.7	t36	1
Allen, Eric, *Phil.*	3	37	12.3	t35	1
Griffin, Don, *S.F.*	3	32	10.7	23	0
Everett, Eric, *T.B.*	3	28	9.3	23	0
Lott, Ronnie, *S.F.*	3	26	8.7	15	0
Washington, James, *Dall.*	3	24	8.0	13	0
Dent, Richard, *Chi.*	3	21	7.0	15	0
McMillian, Audrey, *Minn.*	3	20	6.7	20	0
Woolford, Donnell, *Chi.*	3	18	6.0	9	0
Crockett, Ray, *Det.*	3	17	5.7	9	0
Dimry, Charles, *Atl.*	3	16	5.3	13	0
Jordan, Brian, *Atl.*	3	14	4.7	14	0
Reasons, Gary, *Giants*	3	13	4.3	10	0
Murphy, Mark, *G.B.*	3	6	2.0	4	0
Williams, Perry, *Giants*	3	4	1.3	4	0
Smith, Ben, *Phil.*	3	1	0.3	1	0
Butler, Bobby, *Atl.*	3	0	0.0	0	0

t = touchdown

LEFT: Charles Haley led the NFC in sacks but on this occasion his intended victim is Redskins placekicker Chip Lohmiller.

Chicago rookie free safety Mark Carrier settled in immediately and led the NFL with ten interceptions.

DALLAS COWBOYS

Address Cowboys Center, One Cowboys Parkway, Irving, Texas 75063.
Stadium Texas Stadium, Irving.
Capacity 65,024 *Playing Surface* Texas Turf.
Team Colours Royal Blue, Metallic Silver Blue, and White.
Head Coach Jimmy Johnson – 3rd year.
Championships Division 1970,'71,'73,'76,'77,'78, '79,'81,'85; Conference 1970,'71,'75,'77,'78; Super Bowl 1971,'77.
History NFL 1960-69, NFC 1970-

Tight end Jay Novacek quickly established himself as a starter after being signed from Phoenix as a Plan-B free agent.

After a poor 3-7 start, the Cowboys mounted a spirited rally, winning four straight games only to lose the final two when one victory would have earned the NFC's final wild-card spot. A young squad, already bursting with enthusiasm, has been supercharged by the addition of 12 draftees from the top six rounds alone. If the alarm bells aren't ringing around the league, they should be.

Wading through the knee-deep talent, it is difficult to find an area which wasn't reinforced and perhaps it is the best measure of the confidence in the defensive secondary that it did not receive attention. Having said that, it would appear that only left cornerback Issiac Holt and strong safety Vince Albritton are certain starters. Manny Hendrix may have the edge at right cornerback but several players, with James Washington the possible favourite, will compete to play free safety.

At quarterback, Troy Aikman is unchallenged. Entering his third season, Aikman wears the famous uniform with great stature. He bears the unmistakable stamp of a winner and his injury, early in the Week-Sixteen loss to Philadelphia, was the major factor in the Cowboys' failure to reach the playoffs. The chances are that he'll be throwing to a new combination at wide receiver and it is by no means certain that even Michael Irvin will start. He'll have to re-establish his seniority in a group which includes last year's club leader, Kelvin Martin, 1990 second-round pick Alexander Wright and 1991 first-rounder Alvin Harper. At tight end, Dallas selects from a menu of Jay Novacek, who may be the best receiver at his position in the league, Robert Awalt, who is the classy, dual-purpose type, and Plan-B signing Alfredo Roberts, who muscles opponents around.

Strength in depth at fullback, where a healthy Alonzo Highsmith will vie with last year's starter, Tommie Agee, can only enhance the unquestioned destructive power of running back Emmitt Smith. Together with his medium-range speed and deceptively subtle moves, Smith has the ability to gain extra yardage by breaking tackles. The superior speed of reserve Keith Jones offers an exciting option and means that the Cowboys need not hurry the development of draftee Curvin Richards, who would have been a serious contender for the Heisman Trophy had he stayed in college for his senior year.

Before the draft, head coach Jimmy Johnson saw the offensive line as being unsettled and, certainly, third-rounders James Richards and Eric Williams will be involved in a shuffle which may see Nate Newton revert from right tackle to left guard following the Plan-B loss of starter Crawford Ker. This is suggested by the Plan-B signing of tackle Alan Veingrad, who has started for Green Bay. Center Mark Stepnoski and left tackle Mark Tuinei should remain in place, while there is every confidence in the ability of right guard John Gesek, who came on surprisingly well after having looked vulnerable when he was with the Raiders.

With the arrival of first-round pick Russell Maryland, the competition for places on the defensive line will be severe. Maryland, who was the first selection overall, could start immediately in partnership with awesome right tackle Danny Noonan. At defensive right end, Jim Jeffcoat brings all the experience of his eight pro campaigns to bear. For the defensive left end position, there is really fine pass rushing available in Daniel Stubbs and the fast-developing Tony Tolbert.

Speed has always been the priority in Johnson's teams and he added that in plenty to the linebacking unit with the drafting of Dixon Edwards. The loss of inspirational middle linebacker Eugene Lockhart in a trade makes room for Jack Del Rio, who was expected to challenge seriously in any event. Jesse Solomon should move into Del Rio's former spot on the strong side with all of Ken Norton, Vinson Smith and Edwards competing for the place on the weak side.

Although recognizing a tendency for punter Mike Saxon to tail off towards the end of each season and looking for a little more leg strength on kickoffs from Ken Willis, Johnson does not anticipate making changes.

1991 SCHEDULE OF GAMES

September		
1	at Cleveland	1:00
9	WASHINGTON (Mon.)	8:00
15	PHILADELPHIA	12:00
22	at Phoenix (Sun. night)	5:00
29	NEW YORK GIANTS	12:00
October		
6	vs Green Bay at Milwaukee	12:00
13	CINCINNATI	12:00
20	Open Date	
27	at Detroit	4:00
November		
3	PHOENIX	12:00
10	at Houston	12:00
17	at New York Giants	4:00
24	at Washington	1:00
28	PITTSBURGH (Thanksgiving)	3:00
December		
8	NEW ORLEANS	12:00
15	at Philadelphia	1:00
22	ATLANTA	12:00

1991 Draft

Round	Name	Pos.	Ht.	Wt.	College
1.	Maryland, Russell	DT	6-0	274	Miami
1.	Harper, Alvin	WR	6-3	206	Tennessee
1.	Pritchett, Kelvin*	DT	6-2	281	Mississippi
2.	Edwards, Dixon	LB	6-0	220	Michigan State
3.	Myles, Godfrey	LB	6-1	240	Florida
3.	Richards, James	G	6-4	295	California
3.	Williams, Eric	T	6-5	302	Central State, Ohio
4.	Richards, Curvin	RB	5-9	200	Pittsburgh
4.	Musgrave, Bill	QB	6-2	200	Oregon
4.	Hill, Tony	DE	6-5	241	Tennessee-Chattanooga
4.	Harris, Kevin	DE	6-4	240	Texas Southern
5.	Brownlow, Darrick	LB	5-10	230	Illinois
6.	Sullivan, Mike	G	6-3	278	Miami
7.	Lett, Leon	DT	6-6	272	Emporia State
9.	Mays, Damon	WR	5-8	166	Missouri
10.	Love, Sean	G	6-3	282	Penn State
11.	Boles, Tony	RB	6-0	199	Michigan
12.	Brown, Larry	CB	5-11	190	Texas Christian

* Pritchett was subsequently traded to Detroit

VETERAN ROSTER

No.	Name	Pos.	Ht.	Wt.	NFL Year	College
34	Agee, Tommie	RB	6-0	223	4	Auburn
8	Aikman, Troy	QB	6-4	218	3	UCLA
36	Albritton, Vince	S	6-2	212	8	Washington
31	Ankrom, Scott	DB	6-1	194	2	Texas Christian
89	Awalt, Robert	TE	6-5	238	5	San Diego State
40	Bates, Bill	S	6-1	204	9	Tennessee
44	Brooks, Michael	DB	6-0	195	2	North Carolina State
79	Broughton, Willie	DT	6-5	280	5	Miami
90	Crockett, Willis	LB	6-3	234	2	Georgia Tech
55	Del Rio, Jack	LB	6-4	232	7	Southern California
21	Dixon, James	RB-KR	5-10	184	3	Houston
29	Gant, Kenneth	CB	5-11	181	2	Albany State
63	Gesek, John	G	6-5	283	5	Cal State-Sacramento
66	Gogan, Kevin	T	6-7	311	5	Washington
78	Hamel, Dean	DT	6-3	271	7	Tulsa
50	Harper, Dave	LB	6-1	220	2	Humboldt State
	Harris, Odie	DB	6-0	190	4	Sam Houston State
70	Hellestrae, Dale	G-C	6-5	275	5	Southern Methodist
45	Hendrix, Manny	CB	5-10	185	6	Utah
32	Highsmith, Alonzo	RB	6-1	237	5	Miami
30	Holt, Issiac	CB	6-2	198	7	Alcorn State
20	Horton, Ray	S	5-11	186	9	Washington
	Hudson, Craig	TE	6-3	245	1	Wisconsin
88	Irvin, Michael	WR	6-2	199	4	Miami
77	Jeffcoat, Jim	DE	6-5	264	9	Arizona State
48	Johnston, Daryl	RB	6-2	238	3	Syracuse
97	Jones, Jimmie	DT	6-4	272	2	Miami
26	Jones, Keith	RB	5-10	180	2	Nebraska
83	Martin, Kelvin	WR	5-9	163	5	Boston College
61	Newton, Nate	T	6-3	322	6	Florida A&M
73	Noonan, Danny	DT	6-4	266	5	Nebraska
51	Norton, Ken	LB	6-2	237	4	UCLA
84	Novacek, Jay	TE	6-4	230	7	Wyoming
	Roberts, Alfredo	TE	6-3	246	4	Miami
4	Saxon, Mike	P	6-3	200	7	San Diego State
42	Smagala, Stan	DB	5-10	184	2	Notre Dame
22	Smith, Emmitt	RB	5-9	203	2	Florida
57	Smith, Vinson	LB	6-2	225	3	East Carolina
54	Solomon, Jesse	LB	6-0	235	6	Florida State
53	Stepnoski, Mark	C-G	6-2	266	3	Pittsburgh
18	Stoudt, Cliff	QB	6-4	222	12	Youngstown State
96	Stubbs, Daniel	DE	6-4	264	4	Miami
92	Tolbert, Tony	DE	6-6	254	3	Texas-El Paso
71	Tuinei, Mark	T	6-5	293	9	Hawaii
	Veingrad, Alan	T	6-5	281	5	East Texas State
37	Washington, James	S	6-1	195	4	UCLA
23	Williams, Robert	CB	5-10	186	5	Baylor
1	Willis, Ken	K	5-11	189	2	Kentucky
81	Wright, Alexander	WR	6-0	189	2	Auburn
76	Zimmerman, Jeff	G	6-3	332	4	Florida

NEW YORK GIANTS

Address Giants Stadium, East Rutherford, New Jersey 07073.
Stadium Giants Stadium, East Rutherford, N.J. *Capacity* 77,152 *Playing Surface* AstroTurf.
Team Colours Blue, Red, and White.
Head Coach Ray Handley – 1st year.
Championships Division 1986,'89,'90; Conference 1986,'90; NFL 1927,'34,'38,'56; Super Bowl 1986,'90.
History NFL 1925-69, NFC 1970-

We'll remember the power, the ball-control and the asphyxiating defense. But the lingering image of the 1990 New York Giants is of Bill Parcells, a mix of excitement and calm, of conservatism and dash, the coaching genius whose team marched inexorably to the NFL Championship in Super Bowl XXV. Following his shock resignation in mid-May, assistant Ray Handley will attempt to fill Parcells' shoes.

It is quite remarkable that the Giants' most productive rusher was Ottis Anderson, the blunt instrument at the sharp end, who gained just 784 yards at under 3.5 yards a crack. Even Anderson can not go on for ever and his obvious heir, Rodney Hampton, is ready to bring into action his speed and moves more frequently. Playing mostly as a lead blocker, the style of fullback Maurice Carthon is crucial to the outcome. There is no suggestion that he will be replaced but the Giants had a successor in mind when they drafted Jarrod Bunch in the first round. With the selection of Ed McCaffrey in round three, the club also would have had in mind that, in the passing offense, the top receiver, multi-purpose scatback Dave Meggett, caught just 39 passes. In that discipline, the largest yardage haul was a mere 541. But there is deep speed of the most shocking kind in starting wide receivers Stephen Baker and Mark Ingram. McCaffrey will fill the slot vacated by the departed Odessa Turner. Important to the outcome is the play of tight end Mark Bavaro, who has had knee injuries but, at his best, simply is the best. Encouragingly, reserve tight end Howard Cross made fine progress last season. Perhaps the most surprising aspect of 1990 was the play of reserve quarterback Jeff Hostetler. More elusive than starter Phil Simms, Hostetler showed great poise in handling the pressure as, in double-quick time, he took control of the offense. Common sense suggests that a healthy Simms would resume at the controls but it would be unwise to overlook the possibility of a change in the order.

The collective effort relies on the dominance established by an immensely powerful offensive line. The group formed by John Elliott, William Roberts, Bart Oates, Eric Moore and Doug Riesenberg has few equals. Former first-round pick Brian Williams backs up both at center and guard while 1989 third-rounder Bob Kratch specializes at guard. The drafting of Clarence Jones will boost the depth at tackle.

The Giants' strength on defense is now taken for granted. Careful recruiting has ensured the availability of replacements as senior players leave the arena. The defensive secondary was an area of relative weakness but the signing of free agent cornerback Everson Walls, who was an All-Pro with the Cowboys, completed a unit which has Mark Collins starting at left cornerback, with two hard-hitting safeties, Greg Jackson and Myron Guyton, dominating the middle. One of Perry Williams and former Chicago player Dave Duerson is the fifth player in the nickel package. Linebacking still is a tremendous asset with the fabulous Lawrence Taylor lining up in the position of his choice and ruling supreme. Nominally, he is at right outside linebacker with former Pro Bowler Carl Banks on the left. Another former Cowboy, Steve DeOssie, has fought his way ahead of Gary Reasons to start at left inside linebacker alongside the increasingly effective Pepper Johnson, who led the team in tackles and, together with Taylor, started in the 1991 Pro Bowl.

The three-man defensive line has Leonard Marshall and Eric Dorsey at defensive end with Erik Howard at nose tackle. When they shift to the 4-3, John Washington and Mike Fox come in while Dorsey takes a breather. They form a tough, no-nonsense bunch which gives little away and is particularly tough against the run.

Giants special teams always are well-drilled. Former Miami cornerback Reyna Thompson, who was signed by the Giants as a Plan-B free agent in 1989, won the general-purpose spot on the Pro Bowl roster. Joining him was punter Sean Landeta, who averaged 44.1 gross yards. Who better to round off the unit and kick the winning points in a big game than Matt Bahr, who was yet another steal from the free-agent market?

1991 SCHEDULE OF GAMES

September		
2	SAN FRANCISCO (Mon.)	9:00
8	LOS ANGELES RAMS	1:00
15	at Chicago	12:00
22	CLEVELAND	1:00
29	at Dallas	12:00
October		
6	PHOENIX	4:00
14	at Pittsburgh (Mon.)	9:00
20	Open Date	
27	WASHINGTON (Sun. night)	8:00
November		
4	at Philadelphia (Mon.)	9:00
10	at Phoenix	2:00
17	DALLAS	4:00
24	at Tampa Bay	1:00
December		
1	at Cincinnati	4:00
8	PHILADELPHIA	1:00
15	at Washington	4:00
21	HOUSTON (Sat.)	12:30

LEFT: *John (Jumbo) Elliott is an overpowering force at left tackle and plays a major part when the Giants establish the rushing game as the basis of their offense.*

1991 Draft

Round	Name	Pos.	Ht.	Wt.	College
1.	Bunch, Jarrod	RB	6-2	248	Michigan
2.	McGhee, Kanavis	LB	6-3	257	Colorado
3.	McCaffrey, Ed	WR	6-5	210	Stanford
4.	Jones, Clarence	T	6-5	286	Maryland
5.	Moss, Anthony	LB	6-3	233	Florida State
6.	Miller, Corey	LB	6-1	252	South Carolina
7.	Carter, Simmie	CB	5-11	180	Southern Mississippi
8.	McGriggs, Lamar	S	6-1	199	Western Illinois
9.	Bouldin, Jerry	WR	5-11	192	Mississippi State
10.	Cristobal, Luis	G	6-3	282	Miami
11.	Popson, Ted	TE	6-3	243	Portland State
12.	Wanke, Larry	QB	6-2	223	John Carroll

VETERAN ROSTER

No.	Name	Pos.	Ht.	Wt.	NFL Year	College
51	Abrams, Bobby	LB	6-3	230	2	Michigan
24	Anderson, Ottis	RB	6-2	225	13	Miami
9	Bahr, Matt	K	5-10	175	13	Penn State
85	Baker, Stephen	WR	5-8	160	5	Fresno State
58	Banks, Carl	LB	6-4	235	8	Michigan State
89	Bavaro, Mark	TE	6-4	245	7	Notre Dame
46	Brown, Roger	CB	6-0	196	2	Virginia Tech
44	Carthon, Maurice	RB	6-1	225	7	Arkansas State
6	Cavanaugh, Matt	QB	6-2	210	14	Pittsburgh
25	Collins, Mark	CB	5-10	190	6	Cal State-Fullerton
98	Cooks, Johnie	LB	6-4	251	10	Mississippi State
87	Cross, Howard	TE	6-5	245	3	Alabama
99	DeOssie, Steve	LB	6-2	248	8	Boston College
77	Dorsey, Eric	DE	6-5	280	6	Notre Dame
26	Duerson, Dave	S	6-1	208	9	Notre Dame
76	Elliott, John	T	6-7	305	4	Michigan
93	Fox, Mike	DE	6-6	275	2	West Virginia
29	Guyton, Myron	S	6-1	205	3	Eastern Kentucky
27	Hampton, Rodney	RB	5-11	215	2	Georgia
15	Hostetler, Jeff	QB	6-3	212	7	West Virginia
74	Howard, Erik	NT	6-4	268	6	Washington State
82	Ingram, Mark	WR	5-10	188	5	Michigan State
47	Jackson, Greg	S	6-1	200	3	Louisiana State
79	James, Clint	DE	6-6	270	1	Louisiana State
52	Johnson, Pepper	LB	6-3	248	6	Ohio State
	Kaumeyer, Thom	S	5-11	187	2	Oregon
61	Kratch, Bob	G	6-3	288	3	Iowa
5	Landeta, Sean	P	6-0	200	6	Towson State
57	McGrew, Lawrence	LB	6-6	250	11	Southern California
70	Marshall, Leonard	DE	6-3	285	9	Louisiana State
30	Meggett, Dave	RB-KR	5-7	180	3	Towson State
	Milling, James	WR	5-9	156	3	Maryland
60	Moore, Eric	G	6-5	290	4	Indiana
80	Mrosko, Bob	TE	6-5	270	3	Penn State
65	Oates, Bart	C	6-3	265	7	Brigham Young
55	Reasons, Gary	LB	6-4	234	8	Northwestern State, La.
64	Rehder, Tom	G-T	6-7	290	4	Notre Dame
72	Riesenberg, Doug	T	6-5	275	5	California
66	Roberts, William	G	6-5	280	7	Ohio State
81	Robinson, Stacy	WR	5-11	186	7	North Dakota State
11	Simms, Phil	QB	6-3	214	12	Morehead State
56	Taylor, Lawrence	LB	6-3	243	11	North Carolina
21	Thompson, Reyna	CB	6-0	193	6	Baylor
34	Tillman, Lewis	RB	6-0	195	3	Jackson State
28	Walls, Everson	CB	6-1	194	11	Grambling
73	Washington, John	DE	6-4	275	6	Oklahoma State
36	White, Adrian	S	6-0	200	4	Florida
59	Williams, Brian	C-G	6-5	300	3	Minnesota
23	Williams, Perry	CB	6-2	203	8	North Carolina State

PHILADELPHIA EAGLES

Address Veterans Stadium, Broad St. and Pattison Ave., Philadelphia, Pennsylvania 19148.
Stadium Veterans Stadium, Philadelphia. *Capacity* 65,356 *Playing Surface* AstroTurf-8.
Team Colours Kelly Green, Silver, and White.
Head Coach Rich Kotite – 1st year.
Championships Division 1980,'88; Conference 1980; NFL 1948,'49,'60.
History NFL 1933-69, NFC 1970-

Slowly, gradually, the Eagles are coming together. They've fought their way through difficult periods and managed to reach the playoffs in each of the last three seasons. With two probable starters coming from the draft, the improvement is expected to continue.

The offensive line has been a weakness for some time and, although each year has seen the unit grow stronger, the club found a major new component in top draftee tackle Antone Davis. And it would be unwise to discount the chances of third-rounder Rob Selby. They will join a group which has center David Alexander as the focal point, with Ron Solt and Mike Schad to either side. The supporting pillars, the tackles, are Ron Heller and Reggie Singletary. It would seem that Singletary may be under pressure from the rookies but it is equally possible that there may be some rearranging of personnel.

The offensive backfield boasts a volatile cocktail, with quarterback Randall Cunningham the dominant flavour. The long-striding, elusive Cunningham has led the team in rushing for the last four years, and, with valuable contributions from Heath Sherman, Anthony Toney and Thomas Sanders, in 1990 the Eagles ranked first in the entire NFL. Sherman's electrifying speed is a shock weapon not to be underestimated. This aspect of Cunningham's play is not at the expense of a whole array of passes delivered with touch, timing and power to a starburst of receivers. Fred Barnett and Calvin Williams stream down the sidelines; tight end Keith Jackson thrusts and curls in the medium range and running back Keith Byars fills the gaps, completing an archipelago of targets. The rapid emergence of Williams and Barnett cushioned the loss of injured veteran Mike Quick, and it may be that the emergence of a healthy Mike Bellamy, who was the Eagles' 1990 second-round pick, encourages the ailing Quick to hang up his boots.

Taking its share of bounty from the draft, all three phases of the defense were helped, with safety Jesse Campbell the most likely to break into the starting lineup. However, he will be competing with the tough Andre Waters, who teamed up well with free safety Wes Hopkins last year and will not step aside without a fight. Cornerbacks Eric Allen and Ben Smith are not under threat but some scouts are still not convinced that Smith eases naturally into the position. He can play at safety and there could be some interesting permutations as the Eagles try to make full use of their talent in this, the last line of defense. One option is to use the nickel formation more often, as some teams now do in the face of three- and four-wide receiver sets.

Fourth-rounder William Thomas has a more difficult task attempting to displace either of outside linebackers Seth Joyner and Jessie Small, and more sensibly he is seen as speedy depth following the release of Al Harris. Completing the starting trio, middle linebacker Byron Evans goes from strength to strength.

It is a more-than-reasonable assertion that sixth-round draftee Andy Harmon will not disturb one of the finest four-man defensive lines in the NFL. Injuries to starting defensive tackles Mike Pitts and Jerome Brown slowed the unit, while starting right defensive end Clyde Simmons took time to reach full pace following an Achilles tendon problem. However, All-Pro Reggie White was close to his best, logging 14 sacks to rank second in the NFC and generally presenting opponents with insoluble problems.

With punter John Teltschik injured, the signing of Jeff Feagles off waivers proved to be a wise decision, as he averaged 42 gross yards. However, there will be a two-man battle in camp. There is no obvious challenger to placekicker Roger Ruzek, but it is unsettling that he failed on field goal attempts of 36, 28, 40, 39, 22 and 37 yards.

RIGHT: Reggie White remains the Eagles' most feared defensive lineman and is one of the very best in the NFL. Now and then, he can be kept at bay for a spell, but never for a full game.

1991 SCHEDULE OF GAMES

September		
1	at Green Bay	12:00
8	PHOENIX	1:00
15	at Dallas	12:00
22	PITTSBURGH	1:00
30	at Washington (Mon.)	9:00
October		
6	at Tampa Bay	1:00
13	NEW ORLEANS	1:00
20	Open Date	
27	SAN FRANCISCO	1:00
November		
4	NEW YORK GIANTS (Mon.)	9:00
10	at Cleveland	1:00
17	CINCINNATI	1:00
24	at Phoenix	2:00
December		
2	at Houston (Mon.)	8:00
8	at New York Giants	1:00
15	DALLAS	1:00
22	WASHINGTON	4:00

1991 Draft

Round	Name	Pos.	Ht.	Wt.	College
1.	Davis, Antone	T	6-4	327	Tennessee
2.	Campbell, Jesse	S	6-1	212	North Carolina State
3.	Selby, Rob	T	6-3	291	Auburn
4.	Thomas, William	LB	6-2	207	Texas A&M
5.	Erickson, Craig	QB	6-1	200	Miami
6.	Harmon, Andy	DE	6-4	264	Kent State
7.	Joseph, James	RB	6-0	224	Auburn
8.	Kowalkowski, Scott	LB	6-0	230	Notre Dame
9.	Weatherspoon, Chuck	RB	5-7	229	Houston
10.	Harmon, Eric	G	6-0	282	Clemson
11.	Flores, Mike	DE	6-3	246	Louisville
12.	Beavers, Darrell	S	6-2	230	Morehead State

VETERAN ROSTER

No.	Name	Pos.	Ht.	Wt.	NFL Year	College
72	Alexander, David	C	6-3	282	5	Tulsa
21	Allen, Eric	CB	5-10	188	4	Arizona State
86	Barnett, Fred	WR	6-0	203	2	Arkansas State
81	Bellamy, Mike	WR	6-0	195	2	Illinois
	Booty, John	DB	6-0	182	4	Texas Christian
99	Brown, Jerome	DT	6-2	295	5	Miami
41	Byars, Keith	RB	6-1	238	6	Ohio State
97	Chapura, Dick	DT	6-3	280	4	Missouri
69	Collie, Bruce	G	6-6	275	7	Texas-Arlington
12	Cunningham, Randall	QB	6-4	203	7	Nevada-Las Vegas
78	Darwin, Matt	T	6-4	275	6	Texas A&M
36	Drummond, Robert	RB	6-1	205	3	Syracuse
56	Evans, Byron	LB	6-2	235	5	Arizona
5	Feagles, Jeff	P	6-0	198	4	Miami
90	Golic, Mike	DT	6-5	275	6	Notre Dame
71	Gray, Cecil	G	6-4	264	2	North Carolina
54	Hager, Britt	LB	6-1	222	3	Texas
80	Harris, Rod	WR	5-10	183	3	Texas A&M
73	Heller, Ron	T	6-6	280	8	Penn State
48	Hopkins, Wes	S	6-1	215	8	Southern Methodist
76	Hudson, John	G-C	6-2	265	1	Auburn
88	Jackson, Keith	TE	6-2	250	4	Oklahoma
83	Jackson, Kenny	WR	6-0	180	8	Penn State
46	Jenkins, Izel	CB	5-10	191	4	North Carolina State
	Johnson, Ron	WR	6-3	190	6	Cal State-Long Beach
59	Joyner, Seth	LB	6-2	240	6	Texas-El Paso
94	Kaufusi, Steve	DE	6-4	274	3	Brigham Young
	McKnight, Dennis	C-G	6-4	280	9	Drake
9	McMahon, Jim	QB	6-1	190	10	Brigham Young
47	Moten, Ron	LB	6-1	235	1	Florida
74	Pitts, Mike	DT	6-5	277	9	Alabama
82	Quick, Mike	WR	6-2	195	10	North Carolina State
55	Rose, Ken	LB	6-1	216	5	Nevada-Las Vegas
7	Ruzek, Roger	K	6-1	195	5	Weber State
45	Sanders, Thomas	RB	5-11	203	7	Texas A&M
79	Schad, Mike	G	6-5	290	4	Queens, Canada
23	Sherman, Heath	RB-KR	6-0	190	3	Texas A&I
85	Shuler, Mickey	TE	6-3	231	14	Penn State
96	Simmons, Clyde	DE	6-6	275	6	Western Carolina
68	Singletary, Reggie	T	6-3	285	5	North Carolina State
52	Small, Jessie	LB	6-3	239	3	Eastern Kentucky
26	Smith, Ben	CB	5-11	183	2	Georgia
63	Smith, Daryle	T	6-5	278	4	Tennessee
30	Smith, Otis	CB	5-11	185	1	Missouri
66	Solt, Ron	G	6-3	288	7	Maryland
61	Tamburello, Ben	C-G	6-3	278	4	Auburn
10	Teltschik, John	P	6-2	210	5	Texas
25	Toney, Anthony	RB	6-0	227	6	Texas A&M
43	Vick, Roger	RB	6-3	235	5	Texas A&M
20	Waters, Andre	S	5-11	199	8	Cheyney State
92	White, Reggie	DE	6-5	285	7	Tennessee
89	Williams, Calvin	WR	5-11	181	2	Purdue

PHOENIX CARDINALS

Address P.O. Box 888, Phoenix, Arizona 85001–0888.
Stadium Sun Devil Stadium, Tempe. *Capacity* 72,000 *Playing Surface* Grass.
Team Colours Cardinal Red, Black, and White.
Head Coach Joe Bugel – 2nd year.
Championships Division 1974,'75; NFL 1925,'47.
History NFL 1920-69, NFC 1970-
(They were known as the Chicago Cardinals until 1960, when they moved to St Louis. In 1988, the franchise, still under the same ownership, was transferred to Phoenix.)

Not for some time have the Cardinals had as many areas of strength and, in the draft, they took great care to service the remaining weaknesses. On merit as distinct from hope, then, Phoenix can enter the 1991 season with a wild-card spot as a realistic goal.

There are no problems with the offense that a year's experience will not have helped. Indeed, Phoenix has one of the league's better offensive lines, with Tootie Robbins and the tough Luis Sharpe at tackle, Lance Smith and Derek Kennard at guard, and the powerful Bill Lewis at center. In one sense, it is a measure of the quality of the starters that 1989 first-round pick Joe Wolf has been unable to find a spot, but also it is true that the former Boston College star has not yet settled into a definite rôle.

It was often the earth-moving blocking of Kennard which was exploited by rookie sensation Johnny Johnson, who overshadowed second-round draftee Anthony Thompson to lead the team in rushing. It is not so much that Johnson is better than Thompson but, more, that Johnson is perfect for the system. In seeking to put each player to his best use, Joe Bugel has the kind of problem most head coaches would love. On the other hand, it is crucial to the Cardinals' rushing game that Bugel does use his chosen man correctly, for there is only one running back in the formation, with Walter Reeves as the formal tight end and Tim Jorden the H-back. Both men are essentially blockers and that also is the case for reserve H-back Ron Wolfley.

The absence of a serious pass receiving threat at tight end places greater responsibility on the wide receivers and, here too, the Cardinals pulled out a plum. Third-round draftee Ricky Proehl started only two games, yet he led the team both in receptions and receiving yards. Starting in half of the games, Ernie Jones continued his development at a tremendous pace. It means that the problems involved in the transition from the pairing of Roy Green and J.T. Smith have been solved. Green should retain a spot but Smith has been released.

At quarterback, Timm Rosenbach looks increasingly confident. The mobility which, as a second-year player, helped him out of one or two difficult spots, could soon make a major contribution to the rushing offense.

It was the defense which needed an impact player or two and that priceless commodity may have come in the form of Eric Swann, who did not play collegiate football and, in that sense, must be seen as a major risk. If he does turn out to be as good as expected, the Cardinals have found a future Pro Bowler. Mike Jones has explosive speed and it was only his lack of consistency that saw him still undrafted by the second round. Freddie Joe Nunn is the Cardinals' veteran lineman of great class.

Turning to the linebackers, it has been a mystery that the unit has never quite shown the intensity expected of a collection including former first-round picks Ken Harvey, Anthony Bell and Eric Hill. Last year, however, the switch to a 3-4 formation had the effect of freeing Harvey, who responded with a club-leading ten sacks, one better than Nunn.

Behind them, in the defensive secondary, strong safety Tim McDonald rules supreme as the club's leading tackler and interceptor. And while free safety Lonnie Young underlined his liking for collisions, he will be pressed more strongly by backups Mike Zordich and Marcus Turner. At cornerback, the starting pair of Cedric Mack and Jay Taylor must be pressured by draftees Aeneas Williams and Dexter Davis, both of whom are talented prospects.

Punter Rich Camarillo is coming off a fine year when he was close to earning a third Pro Bowl selection. There's not a great deal wrong with placekicker Al Del Greco but the club signed Plan-B free agent Greg Davis, who is a genuine competitor.

RIGHT: Quarterback Timm Rosenbach came through his first full year as a starter bruised but undaunted.

1991 SCHEDULE OF GAMES

September		
1	at Los Angeles Rams	1:00
8	at Philadelphia	1:00
15	at Washington	1:00
22	DALLAS (Sun. night)	5:00
29	NEW ENGLAND	1:00
October		
6	at New York Giants	4:00
13	at Minnesota	12:00
20	ATLANTA	1:00
27	MINNESOTA	2:00
November		
3	at Dallas	12:00
10	NEW YORK GIANTS	2:00
17	at San Francisco	1:00
24	PHILADELPHIA	2:00
December		
1	Open Date	
8	WASHINGTON	2:00
15	at Denver	2:00
22	NEW ORLEANS	2:00

1991 Draft

Round	Name	Pos.	Ht.	Wt.	College
1.	Swann, Eric	DE	6-3	311	None
2.	Jones, Mike	DE	6-3	274	North Carolina State
3.	Williams, Aeneas	CB	5-10	187	Southern
4.	Davis, Dexter	CB	5-9	175	Clemson
5.	Hammond, Vance	DT	6-5	300	Clemson
6.	Vega, Eduardo	T	6-6	325	Memphis State
7.	Brown, Ivory Lee	RB	6-1	243	Arkansas-Pine Bluff
8.	Amsler, Greg	RB	6-2	236	Tennessee
8.	Evans, Jerry	TE	6-4	255	Toledo
8.	Evans, Scott	DT	6-2	261	Oklahoma
10.	Anderson, Herbie	CB	5-10	184	Texas A&I
11.	LaDuke, Nathan	S	5-9	192	Arizona State
12.	Bridewell, Jeff	QB	6-4	219	Cal-Davis

VETERAN ROSTER

No.	Name	Pos.	Ht.	Wt.	NFL Year	College
55	Bell, Anthony	LB	6-3	235	6	Michigan State
54	Braxton, David	LB	6-1	232	3	Wake Forest
16	Camarillo, Rich	P	5-11	193	11	Washington
37	Centers, Larry	RB	5-11	203	2	Stephen F. Austin
79	Clasby, Bob	DT	6-5	276	5	Notre Dame
	Coleman, Sidney	LB	6-2	250	4	Southern Mississippi
	Davis, Bob	LB	6-0	236	1	Brigham Young
	Davis, Greg	K	5-11	197	5	Citadel
17	Del Greco, Al	K	5-10	195	8	Auburn
	Faulkner, Jeff	DE	6-3	280	3	Southern
26	Field, Amod	WR	5-11	181	1	Montclair State
32	Flagler, Terrence	RB	6-0	200	5	Clemson
20	Flutie, Darren	WR	5-10	187	3	Boston College
81	Green, Roy	WR	6-0	197	13	Henderson, Ark.
56	Harvey, Ken	LB	6-2	228	4	California
	Hill, Derek	WR	6-1	194	3	Arizona
58	Hill, Eric	LB	6-1	251	3	Louisiana State
83	Holmes, Don	WR	5-10	182	6	Mesa, Colorado
80	Jackson, John	WR	5-10	175	2	Southern California
53	Jax, Garth	LB	6-2	236	6	Florida State
39	Johnson, Johnny	RB	6-2	216	2	San Jose State
86	Jones, Ernie	WR	5-11	196	4	Indiana
85	Jorden, Tim	TE	6-2	220	2	Indiana
57	Kauahi, Kani	C	6-2	274	9	Hawaii
70	Kennard, Derek	G	6-3	319	6	Nevada-Reno
51	Lewis, Bill	C	6-7	278	6	Nebraska
30	Little, David	H-B	6-2	226	8	Middle Tennessee State
	Lomack, Tony	WR	5-8	180	2	Florida
29	Lynch, Lorenzo	CB	5-9	200	4	Cal State-Sacramento
46	McDonald, Tim	S	6-2	209	5	Southern California
47	Mack, Cedric	CB	6-0	185	9	Baylor
92	Manley, Dexter	DE	6-3	257	11	Oklahoma State
78	Nunn, Freddie Joe	DE	6-4	250	7	Mississippi
90	Osborne, Eldonta	LB	6-0	226	2	Louisiana Tech
87	Proehl, Ricky	WR	5-10	185	2	Wake Forest
89	Reeves, Walter	TE	6-4	262	3	Auburn
63	Robbins, Tootie	T	6-5	322	10	East Carolina
3	Rosenbach, Timm	QB	6-2	215	3	Washington State
72	Saddler, Rod	DE	6-5	280	5	Texas A&M
67	Sharpe, Luis	T	6-4	290	10	UCLA
61	Smith, Lance	G	6-2	285	7	Louisiana State
69	Smith, Vernice	G	6-2	289	2	Florida A&M
	Stowe, Tyronne	LB	6-1	237	5	Rutgers
27	Taylor, Jay	CB	5-9	175	3	San Jose State
34	Thompson, Anthony	RB	5-11	207	2	Indiana
19	Tupa, Tom	QB-P	6-4	225	4	Ohio State
23	Turner, Marcus	DB	6-0	187	3	UCLA
66	Wahler, Jim	DT	6-3	276	3	UCLA
60	Walker, Jeff	G-T	6-4	286	4	Memphis State
68	Wolf, Joe	T-G	6-5	283	3	Boston College
24	Wolfley, Ron	H-B	6-0	222	7	West Virginia
43	Young, Lonnie	S	6-1	192	7	Michigan State
38	Zordich, Mike	S	5-11	200	5	Penn State

WASHINGTON REDSKINS

Address Redskin Park, P.O. Box 17247, Dulles International Airport, Washington, D.C. 20041.
Stadium Robert F. Kennedy Stadium, Washington. *Capacity* 55,672 *Playing Surface* Grass.
Team Colours Burgundy and Gold.
Head Coach Joe Gibbs – 11th year.
Championships Division 1972,'83,'84,'87; Conference 1972,'82,'83,'87; NFL 1937,'42; Super Bowl 1982,'87.
History NFL 1932-69, NFC 1970-
(Originally named the Boston Braves for the 1932 season only, they were renamed the Boston Redskins until, in 1937, they moved to Washington.)

Under head coach Joe Gibbs, the Redskins always are likely to compete, and it was only their inability to finish off several deep drives which saw them exit at the divisional playoff stage against San Francisco. There have been but minor changes to the squad, which promises to be no less effective in 1991.

The key to Washington's momentum is quarterback Mark Rypien, who has learned the hard way and will be better experienced for the disappointment of the loss to the 49ers. On his day, combining with the 'Posse' of wide receivers Gary Clark, Art Monk and Ricky Sanders, Rypien can destroy opponents. Useful in this department, too, is running back Earnest Byner, whose acquisition in a trade with Cleveland was a master stroke. Led by Clark, the Posse currently ranks as the best trio in the game with Monk as only the third man in league history to have more than 700 career receptions. Unlike some of the teams which use only one running back, the Redskins often field all three wide receivers rather than opting for two tight ends. In the latter position, Don Warren is primarily a blocker.

Byner became only the fifth Redskin in team history to rush for more than 1,000 yards in a season and his haul of 1,219 was good enough to earn a trip to the Pro Bowl. However, a contribution from Gerald Riggs is important if the Redskins wish to shift the emphasis towards a ball-control offense. Also important in this respect is the cohesion of the offensive line, which, last year, made great strides towards re-establishing the level of several years ago when the 'Hogs' ruled. With the NFC's best left tackle, Jim Lachey, and center Jeff Bostic as fixtures, Raleigh McKenzie and Mark Schlereth probably have the edge in the guard positions with Russ Grimm an outstanding backup. At right tackle, reliable veteran Joe Jacoby is sound enough but a healthy Mo Elewonibi could provide strong competition.

The Washington defense does not have a single focus but, if a dominant individual is to be identified by opponents for double-teaming, it is Pro Bowl defensive end Charles Mann. The 4-3 defensive tackles are Darryl Grant and Tracy Rocker, the latter who was looking comfortable before suffering a knee injury halfway through the 1990 campaign. In Rocker's absence, Eric Williams was more than simply a space-filler. With Grant coming to the end, Washington acquired a potential successor in first-round draftee Bobby Wilson. Markus Koch secures the defensive right end position but makes way for Fred Stokes on obvious passing downs.

The emergence of left linebacker Andre Collins may have been the outstanding event for the defense last year. With unquenchable enthusiasm and poise, he catalyzed the unit, relieving the pressure on right linebacker Wilber Marshall. There was a change at middle linebacker, where Kurt Gouveia took over from Greg Manusky midway through the season. The loss of Manusky as a Plan-B free agent left the depth a little thin but it was in the Plan-B system that Matt Millen arrived.

There was a similar process in the defensive secondary, with former Eagle Terry Hoage being signed to counter the loss of starting free safety Todd Bowles. In this case, though, one wonders how the Redskins will replace a player who came second on the team with 110 tackles, had three interceptions, and was considered still to be improving. Alvin Walton, the team leader with 143 tackles, remains at strong safety while at right cornerback there is the reassuring All-Pro speed of Darrell Green. Second-year player Martin Mayhew made outstanding progess, starting 15 games and leading the club with seven interceptions.

Placekicker Chip Lohmiller began to perform like the player whom the club drafted in the 1988 second round as he set a personal best with 131 points, including field goals of 55, 53 and 56 yards. Punter Kelly Goodburn replaced Ralf Mojsiejenko for the final six games but was not the obvious solution to the problem and will be challenged by draftee Cris Shale.

1991 SCHEDULE OF GAMES

September	
1 DETROIT (Sun. night)	8:00
9 at Dallas (Mon.)	8:00
15 PHOENIX	1:00
22 at Cincinnati	1:00
30 PHILADELPHIA (Mon.)	9:00
October	
6 at Chicago	12:00
13 CLEVELAND	1:00
20 Open Date	
27 at New York Giants (Sun. night)	8:00
November	
3 HOUSTON	1:00
10 ATLANTA	1:00
17 at Pittsburgh	1:00
24 DALLAS	1:00
December	
1 at Los Angeles Rams	1:00
8 at Phoenix	2:00
15 NEW YORK GIANTS	4:00
22 at Philadelphia	4:00

Art Monk is only 89 receptions short of equalling Steve Largent's NFL career record of 819.

1991 Draft

Round	Name	Pos.	Ht.	Wt.	College
1.	Wilson, Bobby	DT	6-1	276	Michigan State
3.	Ervins, Ricky	RB	5-7	200	Southern California
6.	Ransom, Dennis	TE	6-3	248	Texas A&M
7.	Cash, Keith	WR	6-4	225	Texas
8.	Spencer, Jimmy	CB	5-9	180	Florida
9.	Bell, Charles	CB	5-10	180	Baylor
10.	Shale, Cris	P	5-10	192	Bowling Green
11.	Gulledge, David	S	6-1	201	Jacksonville State
12.	McCardell, Keenan	WR	5-11	181	Nevada-Las Vegas

VETERAN ROSTER

No.	Name	Pos.	Ht.	Wt.	NFL Year	College
61	Adickes, Mark	G	6-4	275	6	Baylor
53	Bostic, Jeff	C	6-2	260	12	Clemson
82	Brandes, John	TE	6-2	250	5	Cameron, Oklahoma
67	Brown, Ray	T	6-5	280	5	Arkansas State
38	Brown, Tom	RB	6-1	228	2	Pittsburgh
21	Byner, Earnest	RB	5-10	215	8	East Carolina
50	Caldwell, Ravin	LB	6-3	229	5	Arkansas
84	Clark, Gary	WR	5-9	173	7	James Madison
51	Coleman, Monte	LB	6-2	230	13	Central Arkansas
55	Collins, Andre	LB	6-1	230	2	Penn State
12	Conklin, Cary	QB	6-4	215	1	Washington
	Copeland, Danny	S	6-2	212	3	Eastern Kentucky
25	Dupard, Reggie	RB	5-11	205	6	Southern Methodist
27	Edwards, Brad	S	6-2	196	4	South Carolina
	Elewonibi, Mo	T-G	6-4	282	1	Brigham Young
39	Francisco, D'Juan	CB	5-10	185	1	Notre Dame
97	Geathers, James	DE	6-7	290	7	Wichita State
2	Goodburn, Kelly	P	6-2	202	5	Emporia State
54	Gouveia, Kurt	LB	6-1	227	5	Brigham Young
77	Grant, Darryl	DT	6-1	275	11	Rice
28	Green, Darrell	CB	5-8	170	9	Texas A&I
68	Grimm, Russ	G	6-3	275	11	Pittsburgh
	Hoage, Terry	S	6-3	201	8	Georgia
86	Hobbs, Stephen	WR	5-11	195	2	North Alabama
80	Howard, Joe	WR-KR	5-8	170	4	Notre Dame
16	Humphries, Stan	QB	6-2	223	3	Northeast Louisiana
66	Jacoby, Joe	T	6-7	310	11	Louisville
47	Johnson, A.J.	CB	5-8	176	3	Southwest Texas State
88	Johnson, Jimmie	TE	6-2	246	3	Howard
45	Johnson, Sidney	CB	5-9	175	3	California
78	Johnson, Tim	DE-DT	6-3	261	5	Penn State
74	Koch, Markus	DE	6-5	275	6	Boise State
79	Lachey, Jim	T	6-6	290	7	Ohio State
95	Leverenz, Jon	LB	6-2	230	1	Minnesota
8	Lohmiller, Chip	K	6-3	213	4	Minnesota
63	McKenzie, Raleigh	C-G	6-2	270	7	Tennessee
71	Mann, Charles	DE	6-6	270	9	Nevada-Reno
58	Marshall, Wilber	LB	6-1	230	8	Florida
35	Mayhew, Martin	CB	5-8	172	3	Florida State
20	Mays, Alvoid	CB	5-9	180	2	West Virginia
87	Middleton, Ron	TE	6-2	255	6	Auburn
	Millen, Matt	LB	6-2	245	12	Penn State
30	Mitchell, Brian	RB-KR	5-10	195	2	Southwestern Louisiana
81	Monk, Art	WR	6-3	209	12	Syracuse
37	Riggs, Gerald	RB	6-1	232	10	Arizona State
99	Rocker, Tracy	DT	6-3	288	3	Auburn
10	Rutledge, Jeff	QB	6-1	195	13	Alabama
11	Rypien, Mark	QB	6-4	234	5	Washington State
83	Sanders, Ricky	WR	5-11	180	6	Southwest Texas State
69	Schlereth, Mark	G-C	6-3	285	3	Idaho
	Settle, John	RB	5-9	210	5	Appalachian State
76	Simmons, Ed	T	6-5	300	5	Eastern Washington
89	Stanley, Walter	WR-PR	5-9	180	7	Mesa, Colorado
60	Stokes, Fred	DE	6-3	262	5	Georgia Southern
31	Vaughn, Clarence	S	6-0	202	4	Northern Illinois
40	Walton, Alvin	S	6-0	180	6	Kansas
85	Warren, Don	TE	6-4	242	13	San Diego State
	Whisenhunt, Ken	TE	6-3	240	5	Georgia Tech

CHICAGO BEARS

Address Halas Hall, 250 N. Washington, Lake Forest, Illinois 60045.
Stadium Soldier Field, Chicago.
Capacity 66,946 *Playing Surface* Grass.
Team Colours Navy Blue, Orange, and White.
Head Coach Mike Ditka – 10th year.
Championships Division 1984,'85,'86,'87,'88,'90;
Conference 1985;
NFL 1921,'32,'33,'40,'41,'43,'46,'63;
Super Bowl 1985.
History NFL 1920-69, NFC 1970-
(Before 1922, they were known as firstly the Decatur Staleys and then the Chicago Staleys.)

A mix of seasoned veterans and young, improving players launched the Bears to a 9-1 start before they began to shift off course. In the divisional playoffs, a series of minor errors, coupled with a show of wide-ranging versatility by Giants quarterback Jeff Hostetler, saw Chicago beaten by the eventual Super Bowl Champions. It is a solid background against which the Bears embark upon their 72nd NFL campaign.

"Old men with beards and I love 'em all," is how head coach Mike Ditka described the offensive line of tackles Keith Van Horne and Jim Covert, guards Mark Bortz and Tom Thayer, and center Jay Hilgenberg, which has started as a group for the last six seasons. Ditka stated that he wanted a big, tough youngster as backup, and he selected Stan Thomas with his first option. Some scouts feel that Thomas can displace Van Horne at right tackle but others feel that he'll need a year or two to learn the ropes.

It seems certain that third-round pick Chris Gardocki will displace incumbent punter Maury Buford. Not only is Gardocki sound in his primary rôle but, also, he has terrific strength for kickoffs. For the business of splitting the uprights, Kevin Butler is one of the best, particularly on those last-minute character-builders.

When it comes to players who score touchdowns, Chicago is as deep as most teams and better off than many. Senior running back Neal Anderson, who accounted for almost a third of the Bears' total yardage from scrimmage and 13 of the offense's 36 touchdowns, is a low-profile form of Walter Payton. Anderson's starting partner, fullback Brad Muster, is such an outstanding blocker that it is easy to overlook the obvious, namely, that he has the power and explosiveness to maintain the pace were he required to assume the responsibility. The speedy Johnny Bailey is a useful shock weapon.

The philosophies of discipline and consistency extend to the passing offense, directed by the studied care of quarterback Jim Harbaugh, who has become the Bears' career leader in both completion percentage (57.9) and interceptions (1.8%). The pressure from within the club was eased when backup Mike Tomczak was left unprotected in the Plan-B arrangements. As part of the fine-tuning to make the most of Harbaugh's style, last year, the Bears discarded their rotating wide

LEFT: Cornerback Lemuel Stinson had a useful six interceptions and is pictured marking Minnesota wide receiver Anthony Carter.

1991 Draft

Round	Name	Pos.	Ht.	Wt.	College
1.	Thomas, Stan	T	6-5	302	Texas
2.	Zorich, Chris	DT	5-11	267	Notre Dame
3.	Gardocki, Chris	P-K	6-2	193	Clemson
4.	Johnson, Joe	CB	5-8	186	North Carolina State
5.	Morgan, Anthony	WR	6-0	195	Tennessee
6.	Lewis, Darren	RB	5-10	219	Texas A&M
7.	Justin, Paul	QB	6-3	202	Arizona State
8.	Horton, Larry	S	5-10	179	Texas A&M
9.	Stonebreaker, Mike	LB	5-11	226	Notre Dame
10.	Backes, Tom	DE	6-4	223	Oklahoma
11.	Long, Stacy	G	6-2	296	Clemson
12.	Cook, John	DT	6-5	270	Washington

VETERAN ROSTER

No.	Name	Pos.	Ht.	Wt.	NFL Year	College
35	Anderson, Neal	RB	5-11	210	6	Florida
93	Armstrong, Trace	DE	6-4	259	3	Florida
22	Bailey, Johnny	RB-KR	5-8	180	2	Texas A&I
79	Becker, Kurt	G	6-5	269	10	Michigan
62	Bortz, Mark	G	6-6	272	9	Iowa
86	Boso, Cap	TE	6-4	240	5	Illinois
8	Buford, Maury	P	6-0	198	9	Texas Tech
6	Butler, Kevin	K	6-1	190	7	Georgia
20	Carrier, Mark	S	6-1	180	2	Southern California
89	Coley, James	TE	6-3	270	2	Clemson
74	Covert, Jim	T	6-4	278	9	Pittsburgh
54	Cox, Ron	LB	6-2	242	2	Fresno State
82	Davis, Wendell	WR	5-11	188	4	Louisiana State
95	Dent, Richard	DE	6-5	268	9	Tennessee State
37	Douglass, Maurice	DB	5-11	200	6	Kentucky
67	Fontenot, Jerry	G	6-3	272	3	Texas A&M
23	Gayle, Shaun	S	5-11	194	8	Ohio State
29	Gentry, Dennis	WR-KR	5-8	180	10	Baylor
31	Green, Mark	RB	5-11	184	3	Notre Dame
4	Harbaugh, Jim	QB	6-3	220	5	Michigan
63	Hilgenberg, Jay	C	6-3	260	11	Iowa
53	Jones, Dante	LB	6-1	236	4	Oklahoma
88	Kozlowski, Glen	WR	6-1	205	5	Brigham Young
70	Kumerow, Eric	DE-DT	6-7	260	4	Ohio State
46	Lott, James	CB	5-9	181	1	Clemson
76	McMichael, Steve	DT	6-2	268	12	Texas
26	Mangum, John	CB	5-10	173	2	Alabama
84	Morris, Ron	WR	6-1	195	5	Southern Methodist
51	Morrissey, Jim	LB	6-3	227	7	Michigan State
25	Muster, Brad	RB	6-3	231	4	Stanford
36	Paul, Markus	S	6-2	199	3	Syracuse
72	Perry, William	DT	6-2	325	7	Clemson
52	Pruitt, Mickey	LB	6-1	215	4	Colorado
59	Rivera, Ron	LB	6-3	240	8	California
55	Roper, John	LB	6-1	228	3	Texas A&M
30	Rouse, James	RB	6-0	220	2	Arkansas
96	Ryan, Tim	DE	6-4	268	2	Southern California
50	Singletary, Mike	LB	6-0	230	11	Baylor
85	Smith, Quintin	WR	5-10	172	2	Kansas
32	Stinson, Lemuel	CB	5-9	159	4	Texas Tech
49	Tate, David	S	6-0	177	4	Colorado
57	Thayer, Tom	G	6-4	270	7	Notre Dame
80	Thornton, James	TE	6-2	242	4	Cal State-Fullerton
78	Van Horne, Keith	T	6-6	283	11	Southern California
87	Waddle, Tom	WR	6-0	181	3	Boston College
10	Willis, Peter Tom	QB	6-2	188	2	Florida State
73	Wojciechowski, John	G	6-4	270	5	Michigan State

receiver system in favour of full-time starters Wendell Davis and Ron Morris. While each has excellent hands, there was a shortage of speed and this may have arrived with fifth-round draftee Anthony Morgan. Dennis Gentry is a fine third-down specialist. At tight end, James Thornton is a player of great potential, though the local feeling is that he needs to work on his consistency.

Defensively, the squad has no problems except the impossible task of replacing Dan Hampton, one of the greatest at his position in NFL history. Tragically, also, backup Fred Washington was killed in a car accident. Steve McMichael, a former Pro Bowler who shared the defensive right tackle spot as Hampton slowed in 1990, resumes permanently in partnership with William Perry. Two defensive ends of the highest class, Richard Dent and Trace Armstrong, continue to secure the outer limits of the front wall. In the second phase of defense, the NFC's premier middle linebacker, Mike Singletary, reigns supreme, with his lieutenants, Ron Rivera and Jim Morrissey, on the outsides. Dante Jones is Singletary's backup while John Roper and pass rushing specialist Ron Cox platoon with Morrissey and Rivera.

The Bears' secondary may be coming to its best. Shaun Gayle successfully made the switch from free safety to the strong spot, making way for the brilliantly effective rookie, Mark Carrier, who led the NFL with ten interceptions. At left cornerback, Donnell Woolford has come through every test, while Lemuel Stinson is expected to resume on the other corner, having recovered from the knee injury which ended his season on Week Ten. John Mangum and David Tate bring youthful enthusiasm to the nickel formation.

1991 SCHEDULE OF GAMES

September		
1	MINNESOTA	3:00
8	at Tampa Bay	1:00
15	NEW YORK GIANTS	12:00
23	NEW YORK JETS (Mon.)	8:00
29	at Buffalo	1:00
October		
6	WASHINGTON	12:00
13	Open Date	
17	at Green Bay (Thurs. night)	6:30
27	at New Orleans	12:00
November		
3	DETROIT	12:00
11	at Minnesota (Mon.)	8:00
17	at Indianapolis	1:00
24	MIAMI	12:00
28	at Detroit (Thanksgiving)	12:30
December		
8	GREEN BAY	12:00
14	TAMPA BAY (Sat.)	11:30
23	at San Francisco (Mon.)	6:00

DETROIT LIONS

Address Pontiac Silverdome, 1200 Featherstone Road – Box 4200, Pontiac, Michigan 48057.
Stadium Pontiac Silverdome.
Capacity 80,500 *Playing Surface* AstroTurf.
Team Colours Honolulu Blue and Silver.
Head Coach Wayne Fontes – 4th year.
Championships Division 1983; NFL 1935,'52,'53,'57.
History NFL 1930-69, NFC 1970-
(Until 1934, they were known as the Portsmouth (Ohio) Spartans.)

In a year when some scouts expected the Detroit Lions to make a serious bid for honours, injuries and uncertainty in one or two positions placed them on hold. Following reinforcement of the wide receiving corps from the draft, once again, it is easy to be optimistic over the prospects of a club for whom success is long overdue.

The Lions make no secret of their intention to come out throwing the football. They will start four wide receivers though the final arrangement of personnel will not emerge until the preseason. Robert Clark seems assured of one of the spots but the rest of the veterans, which include Aubrey Matthews, Terry Greer, Mike Farr and Jeff Campbell, will have to battle with draftees Herman Moore and Reggie Barrett. Moore and Barrett bring size and power to a group which, by design, featured short, nippy receivers. Critically, for the smooth operation of the 'Silver Stretch' offense, Rodney Peete has been identified as the starting quarterback going into camp. Peete is not likely to unleash very many long-range assaults but he has an accurate arm, he can scramble and he can throw on the run. Furthermore, he's an honest pro, always ready to adapt as the coaches require. However, with Andre Ware waiting his chance, Peete will always be under pressure.

The Lions have opted for a wide-open passing system at a time when, in Barry Sanders, they have the most effective pure runner in the NFC. The 1990 NFL leading rusher, Sanders will make further adjustments to play an increasing part in the passing game, backed up by one of the most seasoned veterans in the league, the great James Wilder.

Reassuringly, Detroit enters the 1991 campaign with a really solid offensive line, featuring tackles Lomas Brown and Harvey Salem, guards Eric Andolsek and Ken Dallafior, and center Kevin Glover. Eric Sanders has been the senior backup at tackle but the intention is to allow Mike Utley the opportunty to make that position his speciality. In line with this thinking, Scott Conover was drafted for depth at guard.

The defense suffered because of injuries to seven starters, often with three or four unavailable at one time. Given a clean bill of health, the Lions will have a respectable defensive line with veterans Dan Owens, Marc Spindler, Mark Duckens and Keith Ferguson in the shakeup to man the defensive end positions, and Pro Bowler Jerry Ball at nose tackle. Major reinforcement has arrived in the shape of first-round draftee Kelvin Pritchett, who can play either end or tackle. In all common sense, outside linebacker Mike Cofer, a former Pro Bowler who has been the Lions' leading sacker for the past four seasons, is essentially a fourth defensive lineman as he takes up a position to rush the passer. George Jamison will start at left outside linebacker, with Dennis Gibson and the inspirational Chris Spielman on the insides. It has been a major disappointment that the inside pairing, which operates with instinctive mutual understanding, has suffered because of injuries which have seen Gibson miss 20-or-so starts over the last two campaigns.

Turning to the secondary, it is a mystery that free safety Bennie Blades has not progressed as expected. Once more, however, injuries may have slowed his development. William White, the secondary's leading tackler both in numbers and force of impact, is secure at strong safety. At left cornerback, Ray Crockett ended the season in charge and is well liked by the coaches. But opponents were quite prepared to take on both Crockett and former Ram LeRoy Irvin, the latter who started all 16 games in 1990. Sheldon White, Bruce McNorton and Bruce Alexander, together with Plan-B signings Melvin Jenkins and Sean Vanhorse, are among the contenders.

Sixth-round draftee Richie Andrews represents expensive competition for placekicker Eddie Murray, but it would be unwise to rule out a former Pro Bowler whose errors last season were attributable to nagging injuries. There's no obvious threat to punter Jim Arnold, but he'll want to regain the form which earned him Pro Bowl spots in both 1988 and 1989.

LEFT: Strong safety William White is seen as the Lions' best open-field tackler.

1991 Draft

Round	Name	Pos.	Ht.	Wt.	College
1.	Moore, Herman	WR	6-3	205	Virginia
1.	Pritchett, Kelvin*	DT	6-2	281	Mississippi
3.	Barrett, Reggie	WR	6-2	215	Texas-El Paso
4.	Scott, Kevin	CB	5-9	175	Stanford
5.	Conover, Scott	G	6-3	286	Purdue
6.	Andrews, Richie	K	5-10	178	Florida State
7.	Thomas, Franklin	TE	6-3	260	Grambling
8.	Jackson, Cedric	RB	5-11	229	Texas Christian
9.	Milburn, Darryl	DE	6-3	256	Grambling
11.	Watkins, Slip	KR	5-8	179	Louisiana State
12.	Alexander, Zeno	LB	6-1	229	Arizona

* Pritchett was drafted by Dallas but traded to Detroit.

VETERAN ROSTER

No.	Name	Pos.	Ht.	Wt.	NFL Year	College
32	Alexander, Bruce	CB	5-9	169	2	Stephen F. Austin
65	Andolsek, Eric	G	6-2	286	4	Louisiana State
6	Arnold, Jim	P	6-3	211	9	Vanderbilt
93	Ball, Jerry	NT	6-1	298	5	Southern Methodist
36	Blades, Bennie	S	6-1	221	4	Miami
75	Brown, Lomas	T	6-4	287	7	Florida
52	Brown, Mark	LB	6-2	240	9	Purdue
87	Campbell, Jeff	WR	5-8	167	2	Colorado
50	Caston, Toby	LB	6-1	243	5	Louisiana State
82	Clark, Robert	WR	5-11	173	4	North Carolina Central
55	Cofer, Michael	LB	6-5	244	9	Tennessee
39	Crockett, Ray	CB	5-9	181	3	Baylor
67	Dallafior, Ken	G-C	6-4	279	7	Minnesota
91	Duckens, Mark	DE	6-4	270	3	Arizona State
81	Farr, Mike	WR	5-10	192	2	UCLA
77	Ferguson, Keith	DE	6-5	276	11	Ohio State
69	Fortin, Roman	T	6-5	270	1	San Diego State
98	Gibson, Dennis	LB	6-2	243	5	Iowa State
53	Glover, Kevin	C-G	6-2	282	7	Maryland
23	Gray, Mel	WR-KR	5-9	162	6	Purdue
74	Graybill, Mike	T	6-7	275	2	Boston University
86	Green, Willie	WR	6-2	179	1	Mississippi
89	Greer, Terry	WR	6-1	192	6	Alabama State
99	Hayworth, Tracy	LB-DE	6-3	250	2	Tennessee
95	Hinckley, Rob	LB	6-4	241	1	Stanford
97	Hunter, Jeff	DE	6-5	285	2	Albany State
47	Irvin, LeRoy	CB	5-11	184	12	Kansas
58	Jamison, George	LB	6-1	228	5	Cincinnati
24	Jenkins, Melvin	CB	5-10	176	5	Cincinnati
57	Jones, Victor	LB	6-2	240	4	Virginia Tech
29	McNorton, Bruce	CB	5-11	175	10	Georgetown, Kentucky
83	Matthews, Aubrey	WR	5-7	165	6	Delta State
3	Murray, Eddie	K	5-10	180	12	Tulane
51	Noga, Niko	LB	6-1	235	8	Hawaii
42	Oldham, Chris	CB	5-9	183	2	Oregon
70	Owens, Dan	DE	6-3	268	2	Southern California
9	Peete, Rodney	QB	6-0	193	3	Southern California
96	Pete, Lawrence	NT	6-0	282	3	Nebraska
4	Pillow, Frank	WR	5-10	170	4	Tennessee State
44	Riley, Eugene	TE	6-2	236	1	Ball State
73	Salem, Harvey	T	6-6	289	9	California
20	Sanders, Barry	RB	5-8	203	3	Oklahoma State
64	Sanders, Eric	T-G	6-7	286	11	Nevada-Reno
54	Spielman, Chris	LB	6-0	247	4	Ohio State
92	Spindler, Marc	DE	6-5	277	2	Pittsburgh
60	Utley, Mike	G-T	6-6	279	3	Washington State
26	Vanhorse, Sean	CB	5-10	180	1	Howard
11	Ware, Andre	QB	6-2	205	2	Houston
28	Welch, Herb	S	5-11	180	7	UCLA
25	White, Sheldon	CB	5-11	188	4	Miami, Ohio
35	White, William	S	5-10	191	4	Ohio State
34	Wilder, James	RB	6-3	225	11	Missouri

1991 SCHEDULE OF GAMES

Date	Game	Time
September		
1	at Washington (Sun. night)	8:00
8	GREEN BAY	1:00
15	MIAMI	1:00
22	at Indianapolis	12:00
29	TAMPA BAY	1:00
October		
6	MINNESOTA	1:00
13	Open Date	
20	at San Francisco	1:00
27	DALLAS	4:00
November		
3	at Chicago	12:00
10	at Tampa Bay	1:00
17	LOS ANGELES RAMS	4:00
24	at Minnesota	12:00
28	CHICAGO (Thanksgiving)	12:30
December		
8	NEW YORK JETS	4:00
15	at Green Bay	12:00
22	at Buffalo	1:00

GREEN BAY PACKERS

Address 1265 Lombardi Avenue, P.O. Box 10628, Green Bay, Wisconsin 54307–0628.
Stadia Lambeau Field, Green Bay, and Milwaukee County Stadium, Milwaukee.
Capacity (Lambeau Field) 59,543, (Milwaukee County Stadium) 56,051. *Playing Surfaces* Grass, both stadia.
Team Colours Dark Green, Gold, and White.
Head Coach Lindy Infante – 4th year.
Championships Division 1972; NFL 1929,'30,'31,'36,'39,'44,'61,'62,'65,'66,'67; Super Bowl 1966,'67.
History NFL 1921-69, NFC 1970-

The Packers are coming off a disappointing season, marred by holdouts and ending with worries over the future health of starting quarterback Don Majkowski. They face a difficult campaign in a very tough division.

Majkowski's shoulder injury has needed surgery and, while Anthony Dilweg has shown himself to be a gritty fighter with a decent arm, he does not yet match up to a healthy Majkowski, for whom greatness was predicted following his excellent 1989 campaign. As insurance, Green Bay signed former Chicago starter Mike Tomczak as a Plan-B free agent. With adequate service from the quarterback position, Sterling Sharpe has shown that he can come close to matching the incomparable Jerry Rice of San Francisco. In 1990, courageously playing with damaged ribs over the final five games, he went over 1,000 yards receiving for the second consecutive time and repeated his Pro Bowl selection. Compared with the silky smooth, highly talented Sharpe, the supporting cast may appear ordinary, but Perry Kemp is a genuine NFL starter of the possession kind while Jeff Query is a third receiver blessed with great speed. Again, tight end Ed West is a reliable veteran.

The cohesiveness on the offensive line was hampered by the early-season holdouts of starting guards Ron Hallstrom and Rich Moran, and by the disappointingly slow progress made by 1989 top pick Tony Mandarich at right tackle. The loss of tackle Alan Veingrad as a 1991 Plan-B free agent saw Green Bay sign three linemen as part of the same procedure. Center James Campen, whose development was a pleasant surprise, and probably Ken Ruettgers will be in harness with Hallstrom, Moran and Mandarich on opening day.

It is no secret that the Packers could use explosive power at running back, and here there are great hopes for 1990 first-round draftee Darrell Thompson. Plan-B signings Allen Rice and Vai Sikahema do bring reliability and speed respectively but, on balance, do not promise any more than incumbents Keith Woodside, Michael Haddix and Herman Fontenot.

With refreshing openness, the Packers announced that they would use the draft to find help for the pass defense and, true to their word, they picked cornerback Vinnie Clark and defensive end Don Davey. Clark and second-year player LeRoy Butler will challenge right cornerback Jerry Holmes for the job of starting in tandem with Mark Lee. Free safety Chuck Cecil should be back from injury to renew a solid partnership with strong safety Mark Murphy, the latter who led the team in tackles and shared the lead with three interceptions. In Cecil's absence, Tiger Greene stood in competently.

If enthusiasm counts for anything, Davey will help a pass rush which depends so much on the mighty Tim Harris, who pounces from the right outside linebacker position. In a sub-par 1990, Harris led the Packers with seven sacks. There are few worries surrounding Scott Stephen, Johnny Holland and Brian Noble who complete the starting set at linebacker and, for the moment,

LEFT: A combination of talent, courage – he played most of the season with injured ribs – and work ethic makes Pro Bowler Sterling Sharpe one of the NFL's finest wide receivers.

VETERAN ROSTER

No.	Name	Pos.	Ht.	Wt.	NFL Year	College
82	Affholter, Erik	WR	6-0	182	1	Southern California
74	Archambeau, Lester	DE	6-4	270	2	Stanford
67	Ard, Billy	G	6-3	273	11	Wake Forest
90	Bennett, Tony	LB	6-2	233	2	Mississippi
83	Bland, Carl	WR	5-11	179	8	Virginia Union
17	Bracken, Don	P	6-1	218	7	Michigan
62	Brock, Matt	DE	6-5	285	3	Oregon
93	Brown, Robert	DE	6-3	270	10	Virginia Tech
51	Bush, Blair	C	6-4	273	14	Washington
36	Butler, LeRoy	CB	6-0	192	2	Florida State
63	Campen, James	C	6-3	275	5	Tulane
26	Cecil, Chuck	S	6-0	188	4	Arizona
	Cheek, Louis	T	6-6	286	4	Texas A&M
	Clark, Greg	LB	6-0	232	4	Arizona State
56	Dent, Burnell	LB	6-1	234	6	Tulane
	Derby, Glenn	T	6-6	290	3	Wisconsin
8	Dilweg, Anthony	QB	6-3	198	3	Duke
	Donelson, Ventson	DB	5-11	180	1	Michigan State
	Douglas, Derrick	RB	5-10	205	1	Louisiana Tech
27	Fontenot, Herman	RB	6-0	205	7	Louisiana State
23	Greene, Tiger	S	6-0	192	7	Western Carolina
35	Haddix, Michael	RB	6-1	230	9	Mississippi State
72	Hall, Mark	DE	6-4	280	3	Southwestern Louisiana
65	Hallstrom, Ron	G	6-6	297	10	Iowa
80	Harris, Jackie	TE	6-3	240	2	Northeast Louisiana
97	Harris, Tim	LB	6-6	258	6	Memphis State
	Hauck, Tim	S	5-11	185	2	Montana
50	Holland, Johnny	LB	6-2	233	5	Texas A&M
44	Holmes, Jerry	CB	6-2	176	10	West Virginia
13	Jacke, Chris	K	6-0	197	3	Texas-El Paso
	Jones, Scott	T	6-5	282	3	Washington
81	Kemp, Perry	WR	5-11	165	5	California, Pa.
10	Kiel, Blair	QB	6-0	203	7	Notre Dame
	Kinchen, Brian	TE	6-2	232	4	Louisiana State
38	Labbe, Rico	S	6-0	210	1	Boston College
	Larson, Kurt	LB	6-4	244	3	Michigan State
22	Lee, Mark	CB	6-0	195	12	Washington
7	Majkowski, Don	QB	6-2	208	5	Virginia
77	Mandarich, Tony	T	6-5	295	3	Michigan State
	Mitchell, Roland	CB	5-11	180	4	Texas Tech
57	Moran, Rich	G	6-2	283	7	San Diego State
37	Murphy, Mark	S	6-2	203	10	West Liberty
79	Nelson, Bob	NT	6-4	275	5	Miami
91	Noble, Brian	LB	6-4	243	7	Arizona State
96	Patterson, Shawn	DE	6-4	270	4	Arizona State
95	Paup, Bryce	LB	6-5	245	2	Northern Iowa
28	Pitts, Ron	CB	5-10	183	6	UCLA
85	Query, Jeff	WR-PR	6-0	167	3	Millikin
	Rice, Allen	RB	5-10	206	8	Baylor
75	Ruettgers, Ken	T	6-5	288	7	Southern California
84	Sharpe, Sterling	WR	6-0	202	4	South Carolina
	Sikahema, Vai	RB-KR	5-9	184	6	Brigham Young
54	Stephen, Scott	LB	6-2	243	5	Arizona State
39	Thompson, Darrell	RB	6-0	215	2	Minnesota
	Tomczak, Mike	QB	6-1	198	7	Ohio State
70	Uecker, Keith	G-T	6-5	295	8	Auburn
87	Weathers, Clarence	WR	5-9	182	9	Delaware State
52	Weddington, Mike	LB	6-4	243	6	Oklahoma
86	West, Ed	TE	6-1	240	8	Auburn
88	Wilson, Charles	WR-KR	5-9	174	2	Memphis State
68	Winter, Blaise	DE	6-4	282	7	Syracuse
29	Woods, Jerry	S	5-8	193	2	Northern Michigan
33	Woodside, Keith	RB	6-0	200	4	Texas A&M
46	Workman, Vince	RB-KR	5-10	195	3	Ohio State

1991 SCHEDULE OF GAMES

September	
1 PHILADELPHIA	12:00
8 at Detroit	1:00
15 TAMPA BAY	12:00
22 at Miami	1:00
29 at Los Angeles Rams	1:00
October	
6 DALLAS at Milwaukee	12:00
13 Open Date	
17 CHICAGO (Thurs. night)	6:30
27 at Tampa Bay	1:00
November	
3 at New York Jets	1:00
10 BUFFALO at Milwaukee	12:00
17 MINNESOTA	12:00
24 INDIANAPOLIS at Milwaukee	12:00
December	
1 at Atlanta	1:00
8 at Chicago	12:00
15 DETROIT	12:00
21 at Minnesota (Sat.)	3:00

1991 Draft

Round	Name	Pos.	Ht.	Wt.	College
1.	Clark, Vinnie	CB	5-11	189	Ohio State
2.	Tuaolo, Esera	NT	6-2	278	Oregon State
3.	Davey, Don	DE	6-3	269	Wisconsin
3.	Webb, Chuck	RB	5-9	209	Tennessee
5.	Fite, Jeff	P	6-0	206	Memphis State
6.	Dean, Walter	RB	5-9	211	Grambling
6.	Garten, Joe	C	6-2	286	Colorado
7.	Blevins, Frank	LB	6-4	225	Oklahoma
7.	Burnette, Reggie	LB	6-1	235	Houston
8.	Walker, Johnny	WR	5-11	188	Texas
9.	Witkowski, Dean	LB	6-1	238	North Dakota
10.	Porter, Rapier	TE	6-3	272	Arkansas-Pine Bluff
11.	Wierenga, J.J.	DE	6-3	273	Central Michigan
12.	Collins, Linzy	WR	6-0	183	Missouri

1990 first-round draftee Tony Bennett will continue to hone his pass-rushing skills.

If Davey adds effervescence, second-round draftee nose tackle Esera Tuaolo brings agility and speed to a unit which has not shown any level of domination. They may just stimulate the best out of starters Matt Brock and Robert Brown, who flank Bob Nelson. The beneficial effects could be felt also by pass rusher Shawn Patterson, who may be the most talented defensive lineman on the roster but has yet to bring his skills into effective focus.

The Packers seem to have no worries over placekicker Chris Jacke, but punter Don Bracken will have to fend off a serious challenge by fifth-round draftee Jeff Fite. In another aspect of special teams play, returning kicks, Green Bay can expect consistent quality from reserve wide receiver Charles Wilson on kickoffs and Query, who handles the punts.

MINNESOTA VIKINGS

Address 9520 Viking Drive, Eden Prairie, Minnesota 55344.
Stadium Hubert H. Humphrey Metrodome, Minneapolis.
Capacity 63,000 *Playing Surface* AstroTurf.
Team Colours Purple, Gold, and White.
Head Coach Jerry Burns – 6th year.
Championships Division 1970,'71,'73,'74,'75,'76, '77,'78,'80,'89; Conference 1973,'74,'76; NFL 1969.
History NFL 1961-69, NFC 1970-

It is one of the unsolved puzzles that the 1990 Minnesota Vikings logged the fourth-worst record in their history. The loss of starting quarterback Wade Wilson was a contributory factor but of equal significance was the absence of defensive tackle Keith Millard, to whom the defense looks for the momentum of its thrust. Both players will be back in 1991 – and so should the Vikings.

Critics point to the 1989 Herschel Walker trade as having hurt the club but, while he has not yet repaid the high cost, last year he rushed for 770 yards at an average of 4.2, caught 35 passes for 315 yards and scored nine touchdowns. In addition, he returned 44 kickoffs for 966 yards. Interestingly, the second-most productive rusher, Rick Fenney, averaged 4.3 yards. Those observations suggest that greater use of the rushing game might bring rewards. On the other hand, the Vikings can point to a group of pass receivers which includes two-time Pro Bowler Anthony Carter, Hassan Jones, an outstanding backup in Cris Carter and tight end Steve Jordan, whose sequence of consecutive Pro Bowl selections is current and stretches back five years. There was no obvious reason for the Vikings to seek further depth but they did, selecting the huge target offered by wide receiver Jake Reed.

Standing in for the injured Wilson, Rich Gannon grew in stature as he adjusted to the tempo. Furthermore, the commitment of this fiery young man, who is prepared to stand up and be counted for those things which he holds dear, is unquestioned. But the steadiness and polish of Wilson are necessary for the most efficient use of the talent and, given his return, the Vikings once more will flourish. Certainly, Minnesota has the key ingredient, an established offensive line. Left tackle Gary Zimmerman has been to three Pro Bowls, left guard Randall McDaniel to two, Kirk Lowdermilk has settled down to become one of the better centers in the league and, in the right side combination of Tim Irwin and Todd Kalis, there is a good blend of experience and youthful promise.

Defensively, Minnesota puts on a frightening show, with each member of the four-man line possessing the speed and penetration to sack the quarterback. The prospect is that Millard will return to team up with defensive left tackle Henry Thomas, operating inside a pair of predatory defensive ends, Chris Doleman and Al Noga. The depth, consisting of Ken Clarke, Thomas Strauthers and Mike Hammerstein, is experienced, if unexciting.

With the retirement of perennial leading tackler Scott Studwell, there was a void at middle linebacker, but his heir apparent, Ray Berry, has started in the past and may be ready to step up permanently. As insurance, Greg Manusky, who started eight games for the Redskins last year, was signed as a Plan-B free agent. On the outsides, Mark Dusbabek has settled in as a starter after his move from Houston as a 1989 Plan-B free agent, while Mike Merriweather has proved his worth many times, most recently as the Vikings' leader in tackles (153) and fumble recoveries (four). Third-round draftee Carlos Jenkins, an outside specialist, comes with a reputation for rushing the passer.

The secondary possesses really fine talent, gathered around the All-Pro excellence of strong safety Joey Browner, who last year ranked second in the club for tackles, had three sacks and intercepted seven passes. Responding to the lead offered by Browner, Darrell Fullington has secured the free safety position, while right cornerback Reggie Rutland has taken well to the responsibility of seniority. Left cornerback Carl Lee has been to the last three Pro Bowls. Audrey McMillian represents the best of the modest depth at cornerback but, for the safety spots, there's an abundance of high-class experience in Ken Stills and Plan-B signings Solomon Wilcots and Felix Wright.

Placekicker Fuad Reveiz likes the Metrodome – his only field goal failure since joining the club halfway through the 1990 campaign was a 40-yarder. And any club would be satisfied with punter Harry Newsome's gross average of 42.3 yards.

LEFT: Outside linebacker Mike Merriweather, who was picked as NFC Player of the Week against Chicago in November, is the catalyst in the Vikings' defense.

1991 SCHEDULE OF GAMES

September		
1	at Chicago	3:00
8	at Atlanta	1:00
15	SAN FRANCISCO	12:00
22	at New Orleans	12:00
29	DENVER (Sun. night)	7:00
October		
6	at Detroit	1:00
13	PHOENIX	12:00
20	at New England	1:00
27	at Phoenix	1:00
November		
3	TAMPA BAY	12:00
11	CHICAGO (Mon.)	8:00
17	at Green Bay	12:00
24	DETROIT	12:00
December		
1	Open Date	
8	at Tampa Bay (Sun. night)	8:00
15	LOS ANGELES RAMS	12:00
22	GREEN BAY	3:00

1991 Draft

Round	Name	Pos.	Ht.	Wt.	College
3.	Jenkins, Carlos	LB	6-3	222	Michigan State
3.	Reed, Jake	WR	6-2	215	Grambling
4.	Baldwin, Randy	RB	5-10	216	Mississippi
5.	Thome, Chris	C	6-4	278	Minnesota
6.	Scott, Todd	CB	5-10	207	Southwestern Louisiana
7.	Reagan, Scotty	DT	6-4	278	Humboldt State
7.	Welborne, Tripp	S	6-0	204	Michigan
8.	Johnson, Reggie	DE	6-2	239	Arizona
9.	Hudson, Gerald	RB	5-8	198	Oklahoma State
10.	Pierce, Brady	T	6-6	294	Wisconsin
11.	Caesar, Ivan	LB	6-1	235	Boston College
12.	Hughes, Darren	WR	5-10	163	Carson-Newman

VETERAN ROSTER

No.	Name	Pos.	Ht.	Wt.	NFL Year	College
21	Allen, Terry	RB	5-10	210	1	Clemson
46	Anderson, Alfred	RB	6-1	214	8	Baylor
50	Berry, Ray	LB	6-2	226	5	Baylor
47	Browner, Joey	S	6-2	228	9	Southern California
81	Carter, Anthony	WR	5-11	178	7	Michigan
80	Carter, Cris	WR	6-3	200	5	Ohio State
71	Clarke, Ken	DT	6-2	280	14	Syracuse
56	Doleman, Chris	DE	6-5	263	7	Pittsburgh
42	Dozier, D.J.	RB	6-0	205	5	Penn State
59	Dusbabek, Mark	LB	6-3	230	3	Minnesota
24	Eilers, Pat	S	5-11	195	2	Notre Dame
31	Fenney, Rick	RB	6-1	231	5	Washington
62	Foote, Chris	C	6-4	266	9	Southern California
29	Fullington, Darrell	S	6-1	195	4	Miami
16	Gannon, Rich	QB	6-3	202	5	Delaware
80	Gustafson, Jim	WR	6-1	174	5	St. Thomas, Minnesota
74	Habib, Brian	T	6-7	288	3	Washington
	Hammerstein, Mike	DE	6-4	272	5	Michigan
25	Hampton, Alonzo	CB	5-10	191	2	Pittsburgh
72	Huffman, David	G	6-6	278	10	Notre Dame
4	Igwebuike, Donald	K	5-9	184	7	Clemson
76	Irwin, Tim	T	6-7	295	11	Tennessee
84	Jones, Hassan	WR	6-0	195	6	Florida State
82	Jones, Mike	TE	6-3	255	2	Texas A&M
83	Jordan, Steve	TE	6-4	240	10	Brown
69	Kalis, Todd	G	6-5	286	4	Arizona State
39	Lee, Carl	CB	6-0	184	9	Marshall
87	Lewis, Leo	WR	5-8	166	11	Missouri
63	Lowdermilk, Kirk	C	6-3	263	7	Ohio State
64	McDaniel, Randall	G	6-3	270	4	Arizona State
26	McMillian, Audrey	CB	6-0	189	6	Houston
	Manusky, Greg	LB	6-1	242	4	Colgate
57	Merriweather, Mike	LB	6-2	222	9	Pacific
75	Millard, Keith	DT	6-5	263	7	Washington State
	Mims, Carl	CB	5-10	180	1	Sam Houston State
	Morris, Jamie	RB	5-7	188	4	Michigan
18	Newsome, Harry	P	6-0	188	7	Wake Forest
99	Noga, Al	DE	6-1	248	4	Hawaii
85	Novoselsky, Brent	TE	6-2	238	4	Pennsylvania
	Pruitt, James	WR	6-3	201	6	Cal State-Fullerton
93	Randle, John	DE	6-1	248	2	Texas A&I
7	Reveiz, Fuad	K	5-11	216	7	Tennessee
48	Rutland, Reggie	CB	6-1	192	5	Georgia Tech
12	Salisbury, Sean	QB	6-5	208	4	Southern California
60	Schreiber, Adam	C-G	6-4	288	8	Texas
30	Smith, Cedric	RB	5-10	223	2	Florida
27	Stills, Ken	S	5-10	186	7	Wisconsin
94	Strauthers, Thomas	DE	6-4	262	8	Jackson State
97	Thomas, Henry	DT	6-2	268	5	Louisiana State
	Vanderbeek, Matt	LB	6-3	258	2	Michigan State
34	Walker, Herschel	RB	6-1	225	6	Georgia
	Walker, Wayne	WR	5-8	162	2	Texas Tech
92	Westbrooks, David	DT	6-4	252	1	Howard
	Wilcots, Solomon	S	5-11	195	5	Colorado
58	Williams, Jimmy	LB	6-3	225	10	Nebraska
11	Wilson, Wade	QB	6-3	210	11	East Texas State
73	Wolfley, Craig	G	6-1	277	12	Syracuse
	Wright, Felix	S	6-2	195	7	Drake
65	Zimmerman, Gary	T	6-6	283	6	Oregon

TAMPA BAY BUCCANEERS

Address One Buccaneer Place, Tampa, Florida 33607.
Stadium Tampa Stadium, Tampa. *Capacity* 74,315 *Playing Surface* Grass.
Team Colours Florida Orange, White, and Red.
Head Coach Richard Williamson – 1st year.
Championships Division 1979,'81.
History AFC 1976, NFC 1977-

Progress for the Buccaneers has been slow as, painstakingly, the pieces have been assembled. They took further steps in the draft, notably by securing the right tackle position with the selection of Charles McRae. They may be ready to make the final leap.

Steady, rather than spectacular, has been the development of quarterback Vinny Testaverde, but always he has improved from year to year and, in 1990, set personal highs with his passer rating of 75.6 and a completion percentage of 55.6 on the way to logging the NFC's best average of 7.72 yards per attempt. By the beginning of the 1991 campaign, the big quarterback, upon whom so much rests, should be ready to light the fuse. As reserve strength of the immediate kind, it is reassuring that former Colts starter Chris Chandler could run the offense with all the efficiency, if not the potential explosiveness, of Testaverde. At wide receiver, starters Mark Carrier and Bruce Hill have shown themselves quite capable of tearing opponents apart, and it is an interesting development that, at the halfway stage last year, tight end Ron Hall was setting a hot pace with his contributions. Again, tailback Gary Anderson is a fine target, slipping out of the backfield. There was a problem with the depth out wide but this may have been eased by the drafting of Florida State's Lawrence Dawsey.

Anderson's main threat is as a rusher and he has every prospect of gaining 1,000 or more yards. Last year, he was on course before being slowed by injuries over the final weeks. His new backup will be Reggie Cobb, who offers a great threat as a runner, and it is because of this and the need for a pure blocker that Cobb has switched from playing fullback. Going into camp, the front runners for the vacancy are Bruce Perkins, Plan-B signing Jamie Lawson and draftee Robert Wilson.

The arrival of McRae to join left tackle Paul Gruber could give Tampa Bay the best pairing in the NFL and is another reason for optimism over Testaverde's prospects. Tom McHale and Ian Beckles man the guard spots well enough, while Randy Grimes is a rock at center. Tony Mayberry is seen as the eventual successor to Grimes.

Excellent drafting, coupled with the refusal of veterans to give way, meant that the Buccaneers were too well-off at linebacker. Even by moving Keith McCants up to defensive end, as is planned, there still would have been a log jam. Accordingly, outside linebacker Winston Moss was traded to the Raiders for draft picks. Ervin Randle and Eugene Marve compete to start at what will be middle linebacker if the Bucs do make the adjustment to a 4-3 defense. Kevin Murphy is expected to start at the right outside position with potential superstar Broderick Thomas on the left.

McCants has developed the size to have a major impact at defensive end in a line completed by stalwart defensive left end Reuben Davis and, almost certainly, defensive tackles Tim Newton and Jim Skow. There was not much help in reserve before the club signed former Cleveland lineman Marlon Jones as a Plan-B free agent.

These are exciting days for a defensive secondary which features right cornerback Wayne Haddix, who, in 1990, set the league alight and earned a Pro Bowl selection by returning three of his seven interceptions for touchdowns. Left cornerback Ricky Reynolds has become a seasoned pro while, in the safety spots, Harry Hamilton and Mark Robinson bear the brunt of the tackling without flinching. With 19 interceptions for big return yardage last year, and promising more of the same, the foursome is a valuable supplement to the offense.

Out of the blue, Steve Christie emerged to give the Buccaneers a credible option when their drives stalled within sensible field goal range. He'll be chasing his own club records in 1991. Punter Mark Royals made a much smaller impact but there are no obvious challengers for his job.

LEFT: Cornerback Wayne Haddix, a 1990 free-agent signing, emerged to lead the Bucs with seven interceptions for 231 return yards and three touchdowns. A Division II All-America, Haddix went undrafted and was discarded after signing for the Giants as a free agent.

1991 Draft

Round	Name	Pos.	Ht.	Wt.	College
1.	McRae, Charles	T	6-6	290	Tennessee
3.	Dawsey, Lawrence	WR	6-0	192	Florida State
3.	Wilson, Robert	RB	5-11	240	Texas A&M
4.	Covington, Tony	CB	5-10	190	Virginia
5.	Bagsby, Terry	LB	6-0	235	East Texas State
5.	Ryan, Tim	G	6-2	275	Notre Dame
6.	Hall, Rhett	DT	6-2	258	California
7.	Tiggle, Calvin	LB	6-0	235	Georgia Tech
8.	Carter, Marty	S	6-1	200	Middle Tennessee State
9.	Taylor, Treamelle	WR	5-8	180	Nevada-Reno
10.	O'Hara, Pat	QB	6-2	200	Southern California
10.	Hickson, Hyland	RB	5-8	217	Michigan State
11.	Sunvold, Mike	DT	6-3	269	Minnesota
12.	Chamblee, Al	LB	6-1	239	Virginia Tech

VETERAN ROSTER

No.	Name	Pos.	Ht.	Wt.	NFL Year	College
40	Anderson, Gary	RB	6-1	190	6	Arkansas
89	Anderson, Jesse	TE	6-2	245	2	Mississippi State
56	Anno, Sam	LB	6-2	235	5	Southern California
75	Bax, Carl	G	6-4	290	3	Missouri
62	Beckles, Ian	G	6-1	295	2	Indiana
69	Bruhin, John	G	6-3	285	4	Tennessee
7	Carlson, Jeff	QB	6-3	215	2	Weber State
88	Carrier, Mark	WR	6-0	185	5	Nicholls State
17	Chandler, Chris	QB	6-4	220	4	Washington
2	Christie, Steve	K	6-0	185	2	William & Mary
33	Cobb, Reggie	RB-KR	6-0	225	2	Tennessee
79	Davis, Reuben	DE	6-4	285	4	North Carolina
76	Dill, Scott	G	6-5	285	4	Memphis State
87	Drewrey, Willie	WR-PR	5-7	170	7	West Virginia
42	Everett, Eric	CB	5-10	170	4	Texas Tech
81	Ford, Chris	WR	6-1	185	2	Lamar
37	Frizzell, William	DB	6-3	206	8	North Carolina Central
60	Grimes, Randy	C	6-4	275	9	Baylor
74	Gruber, Paul	T	6-5	290	4	Wisconsin
45	Haddix, Wayne	CB	6-1	205	4	Liberty
82	Hall, Ron	TE	6-4	245	5	Hawaii
39	Hamilton, Harry	S	6-0	195	8	Penn State
26	Harvey, John	RB	5-11	185	2	Texas-El Paso
84	Hill, Bruce	WR	6-0	180	5	Arizona State
97	Jones, Marlon	DE	6-4	270	3	Central State, Ohio
38	Lawson, Jamie	RB	5-10	240	3	Nicholls State
52	McCants, Keith	LB	6-3	255	2	Alabama
73	McHale, Tom	G	6-4	280	5	Cornell
99	Marve, Eugene	LB	6-2	240	10	Saginaw Valley State
61	Mayberry, Tony	C	6-4	285	2	Wake Forest
59	Murphy, Kevin	LB	6-2	235	6	Oklahoma
96	Newton, Tim	NT	6-0	275	7	Florida
83	Peebles, Danny	WR	5-11	180	3	North Carolina State
32	Perkins, Bruce	RB	6-2	230	2	Arizona State
54	Randle, Ervin	LB	6-1	250	7	Baylor
29	Reynolds, Ricky	CB	5-11	190	5	Washington State
31	Rice, Rodney	CB	5-8	180	3	Brigham Young
90	Robertson, Derrell	DE	6-7	245	1	Mississippi State
30	Robinson, Mark	S	5-11	200	8	Penn State
3	Royals, Mark	P	6-5	215	2	Appalachian State
71	Skow, Jim	DE	6-3	250	6	Nebraska
72	Taylor, Rob	T	6-6	290	6	Northwestern
14	Testaverde, Vinny	QB	6-5	215	5	Miami
51	Thomas, Broderick	LB	6-4	245	3	Nebraska

1991 SCHEDULE OF GAMES

September		
1	at New York Jets	1:00
8	CHICAGO	1:00
15	at Green Bay	12:00
22	BUFFALO	4:00
29	at Detroit	1:00
October		
6	PHILADELPHIA	1:00
13	Open Date	
20	at New Orleans	12:00
27	GREEN BAY	1:00
November		
3	at Minnesota	12:00
10	DETROIT	1:00
17	at Atlanta	1:00
24	NEW YORK GIANTS	1:00
December		
1	at Miami	1:00
8	MINNESOTA (Sun. night)	8:00
14	at Chicago (Sat.)	11:30
22	INDIANAPOLIS	1:00

ATLANTA FALCONS

Address Suwanee Road at I-85, Suwanee, Georgia 30174.
Stadium Atlanta-Fulton County Stadium. *Capacity* 59,643 *Playing Surface* Grass (PAT).
Team Colours Red, Black, White, and Silver.
Head Coach Jerry Glanville – 2nd year; 7th NFL.
Championships Division 1980.
History NFL 1966-69, NFC 1970-

As was widely anticipated, new head coach Jerry Glanville had an enthusing effect on the Falcons, and the apparent modesty of their record should be seen in the context that they play in the only division which has sent two teams to the playoffs in each of the last eight years. This will be their final campaign in Fulton County Stadium before moving to the Georgia Dome. You just wonder if they could depart in style.

Atlanta still have one or two areas of uncertainty, but one of those is not the offensive line, where All-Pros Chris Hinton and Bill Fralic ensure a right-side dominance and former Pro Bowler Mike Kenn continues to give value for money at left tackle. Jamie Dukes has become the unchallenged starting center, and left guard Houston Hoover holds an edge over John Scully. It is a line which opens up enough holes for the powerful Mike Rozier, who may not have breakaway speed but can rattle off four-yard gains all day. The pace and quickness was supposed to arrive with top draftee Steve Broussard and, on occasions, that's what he produced. But Glanville would like to see a greater level of consistency from the power-packed Broussard, not least to hold opposing defensive backs in run-defense positions and give more freedom to one of the most exciting wide receivers in the game.

That player, Andre Rison, tore through his first campaign with the team, gaining 1,208 yards at an average of 14.7 and scoring ten touchdowns. It was good enough to earn him a Pro Bowl starting spot. Michael Haynes is a second starter. Shawn Collins and Floyd Dixon used their opportunities well, but there seems little doubt that first-round draftee Mike Pritchard will be given every chance to make an instant name for himself. The Falcons ask nothing more of their tight ends than to block efficiently and, in Gary Wilkins, they have a tough customer for that responsibility.

It was one of the disappointing aspects of last season that starting quarterback Chris Miller suffered a broken collar-bone in early December when he was going well. A genuine young man who has made solid progress, Miller returns for what promises to be a season of opportunity. There is no immediate threat to Miller, but draftee Brett Favre was too good not to pick in the second round.

Defensively, Atlanta is a mix of excellence and something less than that. Against the run, they ranked third in the NFL. At the heart of things, rookie nose tackle Tory Epps did well, absorbing the initial charges before the finest of reinforcement arrived in the form of inside linebacker Jessie Tuggle, who became the first Falcon to log more than 200 tackles in a season since the great Buddy Curry. Tuggle's inside partner, John Rade, is another of the hard-nosed variety. In contrast, the pass rush is modest, with neither of defensive ends Mike Gann and Tim Green striking terror. They have not been helped by the slow progress of outside linebacker Aundray Bruce, who was the first pick overall in the 1988 draft. On the other hand, 1990 rookie outside linebacker Darion Conner did look good and the other starter, Robert Lyles, is a solid veteran.

Excitement of the electric kind is possible whenever Deion Sanders comes anywhere near the ball, either as a dual-purpose kick returner or as the starting right cornerback. There is every prospect of intense competition for the left cornerback position, with Plan-B free agent Tim McKyer and top draftee Bruce Pickens hard on the heels of the incumbent, 11th-year veteran Bobby Butler. Safeties Brian Jordan and Scott Case filled second and third places respectively on the team tackle list and have developed well as a pairing.

It would appear that former Denver and Minnesota placekicker Rich Karlis will take over from departed Plan-B free agent Greg Davis, but there is continuity in the punting department with the handy Scott Fulhage setting up for his third campaign with the Falcons.

RIGHT: Wide receiver Andre Rison thrived in Atlanta, earning his first Pro Bowl selection.

1991 SCHEDULE OF GAMES

September		
1	at Kansas City	12:00
8	MINNESOTA	1:00
15	at San Diego	1:00
22	LOS ANGELES RAIDERS	1:00
29	NEW ORLEANS	1:00
October		
6	Open Date	
13	SAN FRANCISCO	1:00
20	at Phoenix	1:00
27	LOS ANGELES RAMS	1:00
November		
3	at San Francisco	1:00
10	at Washington	1:00
17	TAMPA BAY	1:00
24	at New Orleans (Sun. night)	7:00
December		
1	GREEN BAY	1:00
8	at Los Angeles Rams	1:00
15	SEATTLE	1:00
22	at Dallas	12:00

1991 Draft

Round	Name	Pos.	Ht.	Wt.	College
1.	Pickens, Bruce	CB	5-9	193	Nebraska
1.	Pritchard, Mike	WR	5-9	182	Colorado
2.	Favre, Brett	QB	6-2	220	Southern Mississippi
4.	Gardner, Moe	DT	6-1	254	Illinois
5.	Goode, James	LB	6-2	246	Oklahoma
6.	Pegram, Erric	RB	5-9	188	North Texas State
7.	Mitchell, Brian	CB	5-9	164	Brigham Young
7.	Tucker, Mark	C-G	6-2	279	Southern California
8.	Austin, Randy	TE	6-2	245	UCLA
9.	Logan, Ernie	DE	6-3	272	East Carolina
10.	Sutton, Walter	WR	5-9	180	Southwest Minnesota
10.	Lucas, Pete	T	6-3	300	Stevens Point, Wis.
11.	Sims, Joe	NT	6-3	301	Nebraska
12.	Christian, Bob	RB	5-10	217	Northwestern

VETERAN ROSTER

No.	Name	Pos.	Ht.	Wt.	NFL Year	College
72	Barnett, Oliver	DE	6-3	288	2	Kentucky
65	Bingham, Guy	C	6-3	260	12	Montana
34	Broussard, Steve	RB	5-7	201	2	Washington State
93	Bruce, Aundray	LB	6-5	248	4	Auburn
77	Bryan, Rick	DE	6-4	265	8	Oklahoma
23	Butler, Bobby	CB	5-11	175	11	Florida State
10	Campbell, Scott	QB	6-0	195	6	Purdue
25	Case, Scott	S	6-0	188	8	Oklahoma
75	Casillas, Tony	NT	6-3	280	6	Oklahoma
85	Collins, Shawn	WR	6-2	207	3	Northern Arizona
56	Conner, Darion	LB	6-2	256	2	Jackson State
86	Dixon, Floyd	WR	5-9	170	6	Stephen F. Austin
	Donaldson, Jeff	S	6-0	190	8	Colorado
64	Dukes, Jamie	C	6-1	285	6	Florida State
	Eaton, Tracey	S	6-1	191	4	Portland State
74	Epps, Tory	NT	6-0	280	2	Memphis State
27	Evers, William	CB	5-10	175	1	Florida A&M
79	Fralic, Bill	G	6-5	280	7	Pittsburgh
17	Fulhage, Scott	P	5-10	193	5	Kansas State
76	Gann, Mike	DE	6-5	270	7	Notre Dame
99	Green, Tim	DE	6-2	245	6	Syracuse
81	Haynes, Michael	WR	6-0	180	4	Northern Arizona
71	Hinton, Chris	T	6-4	300	9	Northwestern
69	Hoover, Houston	G	6-2	290	4	Jackson State
68	Hunter, John	T	6-8	296	3	Brigham Young
43	Johnson, Tracy	RB	6-0	230	3	Clemson
38	Jones, Keith	RB	6-1	210	3	Illinois
40	Jordan, Brian	S	5-11	202	3	Richmond
	Karlis, Rich	K	6-0	180	10	Cincinnati
78	Kenn, Mike	T	6-7	277	14	Michigan
	Le Bel, Harper	TE	6-4	251	3	Colorado State
54	Lyles, Robert	LB	6-1	230	8	Texas Christian
	McKyer, Tim	CB	6-1	177	6	Texas-Arlington
12	Miller, Chris	QB	6-2	200	5	Oregon
	Phillips, Jason	WR	5-7	168	3	Houston
24	Pringle, Mike	RB	5-8	186	2	Cal State-Fullerton
59	Rade, John	LB	6-1	240	9	Boise State
70	Redding, Reggie	T	6-3	281	1	Cal State-Fullerton
95	Reid, Michael	LB	6-2	235	5	Wisconsin
14	Renfroe, Gilbert	QB	6-1	195	1	Tennessee State
80	Rison, Andre	WR	6-0	191	3	Michigan State
	Roland, Benji	NT	6-2	260	2	Auburn
30	Rozier, Mike	RB	5-10	213	7	Nebraska
55	Ruether, Mike	C	6-4	275	6	Texas
91	Salum, Donnie	LB	6-1	235	1	Arizona
21	Sanders, Deion	CB-KR	6-0	187	3	Florida State
61	Scully, John	G	6-6	270	10	Notre Dame
37	Shelley, Elbert	S	5-11	180	5	Arkansas State
83	Simien, Kevin	WR	6-4	202	1	Fort Hays State
89	Thomas, George	WR	5-9	169	3	Nevada-Las Vegas
52	Tippins, Ken	LB	6-1	230	3	Middle Tennessee State
58	Tuggle, Jessie	LB	5-11	230	5	Valdosta State
87	Wilkins, Gary	TE	6-2	235	4	Georgia Tech
	Worthen, Naz	WR-KR	5-8	177	3	North Carolina State

LOS ANGELES RAMS

Address 2327 West Lincoln Avenue, Anaheim, California 92801.
Stadium Anaheim Stadium, Anaheim.
Capacity 69,008 *Playing Surface* Grass.
Team Colours Royal Blue, Gold, and White.
Head Coach John Robinson – 9th year.
Championships Division 1973,'74,'75,'76,'77,'78, '79,'85; Conference 1979; NFL 1945,'51.
History NFL 1937-69, NFC 1970-
(Until 1946, they were known as the Cleveland Rams.)

As usual, the Rams enter the season with an abundance of talent in most areas. But from somewhere, they need to find a knockout punch, be it from an individual or a team effort. Otherwise, this mighty organization may be under pressure to achieve par in what is a difficult division.

It says a lot for the great tradition of Rams offensive lines that, for the first time in five years, the unit sent fewer than three players to the Pro Bowl. There will be changes as the talent is shuffled to accommodate Gerald Perry, who was acquired in a trade with Denver and could start at left tackle, ahead of Irv Pankey. Again, Tom Newberry will shift from left guard to center, challenging Doug Smith and making way for Bern Brostek to offer a bid. Duval Love seems assured of his spot at right guard, with Jackie Slater returning for a 16th NFL year to anchor the line at right tackle. At least, that's what is projected, but a great deal can happen between the start of training camp and opening day.

One thing, the identity of the starting quarterback, is certain, with the high-class Jim Everett resuming ahead of Chuck Long. Everett's starting wide receivers, the fluid Henry Ellard and the speedy Flipper Anderson, will remain intact and there is excellent backup strength in Aaron Cox. But the nature of the passing offense will change with the Plan-B loss of H-back Pete Holohan, who was an important part in the machine. Jim Price will be given the chance to occupy Holohan's spot but the Rams indicate that when they use formations requiring two tight ends, Damone Johnson and Pat Carter will be the likely pairing.

That philosophy has implications for the running backs, where Cleveland Gary has emerged as the primary weapon. Ordinarily, Gary would be operating behind the blocking of fullback Buford McGee, with Robert Delpino a more expressive alternative. Intriguingly, the Rams were prepared to trade away halfback Gaston Green, a former first-round pick of great potential. And one is led to speculate that Marcus Dupree, whose career was thought to be over because of a knee injury, has made better progress than is widely realized.

It has surprised a few observers that the Rams will adopt a 4-3 alignment in 1991. Premier pass rushing outside linebacker Kevin Greene, whose sack total of 46 over the last three seasons is the best in the NFL, will move up to start at defensive right end. Bill Hawkins, a former first-round draftee whose progress has been slowed by injuries, will be tried at defensive left end in competition with Brian Smith and Plan-B free agent signings Karl Wilson and Gerald Robinson. Doug Reed and Alvin Wright are ahead of Mike Piel to start at defensive tackle.

Injuries have been felt severely at linebacker, but there is every prospect that Frank Stams will be fit to play in the middle, with Mike Wilcher on the left and, probably, Fred Strickland rotating with Brett Faryniarz on the right. Second-round draftee Roman Phifer arrives with a reputation for heavy-duty tackling. Only marginally less damaging were the injuries felt in the defensive secondary, but again there is real optimism that All-Pro cornerback Jerry Gray will resume at full speed, joined by top draftee Todd Lyght. This pairing could secure the outside lanes at a stroke. At strong safety, Michael Stewart has the edge over Anthony Newman, and the hope is that Pat Terrell will step into the free safety spot vacated by the loss of Plan-B free agent Vince Newsome.

There seems little doubt that Tony Zendejas, the former Houston placekicker who was signed as a Plan-B free agent, will take over from the departed Mike Lansford, who was lost via the same system. However, for the punting duties, former Pro Bowler Dale Hatcher will face off with incumbent Keith English in a battle which might go the distance.

LEFT: Wide receiver Henry Ellard gives the Rams high-class reliability.

1991 Draft

Round	Name	Pos.	Ht.	Wt.	College
1.	Lyght, Todd	CB	6-0	186	Notre Dame
2.	Phifer, Roman	LB	6-1	220	UCLA
4.	Bailey, Robert	CB	5-9	170	Miami
5.	Young, Robert	DE	6-6	267	Mississippi State
6.	Fort, Neal	T	6-5	279	Brigham Young
7.	Shelton, Tyrone	RB	5-10	215	William and Mary
8.	Tyrance, Pat	LB	6-1	240	Nebraska
9.	Fields, Jeff	NT	6-2	294	Arkansas State
11.	Crews, Terry	LB	6-2	241	Western Michigan
12.	Pahukoa, Jeff	T	6-2	301	Washington
12.	Thompson, Ernie	RB	6-0	240	Indiana

VETERAN ROSTER

No.	Name	Pos.	Ht.	Wt.	NFL Year	College
83	Anderson, Willie	WR	6-0	175	4	UCLA
	Bailey, Stacey	WR	6-1	163	10	San Jose State
42	Berry, Latin	CB	5-10	196	2	Oregon
57	Bethune, George	LB	6-4	240	3	Alabama
61	Brostek, Bern	C	6-3	300	2	Washington
59	Butcher, Paul	LB	6-0	230	5	Wayne State
88	Carter, Pat	TE	6-4	250	4	Florida State
84	Cox, Aaron	WR	5-10	178	4	Arizona State
72	Cox, Robert	T	6-5	285	6	UCLA
39	Delpino, Robert	RB	6-0	205	4	Missouri
34	Dupree, Marcus	RB	6-2	225	2	Southern Mississippi
80	Ellard, Henry	WR	5-11	182	9	Fresno State
8	English, Keith	P	6-3	220	2	Colorado
11	Everett, Jim	QB	6-5	212	6	Purdue
89	Faison, Derrick	WR	6-4	200	2	Howard
51	Faryniarz, Brett	LB	6-3	235	4	San Diego State
43	Gary, Cleveland	RB	6-0	226	3	Miami
25	Gray, Jerry	CB	6-0	185	7	Texas
91	Greene, Kevin	LB	6-3	250	7	Auburn
	Hatcher, Dale	P	6-2	220	6	Clemson
70	Hawkins, Bill	DT	6-6	266	3	Miami
20	Henley, Darryl	CB-PR	5-9	172	3	UCLA
86	Johnson, Damone	TE	6-4	250	6	Cal Poly-SLO
52	Kelm, Larry	LB	6-4	240	5	Texas A&M
	Lilly, Sammy	CB	5-9	175	3	Georgia Tech
16	Long, Chuck	QB	6-4	221	6	Iowa
67	Love, Duval	G	6-3	287	7	UCLA
24	McGee, Buford	RB	6-0	210	8	Mississippi
71	Milinichik, Joe	G	6-5	275	5	North Carolina State
66	Newberry, Tom	G	6-2	285	6	Wisconsin-LaCrosse
26	Newman, Anthony	S	6-0	199	4	Oregon
	Pagel, Mike	QB	6-2	220	10	Arizona State
75	Pankey, Irv	T	6-5	295	12	Penn State
	Perry, Gerald	T	6-6	305	4	Southern
95	Piel, Mike	DT	6-4	263	3	Illinois
	Price, Jim	H-B	6-4	247	1	Stanford
93	Reed, Doug	DT	6-3	265	8	San Diego State
	Robinson, Gerald	DE	6-3	262	4	Auburn
	Sanders, Glenell	LB	6-0	224	2	Louisiana Tech
78	Slater, Jackie	T	6-4	287	16	Jackson State
96	Smith, Brian	DT	6-6	242	3	Auburn
56	Smith, Doug	C	6-3	272	14	Bowling Green
50	Stams, Frank	LB	6-2	240	3	Notre Dame
23	Stewart, Michael	S	6-0	195	5	Fresno State
53	Strickland, Fred	LB	6-2	250	4	Purdue
	Tatupu, Mosi	RB	6-0	227	14	Southern California
37	Terrell, Pat	S	6-0	195	2	Notre Dame
	Thomas, Rodney	CB	5-10	190	4	Brigham Young
54	Wilcher, Mike	LB	6-3	245	9	North Carolina
	Wilson, Karl	DE	6-4	275	5	Louisiana State
99	Wright, Alvin	NT	6-2	285	6	Jacksonville State
	Zendejas, Tony	K	5-8	165	7	Nevada-Reno

1991 SCHEDULE OF GAMES

Date	Opponent	Time
September		
1	PHOENIX	1:00
8	at New York Giants	1:00
15	at New Orleans (Sun. night)	7:00
22	at San Francisco	1:00
29	GREEN BAY	1:00
October		
6	Open Date	
13	SAN DIEGO	1:00
20	at Los Angeles Raiders	1:00
27	at Atlanta	1:00
November		
3	NEW ORLEANS	1:00
10	KANSAS CITY	1:00
17	at Detroit	4:00
25	SAN FRANCISCO (Mon.)	6:00
December		
1	WASHINGTON	1:00
8	ATLANTA	1:00
15	at Minnesota	12:00
22	at Seattle (Sun. night)	5:00

NEW ORLEANS SAINTS

Address 1500 Poydras Street, New Orleans, Louisiana 70112.
Stadium Louisiana Superdome, New Orleans. *Capacity* 69,065 *Playing Surface* AstroTurf.
Team Colours Old Gold, Black, and White.
Head Coach Jim Mora – 6th year.
Championships None.
History NFL 1967-69, NFC 1970-

With their restricted number of draft picks and only a few changes resulting from the Plan-B market, the Saints' roster will have a familiar look entering the 1991 campaign. It ought to be good enough for New Orleans to make a run once again at the playoffs.

The front office might point out that its 1991 first-round pick had been used to find a player who already has spent a season settling in with the team. That player, former Dallas quarterback Steve Walsh, started 11 of the 13 games for which he was available. It is too early to assess his value but he has the class background which comes with any former University of Miami starter. Interestingly, there is the possibility that former starter Bobby Hebert, who withdrew into the background after failure to reach contractual agreement, may return. Walsh was not helped by what the Saints regard as 'disappointment' at wide receiver, where Brett Perriman lagged some way behind Eric Martin in productivity. Confirming that view, New Orleans selected wide receiver Wesley Carroll with their top option and he will be given every opportunity to win a starting spot, partnering the highly respected and well-established Martin. Backup Floyd Turner also could be a factor as a third receiver after averaging 18.9 yards and scoring four touchdowns last year. You have to like tight end Hoby Brenner – even his name sounds reliable – who lends his considerable bulk to the business of blocking and can slip into the open to catch a few passes.

Largely unheralded around the league, New Orleans has one of the best offensive lines. Even protecting a young quarterback, with all the uncertainties that ensue, only 20 sacks were given up. Again, the rushing offense averaged four yards per carry. Somebody ought to begin making posters showing tackles Kevin Haverdink and Stan Brock, guards Jim Dombrowski and Steve Trapilo, and center Joel Hilgenberg. For ten games last year, the line missed its favourite running back, Dalton Hilliard, who suffered a knee injury. He returned for the wild card game but it is not clear if he will regain his full powers. Much will depend upon the development of the immensely powerful Craig Heyward, who could be a franchise back, while a return to full confidence by Rueben Mayes could solve every problem.

Again, the Saints were true to their postseason analysis when they sought help, albeit in the fifth round, by selecting cornerback Reginald Jones. They do have an established starting quartet in cornerbacks Robert Massey and Toi Cook, free safety Gene Atkins and strong safety Brett Maxie. However, the feeling is that 1990 second-round draftee Vince Buck will have to be found more playing time, though his future rôle has not been clarified. Certainly, 1990 was a good year for defense, with the unit conceding the fewest points (275) in a Saints 16-game regular season. One reason is the continuing authority at linebacker, where currently the tradition is maintained by outside specialists Rickey Jackson and Pat Swilling, with Sam Mills and Vaughan Johnson on the insides. DeMond Winston, James Williams and Brian Forde await their opportunities.

There was an excellent addition to the pass rush in the form of top draftee defensive end Renaldo Turnbull, who broke Jackson's rookie sack record with nine. Wayne Martin returns from injury to man the defensive left end position, with steady veteran Jim Wilks at right end, meaning that Turnbull can be kept on hold until it is time to go after the passer. Robert Goff, who started ten games at nose tackle, was an excellent bargain in an early September trade with Tampa Bay.

Placekicker Morten Andersen had his critics but Andersen's response was a fifth Pro Bowl selection. He is generally regarded as the best in the NFC. Tommy Barnhardt had a useful season, his second with New Orleans after being signed as a 1989 free agent. Barnhardt averaged 42.7 yards with his punts to rank sixth in the NFL.

LEFT: Specialist pass rusher Renaldo Turnbull set a Saints rookie record with nine sacks.

1991 Draft

Round	Name	Pos.	Ht.	Wt.	College
2.	Carroll, Wesley	WR	6-0	176	Miami
5.	Jones, Reginald	DB	6-0	198	Memphis State
6.	McAfee, Fred	RB	5-10	190	Mississippi College
7.	Haynes, Hayward	G	6-2	290	Florida State
8.	Wainright, Frank	TE	6-2	240	Northern Colorado
9.	Wallace, Anthony	RB	5-11	192	California
11.	Ross, Scott	LB	6-1	237	Southern California
12.	Drabczak, Mark	G	6-4	283	Minnesota

VETERAN ROSTER

No.	Name	Pos.	Ht.	Wt.	NFL Year	College
86	Alphin, Gerald	WR	6-3	220	2	Kansas State
7	Andersen, Morten	K	6-2	221	10	Michigan State
28	Atkins, Gene	S	6-1	200	5	Florida A&M
6	Barnhardt, Tommy	P	6-2	207	5	North Carolina
85	Brenner, Hoby	TE	6-5	245	11	Southern California
67	Brock, Stan	T	6-6	292	12	Colorado
16	Buck, Mike	QB	6-3	227	2	Maine
26	Buck, Vince	CB	6-0	198	2	Central State, Ohio
41	Cook, Toi	CB	5-11	188	5	Stanford
71	Cooper, Richard	T	6-4	285	2	Tennessee
72	Dombrowski, Jim	G	6-5	298	6	Virginia
89	Early, Quinn	WR	6-0	190	4	Iowa
22	Fenerty, Gill	RB	6-0	205	2	Holy Cross
52	Forde, Brian	LB	6-3	225	4	Washington State
11	Fourcade, John	QB	6-1	215	5	Mississippi
91	Goff, Robert	NT	6-3	270	4	Auburn
66	Griffith, Brent	T	6-6	300	1	Minnesota-Duluth
74	Haverdink, Kevin	T	6-5	285	3	Western Michigan
3	Hebert, Bobby	QB	6-4	215	6	Northwestern State, La.
34	Heyward, Craig	RB	5-11	260	4	Pittsburgh
61	Hilgenberg, Joel	C	6-2	252	8	Iowa
87	Hill, Lonzell	WR	5-11	189	5	Washington
21	Hilliard, Dalton	RB	5-8	204	6	Louisiana State
57	Jackson, Rickey	LB	6-2	243	11	Pittsburgh
53	Johnson, Vaughan	LB	6-3	235	6	North Carolina State
23	Jordan, Buford	RB	6-0	223	6	McNeese State
62	Leggett, Brad	C	6-4	270	2	Southern California
24	Mack, Milton	CB	5-11	182	5	Alcorn State
42	Manoa, Tim	RB	6-1	245	4	Penn State
84	Martin, Eric	WR	6-1	207	7	Louisiana State
93	Martin, Wayne	DE	6-5	275	3	Arkansas
40	Massey, Robert	CB	5-10	182	3	North Carolina Central
39	Maxie, Brett	S	6-2	194	7	Texas Southern
36	Mayes, Rueben	RB	5-11	200	5	Washington State
69	Miller, Les	NT	6-7	300	5	Fort Hays State
51	Mills, Sam	LB	5-9	225	6	Montclair State
35	Morse, Bobby	RB-PR	5-10	213	4	Michigan State
15	Newman, Pat	WR	5-11	189	1	Utah State
80	Perriman, Brett	WR	5-9	180	4	Miami
83	Scales, Greg	TE	6-4	253	4	Wake Forest
96	Simmons, Michael	DE	6-4	269	2	Mississippi State
99	Smeenge, Joel	DE	6-5	250	2	Western Michigan
33	Spears, Ernest	S	5-11	192	2	Southern California
56	Swilling, Pat	LB	6-3	242	6	Georgia Tech
37	Thompson, Bennie	S	6-0	200	2	Grambling
82	Tice, John	TE	6-5	249	9	Maryland
65	Trapilo, Steve	G	6-5	281	5	Boston College
97	Turnbull, Renaldo	DE	6-4	248	2	West Virginia
88	Turner, Floyd	WR	5-11	188	3	Northwestern State, La.
4	Walsh, Steve	QB	6-2	200	3	Miami
50	Wheeler, Todd	C	6-4	269	1	Georgia
94	Wilks, Jim	DE-NT	6-5	275	11	San Diego State
90	Williams, James	LB	6-0	230	2	Mississippi State
92	Winston, DeMond	LB	6-2	239	2	Vanderbilt

1991 SCHEDULE OF GAMES

September		
1	SEATTLE	12:00
8	at Kansas City	12:00
15	L.A. RAMS (Sun. night)	7:00
22	MINNESOTA	12:00
29	at Atlanta	1:00
October		
6	Open Date	
13	at Philadelphia	1:00
20	TAMPA BAY	12:00
27	CHICAGO	12:00
November		
3	at Los Angeles Rams	1:00
10	SAN FRANCISCO	12:00
17	at San Diego	1:00
24	ATLANTA (Sun. night)	7:00
December		
1	at San Francisco	1:00
8	at Dallas	12:00
16	L.A. RAIDERS (Mon.)	8:00
22	at Phoenix	2:00

SAN FRANCISCO 49ers

Address 4949 Centennial Boulevard, Santa Clara, California 95054.
Stadium Candlestick Park, San Francisco. *Capacity* 65,729 *Playing Surface* Grass.
Team Colours Forty Niners Gold and Scarlet.
Head Coach George Seifert – 3rd year.
Championships Division 1970,'71,'72,'81,'83,'84, '86,'87,'88,'89,'90; Conference 1981,'84,'88,'89; Super Bowl 1981,'84,'88,'89.
History AAFC 1946-49, NFL 1950-69, NFC 1970-

The 49ers may no longer wear the aura of invincibility, but it is worth remembering that they were just four seconds away from contesting a third consecutive Super Bowl. Less than three minutes earlier, they had been driving for what seemed to be an insurance score when Roger Craig saw the ball stripped away. Craig is no longer with the team and neither is All-Pro free safety Ronnie Lott – they have been signed by the Raiders as Plan-B free agents – but it would be unwise to interpret these events as signalling the first stages in the fall of a dynasty.

It was good news for San Francisco that reserve quarterback Steve Young decided to remain with the club. He may have to soldier on, champing at the bit in the shadow of Joe Montana, but his day will come. For the moment, Montana is peerless, not perhaps in the context of the NFL overall but, certainly, in the offensive system which was designed around him and which, despite the changes in personnel, remains essentially constant in philosophy. Jerry Rice, the NFL's premier wide receiver, returns to continue his assault on the all-time receiving records and, were it not for the presence of Rice, the other starter, John Taylor, might be making his bid for a place in history. Mike Wilson has been released but backup Mike Sherrard is of 49ers quality. The presence of a classy receiver in tight end Brent Jones gives the offense potential scatter-gun effectiveness on every down.

Strangely, the rushing game fell away in 1990, and it would seem that fullback Tom Rathman needs a foil to operate at his best. He will have that in second-year player Dexter Carter, who could be a great one. And while draftee Ricky Watters is not the sort to carve out his own daylight, he certainly can exploit every gap that his linemen can create. In that respect, the 49ers are very comfortable with a well-experienced line which can shove opponents around. The unit will have Bubba Paris and Steve Wallace at tackle, Harris Barton and Guy McIntyre at guard, and Jesse Sapolu at center. The 49ers placed a high value on former Miami Pro Bowl guard Roy Foster, who was signed as a Plan-B free agent.

On defense, there will be changes at inside linebacker and free safety following the Plan-B losses of Matt Millen and Lott. The 49ers signed three linebackers by the same system and used the draft in rounds two and four for further choice. These, together with LeRoy Etienne, will battle for the right to start alongside Keith DeLong. The outside linebackers are Bill Romanowski, who is excellent against the run, and Charles Haley, who is among the NFL's elite as a pass rusher. The loss of Keena Turner was another reason for seeking fresh talent. Such is the quality in depth for the defensive line that the starting trio, ends Pierce Holt and Kevin Fagan, and nose tackle Michael Carter, is not that far ahead of the reserves, Dennis Brown, Larry Roberts and Jim Burt. As a 1990 rookie, Brown made his mark with six sacks.

The secondary will feel the departure of Lott, whose loss the club may come to see as an error of judgement. However, the 49ers' front office houses some shrewd fellows. Their signing of strong safety Dave Waymer, who was said to be past his best, turned up trumps when the former Saint grabbed a club-leading seven interceptions. So it would be no surprise were former Washington starter Todd Bowles, a 1991 Plan-B free agent signing, to move into Lott's position and be a success. The corners are in the first-class custodianship of Darryl Pollard and Don Griffin.

Despite often being left with the responsibility for hitting a distant target, Mike Cofer's placekicking is a little better than par. Again, the 49ers' acceptance of Barry Helton's modest punting average may confirm their requirement that he punts for position rather than distance.

RIGHT: Dexter Carter is expected to be the 49ers' main strike weapon at running back.

1991 SCHEDULE OF GAMES

September		
2	at New York Giants (Mon.)	9:00
8	SAN DIEGO	1:00
15	at Minnesota	12:00
22	LOS ANGELES RAMS	1:00
29	at Los Angeles Raiders	1:00
October		
6	Open Date	
13	at Atlanta	1:00
20	DETROIT	1:00
27	at Philadelphia	1:00
November		
3	ATLANTA	1:00
10	at New Orleans	12:00
17	PHOENIX	1:00
25	at Los Angeles Rams (Mon.)	6:00
December		
1	NEW ORLEANS	1:00
8	at Seattle	1:00
14	KANSAS CITY (Sat.)	1:00
23	CHICAGO (Mon.)	6:00

1991 Draft

Round	Name	Pos.	Ht.	Wt.	College
1.	Washington, Ted	DT	6-4	303	Louisville
2.	Watters, Ricky	RB	6-1	212	Notre Dame
2.	Johnson, John	LB	6-3	225	Clemson
4.	Donahue, Mitch	LB	6-2	255	Wyoming
5.	Hanks, Merton	DB	6-1	177	Iowa
5.	Boatswain, Harry	T	6-4	295	New Haven
6.	Bowles, Scott	T	6-5	280	North Texas State
7.	Canley, Sheldon	RB	5-8	195	San Jose State
8.	Hargain, Tony	WR	6-0	188	Oregon
9.	Riddick, Louis	S	6-1	216	Pittsburgh
10.	Holdbrooks, Byron	NT	6-4	265	Alabama
11.	Slaughter, Bobby	WR	5-11	175	Louisiana Tech
12.	Confer, Cliff	DE	6-3	278	Michigan State

VETERAN ROSTER

No.	Name	Pos.	Ht.	Wt.	NFL Year	College
79	Barton, Harris	T	6-4	280	5	North Carolina
13	Bono, Steve	QB	6-4	215	7	UCLA
	Bowles, Todd	S	6-2	203	6	Temple
31	Brooks, Chet	S	5-11	191	4	Texas A&M
96	Brown, Dennis	DE	6-4	290	2	Washington
	Brown, Steve	CB-S	5-11	190	9	Oregon
64	Burt, Jim	NT	6-1	270	11	Miami
52	Caliguire, Dean	C	6-2	282	1	Pittsburgh
35	Carter, Dexter	RB-KR	5-9	170	2	Florida State
95	Carter, Michael	NT	6-2	285	8	Southern Methodist
6	Cofer, Mike	K	6-1	160	4	North Carolina State
38	Cox, Greg	LB-S	6-0	217	4	San Jose State
25	Davis, Eric	CB	5-11	178	2	Jacksonville State
59	DeLong, Keith	LB	6-2	235	3	Tennessee
50	Etienne, LeRoy	LB	6-2	245	2	Nebraska
75	Fagan, Kevin	DE	6-3	260	5	Miami
	Foster, Roy	G	6-4	284	10	Southern California
29	Griffin, Don	CB	6-0	176	6	Middle Tennessee State
94	Haley, Charles	LB-DE	6-5	230	6	James Madison
57	Harrison, Martin	LB	6-5	240	1	Washington
9	Helton, Barry	P	6-3	205	4	Colorado
30	Henderson, Keith	RB	6-1	220	3	Georgia
78	Holt, Pierce	DE	6-4	280	4	Angelo State
40	Jackson, Johnny	S	6-1	204	3	Houston
84	Jones, Brent	TE	6-4	230	5	Santa Clara
	Jordan, Darin	LB	6-1	240	2	Northeastern
45	Lewis, Kevin	CB	5-11	173	2	Northwestern State, La.
83	Lewis, Ronald	WR	5-11	173	2	Florida State
62	McIntyre, Guy	G	6-3	265	8	Georgia
16	Montana, Joe	QB	6-2	195	13	Notre Dame
77	Paris, Bubba	T	6-6	299	9	Michigan
72	Pollack, Frank	T-G	6-4	277	2	Northern Arizona
26	Pollard, Darryl	CB	5-11	187	5	Weber State
	Radloff, Wayne	C	6-5	277	6	Georgia
44	Rathman, Tom	RB	6-1	232	6	Nebraska
80	Rice, Jerry	WR	6-2	200	7	Mississippi Valley State
91	Roberts, Larry	DE	6-3	275	6	Alabama
	Robinson, Jeroy	LB	6-1	241	2	Texas A&M
53	Romanowski, Bill	LB	6-4	231	4	Boston College
61	Sapolu, Jesse	C-G	6-4	260	6	Hawaii
88	Sherrard, Mike	WR	6-2	187	4	UCLA
63	Siglar, Ricky	G-T	6-7	296	2	San Jose State
24	Sydney, Harry	RB	6-0	217	5	Kansas
82	Taylor, John	WR	6-1	185	5	Delaware State
60	Thomas, Chuck	C-G	6-3	280	6	Oklahoma
23	Tillman, Spencer	RB	5-11	206	5	Oklahoma
74	Wallace, Steve	T	6-5	276	6	Auburn
89	Walls, Wesley	TE	6-5	246	3	Mississippi
99	Walter, Michael	LB	6-3	238	9	Oregon
	Washington, Chris	LB	6-4	240	7	Iowa State
43	Waymer, Dave	S	6-1	188	12	Notre Dame
	Whitmore, David	S	6-0	235	2	Stephen F. Austin
81	Williams, Jamie	TE	6-4	245	9	Nebraska
8	Young, Steve	QB	6-2	200	7	Brigham Young

Chapter Seven

How The Season Works

The National Football League consists of 28 teams divided into two **Conferences**, the American Football Conference (AFC) and the National Football Conference (NFC). Each conference has 14 teams, and is subdivided into two five-team **Divisions** and one four-team **Division**. These are essentially based on sensible geographical considerations but also take into account the traditional rivalries which were in existence when the expanded NFL was restructured in 1970. The teams are listed below in order of their final 1990 division standings since this is of importance in arriving at a team's schedule (fixture list) for 1991.

The Schedule

When considering a team's schedule, it's best to set aside the four teams who each finished the 1989 season in fifth place in their divisions. Looking at the remaining 24, every team plays 12 games against others from its own conference. Again, excluding the four fifth-placed teams, every team will play four games against teams from the rival conference (known as Interconference games), specifically to allow fans in the cities of one conference the opportunity of seeing the star players and teams of the other conference. The

American Football Conference

Eastern Division

		W	L	T
Buffalo	AE-1	13	3	0
Miami	AE-2	12	4	0
Indianapolis	AE-3	7	9	0
N.Y. Jets	AE-4	6	10	0
New England	AE-5	1	15	0

Central Division

		W	L	T
Cincinnati	AC-1	9	7	0
Houston	AC-2	9	7	0
Pittsburgh	AC-3	9	7	0
Cleveland	AC-4	3	13	0

Western Division

		W	L	T
L.A. Raiders	AW-1	12	4	0
Kansas City	AW-2	11	5	0
Seattle	AW-3	9	7	0
San Diego	AW-4	6	10	0
Denver	AW-5	5	11	0

National Football Conference

Eastern Division

		W	L	T
N.Y. Giants	NE-1	13	3	0
Philadelphia	NE-2	10	6	0
Washington	NE-3	10	6	0
Dallas	NE-4	7	9	0
Phoenix	NE-5	5	11	0

Central Division

		W	L	T
Chicago	NC-1	11	5	0
Tampa Bay	NC-2	6	10	0
Detroit	NC-3	6	10	0
Green Bay	NC-4	6	10	0
Minnesota	NC-5	6	10	0

Western Division

		W	L	T
San Francisco	NW-1	14	2	0
New Orleans	NW-2	8	8	0
L.A. Rams	NW-3	5	11	0
Atlanta	NW-4	5	11	0

structure of a team's schedule depends on whether it plays in a four-team or a five-team division.

Four-Team Division

A typical schedule, e.g., for the Atlanta Falcons, appears below. It is set out, deliberately not in chronological order but to emphasize that the schedule has a quite definite structure.

Atlanta Falcons (NFC West)

Los Angeles Rams	NFC West	Home
Los Angeles Rams	NFC West	Away
New Orleans Saints	NFC West	Home
New Orleans Saints	NFC West	Away
San Francisco 49ers	NFC West	Home
San Francisco 49ers	NFC West	Away
Green Bay Packers	NFC Central	Home
Tampa Bay Buccaneers	NFC Central	Home
Minnesota Vikings	NFC Central	Home
Dallas Cowboys	NFC East	Away
Phoenix Cardinals	NFC East	Away
Washington Redskins	NFC East	Away
Los Angeles Raiders	AFC West	Home
Seattle Seahawks	AFC West	Home
Kansas City Chiefs	AFC West	Away
San Diego Chargers	AFC West	Away

The Falcons will always play their division rivals, the Los Angeles Rams, New Orleans and San Francisco, both home and away. The flavour of intra-conference competition is maintained by six games, every year, against teams from outside their division but within their conference. There will always be three games against the NFC East and three against the NFC Central. Again, every year, there will be four games against teams from a particular division of the rival conference, based on a three-year cycle. In 1991, they play the AFC West; in 1992, they will play teams from the AFC East and in 1993, the AFC Central. For every NFL team, a complete list of opponents, other than those within a team's own division, is arrived at by applying the following formula. The letters and numbers refer to Conference, Division and final standing in that division. Thus, the Dallas Cowboys, who are in the National Conference Eastern Division and finished fourth in that division, are identified as NE-4. Equally, the Pittsburgh Steelers, who are in the American Conference Central Division and finished third in that division, are labelled AC-3.

AFC EAST-AE

AE-1		AE-2		AE-3		AE-4		AE-5	
H	**A**	**H**	**A**	**H**	**A**	**H**	**A**	**H**	**A**
AC-1	AW-1	AC-2	AW-2	AC-3	AW-3	AC-2	AW-3	AC-2	AC-1
AC-3	AW-2	AC-1	AW-4	AC-4	AW-1	AW-4	AC-4	AC-4	AC-3
NC-1	NC-2	NC-2	NC-1	NC-1	NC-2	NC-2	NC-1	AW-5	AW-5
NC-3	NC-4	NC-4	NC-3	NC-3	NC-4	NC-4	NC-3	NC-5	NE-5

AFC CENTRAL-AC

AC-1		AC-2		AC-3		AC-4	
H	**A**	**H**	**A**	**H**	**A**	**H**	**A**
AW-1	AE-1	AW-1	AE-2	AE-5	AE-1	AE-4	AE-3
AE-5	AE-2	AW-2	AE-4	AW-3	AE-3	AW-2	AE-5
AW-3	AW-5	AW-5	AE-5	AW-4	AW-5	AW-5	AW-4
NE-1	NE-2	NE-2	NE-1	NE-1	NE-2	NE-2	NE-1
NE-3	NE-4	NE-4	NE-3	NE-3	NE-4	NE-4	NE-3

AFC WEST-AW

AW-1		AW-2		AW-3		AW-4		AW-5	
H	**A**	**H**	**A**	**H**	**A**	**H**	**A**	**H**	**A**
AE-1	AC-1	AE-2	AC-2	AE-3	AC-3	AE-2	AE-4	AC-1	AC-2
AE-3	AC-2	AE-1	AC-4	AE-4	AC-1	AC-4	AC-3	AC-3	AC-4
NW-1	NW-2	NW-2	NW-1	NW-1	NW-2	NW-2	NW-1	AE-5	AE-5
NW-3	NW-4	NW-4	NW-3	NW-3	NW-4	NW-4	NW-3	NE-5	NC-5

NFC EAST-NE

NE-1 H	NE-1 A	NE-2 H	NE-2 A	NE-3 H	NE-3 A	NE-4 H	NE-4 A	NE-5 H	NE-5 A
NW-1	NC-1	NW-2	NC-2	NC-3	NC-1	NW-2	NC-3	NC-5	NC-5
NW-3	NC-2	NW-1	NC-4	NW-4	NW-3	NW-4	NC-4	NW-2	NW-1
AC-2	AC-1	AC-1	AC-2	AC-2	AC-1	AC-1	AC-2	NW-4	NW-3
AC-4	AC-3	AC-3	AC-4	AC-4	AC-3	AC-3	AC-4	AE-5	AW-5

NFC CENTRAL-NC

NC-1 H	NC-1 A	NC-2 H	NC-2 A	NC-3 H	NC-3 A	NC-4 H	NC-4 A	NC-5 H	NC-5 A
NE-1	NW-1	NE-1	NW-4	NE-4	NE-3	NE-2	NW-3	NE-5	NE-5
NE-3	NW-2	NE-2	NW-2	NW-3	NW-1	NE-4	NW-4	NW-1	NW-2
AE-2	AE-1	AE-1	AE-2	AE-2	AE-1	AE-1	AE-2	NW-3	NW-4
AE-4	AE-3	AE-3	AE-4	AE-4	AE-3	AE-3	AE-4	AW-5	AE-5

NFC WEST-NW

NW-1 H	NW-1 A	NW-2 H	NW-2 A	NW-3 H	NW-3 A	NW-4 H	NW-4 A
NC-1	NC-5	NC-1	NE-2	NC-4	NC-3	NC-2	NE-3
NC-3	NE-1	NC-2	NE-4	NE-3	NC-5	NC-4	NE-4
NE-5	NE-2	NC-5	NE-5	NE-5	NE-1	NC-5	NE-5
AW-2	AW-1	AW-1	AW-2	AW-2	AW-1	AW-1	AW-2
AW-4	AW-3	AW-3	AW-4	AW-4	AW-3	AW-3	AW-4

Five-Team Division (Top Four Teams Only)

In the AFC West the schedules for the top four teams have identical structure and include home and away games against the other four teams in the division. Each of the top four teams plays two games against AFC Central teams and two against the AFC East. Also, they play the top four teams in the NFC West as part of their three-year cycle of interconference games. In 1992, they will play teams from the NFC East and in 1993, the NFC Central. Below is the schedule for Kansas City.

Kansas City Chiefs (AFC West)

Denver Broncos	AFC West	Home
Denver Broncos	AFC West	Away
Los Angeles Raiders	AFC West	Home
Los Angeles Raiders	AFC West	Away
San Diego Chargers	AFC West	Home
San Diego Chargers	AFC West	Away
Seattle Seahawks	AFC West	Home
Seattle Seahawks	AFC West	Away
Buffalo Bills	AFC East	Home
Miami Dolphins	AFC East	Home
Cleveland Browns	AFC Central	Away
Houston Oilers	AFC Central	Away
Atlanta Falcons	NFC West	Home
Los Angeles Rams	NFC West	Away
New Orleans Saints	NFC West	Home
San Francisco 49ers	NFC West	Away

Fifth-Placed Teams

In the AFC, the two fifth-placed teams will each play eight games against teams from their own division and will always play single games against each of the four AFC Central division teams. In the NFC, the two fifth-placed teams each play eight games against teams within their own division and will always play single games against the four NFC West teams. Each of the four fifth-placed teams is guaranteed home and away games against the other fifth-placed team in its own conference, and single games against the two fifth-placed teams from the rival conference. The schedule structures for all four teams are set out as follows:

New England Patriots (AE-5)

AFC East		8 games
AFC Central		4 games
Denver	(AW-5)	Home
Denver	(AW-5)	Away
Minnesota	(NC-5)	Home
Phoenix	(NE-5)	Home

Denver Broncos (AW-5)

AFC West		8 games
AFC Central		4 games
New England	(AE-5)	Home
New England	(AE-5)	Away
Minnesota	(NC-5)	Away
Phoenix	(NE-5)	Home

Phoenix (NE-5)

NFC East		8 games
NFC West		4 games
Minnesota	(NC-5)	Home
Minnesota	(NC-5)	Away
Denver	(AW-5)	Away
New England	(AE-5)	Home

Minnesota (NC-5)

NFC Central		8 games
NFC West		4 games
Phoenix	(NE-5)	Home
Phoenix	(NE-5)	Away
Denver	(AW-5)	Home
New England	(AE-5)	Away

The Playoffs

On completion of the regular season, each conference holds an elimination competition known as the Playoffs. Under a playoff format introduced for the 1990 season, the teams involved will be the three division winners and three Wild Card teams, namely, those three, other than the division winners, who have the best won-lost-tied records. In 1991, the three Wild Cards, together with the division winner with the poorest record, will contest the first round of the playoffs, the victors joining the two division winners with the better records in the conference semi-finals. Operating on the best-versus-worst principle, the team with the best record will play the team which has the poorest record.

Home-Field Advantage in the Playoffs

The game site is determined on the best-versus-worst principle, with the team which has the better won-lost-tied record always given home-field advantage. Taking the AFC as the example, in the 1990 playoffs the pecking order of teams was a follows:

	W	L	T
Buffalo*	13	3	0
L.A. Raiders*	12	4	0
Cincinnati*	9	7	0
Miami**	12	4	0
Kansas City**	11	5	0
Houston**	9	7	0

* Division Champions
**Wild Card teams

Tie-Breaking Procedures

Ties are broken by the following list of criteria:

Teams in the same division

A: *Two teams*

1. Head-to-head (best record in games played between the two teams)
2. Best record in games played within the division
3. Best record in games played within the conference
4. Best record in common games
5. Best net points scored in division games (just like goal difference in soccer)
6. Best net points in all games

B: *Three or More Teams* (if two teams remain tied after all other teams are eliminated, the tie-breaking procedure reverts to A:1.)

1. Head-to-head (best record in games played between the teams)
2. Best record in games played within the division
3. Best record in games played within the conference
4. Best record in common games
5. Best net points in division games
6. Best net points in all games

Tie-Breakers for the Wild Card places

(a) If the teams are from the same division, the division tie-breaker is applied.
(b) If the teams are from different divisions, the following procedure is adopted:

C: *Two Teams*

1. Head-to-head (if they have played each other)
2. Best record in games played within the conference
3. Best record in common games (minimum of four)
4. Best average net points in conference games
5. Best net points in all games

D: *Three or More Teams* (If two teams remain tied after all other teams are eliminated, the tie-breaking procedure reverts to A:1, or C:1, whichever is applicable.)

1. Head-to-head sweep (this applies only if one team has either beaten or lost to all the others)
2. Best record in games played within the conference
3. Best record in common games (minimum of four)
4. Best average net points in conference games
5. Best net points in all games

1990 Tie-Breakers

Cincinnati-Houston-Pittsburgh (division title): B:1; Order: Cincinnati (3-1), Houston (2-2), Pittsburgh (1-3).
Houston-Seattle-Pittsburgh (third wild-card place): D:2; Order: Houston (8-4), Seattle (7-5), Pittsburgh (6-6).
Philadelphia-Washington (home-field advantage): A:2; Order: Philadelphia (5-3), Washington (4-4).

CHAPTER EIGHT

1991 NATIONAL FOOTBALL LEAGUE SCHEDULE

(All times local)

FIRST WEEK

Sunday, September 1	**Kickoff**
Atlanta at Kansas City	12:00
Cincinnati at Denver	2:00
Dallas at Cleveland	1:00
Detroit at Washington	8:00
Los Angeles Raiders at Houston	3:00
Miami at Buffalo	4:00
Minnesota at Chicago	3:00
New England at Indianapolis	3:00
Philadelphia at Green Bay	12:00
Phoenix at Los Angeles Rams	1:00
San Diego at Pittsburgh	4:00
Seattle at New Orleans	12:00
Tampa Bay at New York Jets	1:00
Monday, September 2	
San Francisco at New York Giants	9:00

SECOND WEEK

Sunday, September 8	
Chicago at Tampa Bay	1:00
Cleveland at New England	1:00
Denver at Los Angeles Raiders	1:00
Green Bay at Detroit	1:00
Houston at Cincinnati	8:00
Indianapolis at Miami	1:00
Los Angeles Rams at New York Giants	1:00
Minnesota at Atlanta	1:00
New Orleans at Kansas City	12:00
New York Jets at Seattle	1:00
Phoenix at Philadelphia	1:00
Pittsburgh at Buffalo	1:00
San Diego at San Francisco	1:00
Monday, September 9	
Washington at Dallas	8:00

THIRD WEEK

Sunday, September 15	
Atlanta at San Diego	1:00
Buffalo at New York Jets	4:00
Cincinnati at Cleveland	1:00
Indianapolis at Los Angeles Raiders	1:00
Los Angeles Rams at New Orleans	7:00
Miami at Detroit	1:00
New England at Pittsburgh	1:00
New York Giants at Chicago	12:00
Philadelphia at Dallas	12:00
Phoenix at Washington	1:00
San Francisco at Minnesota	12:00
Seattle at Denver	2:00
Tampa Bay at Green Bay	12:00
Monday, September 16	
Kansas City at Houston	8:00

FOURTH WEEK

Sunday, September 22	
Buffalo at Tampa Bay	4:00
Cleveland at New York Giants	1:00
Dallas at Phoenix	5:00
Detroit at Indianapolis	12:00
Green Bay at Miami	1:00
Houston at New England	1:00
Los Angeles Raiders at Atlanta	1:00
Los Angeles Rams at San Francisco	1:00
Minnesota at New Orleans	12:00
Pittsburgh at Philadelphia	1:00
San Diego at Denver	2:00
Seattle at Kansas City	3:00
Washington at Cincinnati	1:00
Monday, September 23	
New York Jets at Chicago	8:00

FIFTH WEEK

Open Date: Four AFC Central teams

Sunday, September 29	
Chicago at Buffalo	1:00
Denver at Minnesota	7:00
Green Bay at Los Angeles Rams	1:00
Indianapolis at Seattle	1:00
Kansas City at San Diego	1:00
Miami at New York Jets	4:00
New England at Phoenix	1:00

New Orleans at Atlanta	1:00
New York Giants at Dallas	12:00
San Francisco at Los Angeles Raiders	1:00
Tampa Bay at Detroit	1:00

Monday, September 30

Philadelphia at Washington	9:00

SIXTH WEEK

Open Date: Four NFC West teams

Sunday, October 6

Dallas vs. Green Bay at Milwaukee	12:00
Denver at Houston	12:00
Miami at New England	1:00
Minnesota at Detroit	1:00
New York Jets at Cleveland	1:00
Philadelphia at Tampa Bay	1:00
Phoenix at New York Giants	4:00
Pittsburgh at Indianapolis	7:00
San Diego at Los Angeles Raiders	1:00
Seattle at Cincinnati	1:00
Washington at Chicago	12:00

Monday, October 7

Buffalo at Kansas City	8:00

SEVENTH WEEK

Open Date: Four NFC Central and Two AFC Fifth-Placed teams

Sunday, October 13

Cincinnati at Dallas	12:00
Cleveland at Washington	1:00
Houston at New York Jets	4:00
Indianapolis at Buffalo	1:00
Los Angeles Raiders at Seattle	4:30
Miami at Kansas City	3:00
New Orleans at Philadelphia	1:00
Phoenix at Minnesota	12:00
San Diego at Los Angeles Rams	1:00
San Francisco at Atlanta	1:00

Monday, October 14

New York Giants at Pittsburgh	9:00

EIGHTH WEEK

Open Date: Four NFC East teams

Thursday, October 17

Chicago at Green Bay	6:30

Sunday, October 20

Atlanta at Phoenix	1:00
Cleveland at San Diego	1:00
Detroit at San Francisco	1:00
Houston at Miami	1:00
Kansas City at Denver	2:00
Los Angeles Rams at Los Angeles Raiders	1:00
Minnesota at New England	1:00
New York Jets at Indianapolis	12:00
Seattle at Pittsburgh	1:00
Tampa Bay at New Orleans	12:00

Monday, October 21

Cincinnati at Buffalo	9:00

NINTH WEEK

Open Date: Four AFC East teams

Sunday, October 27

Chicago at New Orleans	12:00
Cincinnati at Houston	12:00
Dallas at Detroit	4:00
Denver at New England	1:00
Green Bay at Tampa Bay	1:00
Los Angeles Rams at Atlanta	1:00
Minnesota at Phoenix	2:00
Pittsburgh at Cleveland	1:00
San Diego at Seattle	1:00
San Francisco at Philadelphia	1:00
Washington at New York Giants	8:00

Monday, October 28

Los Angeles Raiders at Kansas City	8:00

TENTH WEEK

Open Date: Four AFC West teams

Sunday, November 3

Atlanta at San Francisco	1:00
Cleveland at Cincinnati	1:00
Detroit at Chicago	12:00
Green Bay at New York Jets	1:00
Houston at Washington	1:00
Miami at Indianapolis	4:00
New England at Buffalo	1:00
New Orleans at Los Angeles Rams	1:00
Phoenix at Dallas	12:00
Pittsburgh at Denver	6:00
Tampa Bay at Minnesota	12:00

Monday, November 4

New York Giants at Philadelphia	9:00

ELEVENTH WEEK

Sunday, November 10

Atlanta at Washington	1:00
Buffalo vs. Green Bay at Milwaukee	12:00
Dallas at Houston	12:00
Detroit at Tampa Bay	1:00
Indianapolis at New York Jets	1:00
Kansas City at Los Angeles Rams	1:00
Los Angeles Raiders at Denver	2:00
New England at Miami	8:00
New York Giants at Phoenix	2:00
Philadelphia at Cleveland	1:00
Pittsburgh at Cincinnati	1:00
San Francisco at New Orleans	12:00
Seattle at San Diego	1:00

Monday, November 11

Chicago at Minnesota	8:00

TWELFTH WEEK

Sunday, November 17

Chicago at Indianapolis	1:00
Cincinnati at Philadelphia	1:00
Cleveland at Houston	7:00

Dallas at New York Giants	4:00
Denver at Kansas City	12:00
Los Angeles Rams at Detroit	4:00
Minnesota at Green Bay	12:00
New Orleans at San Diego	1:00
New York Jets at New England	1:00
Phoenix at San Francisco	1:00
Seattle at Los Angeles Raiders	1:00
Tampa Bay at Atlanta	1:00
Washington at Pittsburgh	1:00

Monday, November 18

Buffalo at Miami	9:00

THIRTEENTH WEEK

Sunday, November 24

Atlanta at New Orleans	7:00
Buffalo at New England	1:00
Dallas at Washington	1:00
Denver at Seattle	1:00
Detroit at Minnesota	12:00
Houston at Pittsburgh	1:00
Indianapolis vs. Green Bay at Milwaukee	12:00
Kansas City at Cleveland	1:00
Los Angeles Raiders at Cincinnati	1:00
Miami at Chicago	12:00
New York Giants at Tampa Bay	1:00
Philadelphia at Phoenix	2:00
San Diego at New York Jets	4:00

Monday, November 25

San Francisco at Los Angeles Rams	6:00

FOURTEENTH WEEK

Open Date: Two NFC Fifth-Placed teams

Thursday, November 28

Chicago at Detroit	12:30
Pittsburgh at Dallas	3:00

Sunday, December 1

Cleveland at Indianapolis	1:00
Green Bay at Atlanta	1:00
Kansas City at Seattle	1:00
Los Angeles Raiders at San Diego	5:00
New England at Denver	2:00
New Orleans at San Francisco	1:00
New York Giants at Cincinnati	4:00
New York Jets at Buffalo	1:00
Tampa Bay at Miami	1:00
Washington at Los Angeles Rams	1:00

Monday, December 2

Philadelphia at Houston	8:00

FIFTEENTH WEEK

Sunday, December 8

Atlanta at Los Angeles Rams	1:00
Buffalo at Los Angeles Raiders	1:00
Denver at Cleveland	1:00
Green Bay at Chicago	12:00
Indianapolis at New England	1:00
Minnesota at Tampa Bay	8:00
New Orleans at Dallas	12:00
New York Jets at Detroit	4:00
Philadelphia at New York Giants	1:00
Pittsburgh at Houston	12:00
San Diego at Kansas City	12:00
San Francisco at Seattle	1:00
Washington at Phoenix	2:00

Monday, December 9

Cincinnati at Miami	9:00

SIXTEENTH WEEK

Saturday, December 14

Kansas City at San Francisco	1:00
Tampa Bay at Chicago	11:30

Sunday, December 15

Buffalo at Indianapolis	8:00
Cincinnati at Pittsburgh	1:00
Dallas at Philadelphia	1:00
Detroit at Green Bay	12:00
Houston at Cleveland	1:00
Los Angeles Rams at Minnesota	12:00
Miami at San Diego	1:00
New England at New York Jets	1:00
New York Giants at Washington	4:00
Phoenix at Denver	2:00
Seattle at Atlanta	1:00

Monday, December 16

Los Angeles Raiders at New Orleans	8:00

SEVENTEENTH WEEK

Saturday, December 21

Green Bay at Minnesota	3:00
Houston at New York Giants	12:30

Sunday, December 22

Atlanta at Dallas	12:00
Cleveland at Pittsburgh	1:00
Denver at San Diego	1:00
Detroit at Buffalo	1:00
Indianapolis at Tampa Bay	1:00
Kansas City at Los Angeles Raiders	1:00
Los Angeles Rams at Seattle	5:00
New England at Cincinnati	1:00
New Orleans at Phoenix	2:00
New York Jets at Miami	1:00
Washington at Philadelphia	4:00

Monday, December 23

Chicago at San Francisco	6:00

POSTSEASON

Saturday, Dec. 28	AFC and NFC First Round Playoffs
Sunday, Dec. 29	AFC and NFC First Round Playoffs
Saturday, Jan. 4	AFC and NFC Divisional Playoffs
Sunday, Jan. 5	AFC and NFC Divisional Playoffs
Sunday, Jan. 12	AFC and NFC Championship Games
Sunday, Jan. 26	Super Bowl XXVI at Metrodome, Minneapolis, Minnesota
Sunday, Feb. 2	AFC-NFC Pro Bowl at Honolulu, Hawaii

ALL-TIME SERIES RECORDS

	Buffalo	Indianapolis	Miami	New England	N.Y. Jets	Cincinnati	Cleveland	Houston	Pittsburgh	Denver	Kansas City	L.A. Raiders	San Diego	Seattle
Buffalo		21-19-1	15-35-1	28-33-1	33-28-0	6-11-0	3-8-0	12-19-0	5-6-0	15-10-1	15-12-1	14-13-0	9-17-2	1-3-0
Indianapolis	19-21-1		13-30-0	18-23-0	23-19-0	7-5-0	7-13-0	6-6-0	4-10-0	2-8-0	4-6-0	3-4-0	5-6-0	2-0-0
Miami	35-15-1	30-13-0		29-21-0	27-23-1	9-3-0	6-4-0	10-11-0	9-5-0	5-2-1	8-9-0	4-16-1	6-9-0	4-2-0
New England	33-28-1	23-18-0	21-29-0		27-34-1	7-5-0	2-7-0	16-14-1	3-7-0	12-15-0	7-12-3	13-13-1	13-12-2	6-4-0
N.Y. Jets	28-33-0	19-23-0	23-27-1	34-27-1		8-6-0	5-9-0	12-15-1	1-11-0	11-10-1	13-14-1	11-13-2	8-16-1	3-7-0
Cincinnati	11-6-0	5-7-0	3-9-0	5-7-0	6-8-0		22-19-0	25-19-1	21-20-0	6-9-0	9-10-0	5-15-0	9-11-0	6-4-0
Cleveland	8-3-0	13-7-0	4-6-0	7-2-0	9-5-0	19-22-0		26-16-0	49-33-0	5-12-0	6-6-2	2-10-0	5-7-1	3-8-0
Houston	19-12-0	6-6-0	11-10-0	14-16-1	15-12-1	19-25-1	16-26-0		15-29-0	19-11-1	14-22-0	12-22-0	15-17-1	4-4-0
Pittsburgh	6-5-0	10-4-0	5-9-0	7-3-0	11-1-0	20-21-0	33-49-0	29-15-0		7-10-1	12-5-0	6-10-0	11-5-0	4-3-0
Denver	10-15-1	8-2-0	2-5-1	15-12-0	10-11-1	9-6-0	12-5-0	11-19-1	10-7-1		25-36-0	19-41-2	31-30-1	16-12-0
Kansas City	12-15-1	6-4-0	9-8-0	12-7-3	14-13-1	10-9-0	6-6-2	22-14-0	5-12-0	36-25-0		26-35-2	29-31-1	13-12-0
L.A. Raiders	13-14-0	4-3-0	16-4-1	13-13-1	13-11-2	15-5-0	10-2-0	22-12-0	10-6-0	41-19-2	35-26-2		40-21-2	13-15-0
San Diego	17-9-2	6-5-0	9-6-0	12-13-2	16-8-1	11-9-0	7-5-1	17-15-1	5-11-0	30-31-1	31-29-1	21-40-2		11-13-0
Seattle	3-1-0	0-2-0	2-4-0	4-6-0	7-3-0	4-6-0	8-3-0	4-4-0	3-4-0	12-16-0	12-13-0	15-13-0	13-11-0	
Dallas	3-1-0	6-3-0	2-5-0	6-0-0	4-1-0	2-2-0	9-16-0	4-2-0	11-13-0	3-2-0	2-2-0	1-3-0	4-1-0	3-1-0
N.Y. Giants	3-3-0	4-7-0	1-1-0	3-1-0	3-3-0	0-3-0	16-26-2	3-0-0	41-26-3	4-2-0	5-1-0	2-3-0	4-2-0	4-2-0
Philadelphia	4-2-0	5-6-0	2-5-0	5-2-0	4-0-0	0-5-0	11-30-1	4-0-0	43-25-3	4-2-0	1-0-0	3-3-0	2-3-0	3-1-0
Phoenix	3-3-0	6-4-0	0-6-0	5-1-0	2-1-0	1-3-0	10-31-3	3-2-0	21-29-3	0-2-1	1-3-1	1-2-0	1-4-0	3-0-0
Washington	4-2-0	6-16-0	3-5-0	4-1-0	4-0-0	3-2-0	8-32-1	2-3-0	41-27-3	3-3-0	1-2-0	2-5-0	5-0-0	4-1-0
Chicago	3-1-0	15-21-0	1-4-0	3-3-0	2-1-0	2-2-0	3-7-0	2-3-0	15-4-1	5-4-0	3-2-0	3-4-0	1-4-0	2-4-0
Detroit	1-1-1	16-17-2	1-2-0	2-2-0	2-3-0	2-3-0	13-4-0	2-3-0	13-10-1	3-4-0	3-4-0	2-5-0	3-2-0	1-4-0
Green Bay	1-3-0	18-18-1	0-6-0	2-2-0	1-4-0	2-4-0	8-5-0	2-3-0	16-11-0	1-4-1	2-3-1	2-5-0	3-1-0	3-3-0
Minnesota	4-2-0	6-12-1	1-5-0	2-2-0	1-3-0	3-3-0	7-3-0	3-2-0	6-5-0	4-2-0	2-3-0	2-6-0	3-3-0	2-3-0
Tampa Bay	4-1-0	1-4-0	1-3-0	0-3-0	1-4-0	1-3-0	0-4-0	1-3-0	0-4-0	0-2-0	2-4-0	0-2-0	0-4-0	0-2-0
Atlanta	3-2-0	0-10-0	1-4-0	3-3-0	2-3-0	2-5-0	1-8-0	5-2-0	1-8-0	3-4-0	0-2-0	2-4-0	2-1-0	0-4-0
L.A. Rams	3-2-0	16-20-2	1-4-0	2-3-0	4-2-0	2-4-0	8-9-0	4-2-0	13-5-2	3-3-0	3-0-0	2-4-0	2-2-0	4-0-0
New Orleans	2-2-0	2-3-0	1-4-0	1-5-0	2-4-0	4-3-0	3-8-0	3-3-1	5-5-0	1-4-0	2-2-0	1-3-1	1-3-0	2-2-0
San Francisco	2-2-0	16-21-0	2-4-0	5-1-0	5-1-0	7-1-0	6-8-0	5-2-0	7-7-0	3-4-0	3-1-0	2-4-0	2-3-0	3-1-0